IMAGES
of America

EARLY MENDOCINO COAST

ON THE COVER: Picnic excursion trains gave loggers and mill workers and their families something to look forward to. Patriotic bunting decorating the cars may indicate a Fourth of July outing. Logging companies maintained picnic grounds in unlogged groves of trees. This train is from the Albion Lumber Company and is headed out toward Anderson Valley. (Courtesy of Robert Lee.)

IMAGES of America
EARLY MENDOCINO COAST

Katy M. Tahja

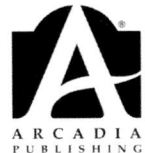

Copyright © 2008 by Katy M. Tahja
ISBN 978-0-7385-5946-9

Published by Arcadia Publishing
Charleston, South Carolina

Printed in the United States of America

Library of Congress Catalog Card Number: 2008922710

For all general information contact Arcadia Publishing at:
Telephone 843-853-2070
Fax 843-853-0044
E-mail sales@arcadiapublishing.com
For customer service and orders:
Toll-Free 1-888-313-2665

Visit us on the Internet at www.arcadiapublishing.com

To Robert and Lila Lee of Ukiah, California. Robert's outstanding collection of thousands of photographs was a delight to access, and Lila's encyclopedic knowledge of Mendocino County history was invaluable. They are both treasures in our community of local history lovers.

Contents

Acknowledgments		6
Introduction		7
1.	First Comers and the South Coast: 35 Miles Gualala to Cuffey's Cove	9
2.	Middle Coast: 14 Miles Navarro River to Little River	39
3.	Mendocino and Environs: 10 Miles Mendocino to Fort Bragg	67
4.	North Coast and Lost Coast: 50 Miles Cleone to Needle Rock	111

Acknowledgments

Because photographs have been shared by historic preservation groups in Mendocino County for decades, those in this book have come from a wide variety of sources. Thanks to photograph historian Robert Lee for the majority of the images. Thanks also to Bob Lorentzen, author of several excellent books on Mendocino including *The Mendocino Glove Box Guide*; Bruce Levene; the California history section of the California State Library; the Mendocino County Historical Society; the Kelley House Museum; the Mendocino County Museum; the Skunk Train; the Little River Inn; and the Howard Creek Ranch.

As the world's slowest typist, I thank Sally Young and Jane Oros for word processing skills. As a self-proclaimed "computer dweeb," I also thank Jane Oros for technical computer solutions to the problems I experienced.

And loving thanks to my husband, David, who put up for months with research materials stacked in teetering piles around my living room chair. He patiently dealt with my interruptions while he read in the evenings and I researched and called out: "Hey, listen to this! Did you know. . ."

Introduction

While driving the Shoreline Highway along 106 miles of Mendocino County coast, a traveler today might wonder, "What brought people here in the first place?"

It was not the sweeping vistas of surf and sand or good farmlands. There was no gold to be found as in the Sierra. No easy paths traversed the county for travel; there were only dense forests, deep canyons, and wide rivers. So what brought the very first white settlers to the fog-shrouded coast? A search for a shipwreck!

In 1850, a schooner called the *Frolic* ran aground on the rocks at Point Cabrillo between Fort Bragg and Mendocino. The crew sailed a leaky lifeboat back to San Francisco and reported that their ship full of trade goods from the Orient, including silks and porcelain, was waiting to be salvaged.

A San Francisco entrepreneur named Harry Meiggs sent Jerome Ford to find the wreck site and recover the trade goods. It was too late, for he arrived on the Mendocino Coast to find Pomo natives wearing silk shawls, eating preserved ginger, and making beads from broken porcelain pottery.

Jerome Ford returned to San Francisco to tell Meiggs the trade goods were gone but he had found something more valuable: trees. There were huge, vast forests of tall trees growing right down to the water's edge.

San Francisco and the entire Bay Area were booming after the Gold Rush, and building materials brought premium prices. Ford came back to Mendocino with the first of many sawmills that would be built from Gualala, near the Sonoma County border, to Needle Rock, just below the Humboldt County line.

Each new sawmill had a shipping point, since no inland roads or railroads connected to the coast. These early loggers had no idea the trees they looked at were 500, 1,000, even 2,000 years old. And they thought, with the forests being so huge, logging could last forever. It did not.

Today's Shoreline Highway passes fern-covered canyons, quaint bed-and-breakfasts, and art-centered villages. A century ago, all these places had a lumber mill, a logging railroad, or a shipping point.

Back then, everything revolved around the timber industry. If a person was not chopping down a tree, he was hunting game for a logging camp cookhouse. A man could grow hay to feed the oxen that pulled the logs through the woods or later be the engineer behind the controls of a logging locomotive.

One hundred years ago, the Mendocino Coast was a working industrial landscape. Mechanical contrivances sprouted off the headlands to get the lumber onto the ships for transit. More mechanical wonders got the cut lumber from the sawmill to the coast. Human ingenuity and hard work took a standing tree with enough lumber for five houses and turned it into piles of boards bound together for shipment.

As with any settlement pattern, the native people got shoved aside as thousands of young men arrived to fell trees and work in mills. These men were followed by wives, families, and women of ill-repute. Farms were established on logged-over lands as crossroads villages and mill towns appeared.

A century ago, the closer to San Francisco a landing was, the busier it was. Booming economies gave place names to more than 80 spots on the coast, and names changed. Is it possible that one town was alternately named Fish Rock, Ferguson's Cove, and Haven's Anchorage? Who named Nip and Tuck or Rough and Ready? Some questions will never have answers. Were the Russians at Russian Gulch? Who signaled what at Signal Port? Greenwood became a town with two names: traditionally called Greenwood, when the townspeople asked for a post office, they were told the name already belonged to a town in the Sierra, so they used the name Elk. But everyone still called the place Greenwood. Some place names are new. Whiskey Shoals is named for the area rumrunners who smuggled booze on shore during Prohibition. Irish Beach is a vacation home community. Others names are older: Kibesillah and Abalobidiah, for example, are from native cultures.

But many old places, once full of life and commerce, have vanished. Visitors might see a sign on a fence post or a road name but nothing remains of the town. Photographs in this book, though, give glimpses of the Mendocino Coast's past.

Boom-and-bust cycles in timber products caused places to appear then vanish as if by magic. It took decades for residents to realize the forest was not coming back after a second or third cutting, and the visitors who did come did not want to look at cut-over forest. They liked trees.

Tourists needed a place to stay, and they enjoyed interesting restaurants. Travelers spent money in gift shops and art galleries. The same lighthouses that used to guide lumber schooners up and down the coast for a century were now beacons for history lovers. Logging is gone, and tourism has taken its place. The Mendocino Coast went from an extractive economy to an amenities-based economy.

The opening of the Golden Gate Bridge started the tourism industry. The Redwood Empire Association began to extol the virtues of visiting the North Coast. It took years to get roads into the state highway system. There was no road from Gualala to Ukiah 100 years ago. It took until 1925 to get a state highway from Westport to Leggett and Highway 101. In the 1930s, the state coated the gravel and dirt roads with oil, and later, asphalt. It was the 1950s before there was pavement from Mendocino to Point Arena.

Starting with the native peoples, the historic photographs here are arranged from the Sonoma County line going north up the Shoreline Highway toward Humboldt County. A diversion at milepost 90.88 takes travelers to a part of the Mendocino Coast that most people never visit. It's a local secret, a magic, empty place, a Lost Coast. Right up on the Humboldt County line, Bear Harbor, Needle Rock, and miles of empty coastline make up this forgotten coast. Thought it's hard to get to, it's worth the side trip.

So take a drive up the Mendocino Coast, referring to this book, and mile by mile, have a peek at what it was like in yesteryear. And as a favor to other motorists, pull all the way off the Shoreline Highway into turnouts to enjoy the views.

One

First Comers and the South Coast
35 Miles
Gualala to Cuffey's Cove

Long before the arrival of white settlers, the native Pomo and Yuki peoples lived a life of abundance. While seasonal village sites and place names existed along the coast, most early people lived in the interior of the county, closer to acorns, their main food source. Trips to the coast occurred to catch salmon, abalone, mussels, crabs, and to gather seaweed. Sea lion and whale meat was savored if available on the shore. Homes were cone-like dwellings of bark. Clothing was limited to grass skirts and fur-skin capes. Rough seas and rugged terrain protected native cultures on the North Coast until the Russians arrived to hunt for furs in 1812. The Gold Rush in 1849 brought more explorers north, and by the 1850s, the good life was gone. Natives were restricted to reservations, enslaved, or, if lucky, put to work doing menial jobs for settlers. The one traditional skill that survived was basketry; it was admired by European cultures.

From Gualala north, settlements spread up the coast. The South Coast in particular seemed to have a shipping point to export wood products every few miles. Called "dog holes" because they were often so small that a dog would have trouble turning around in such a tight space, these tiny ports led to the creation of short, shallow lumber schooners with crews of four.

Because there were so many creeks and rivers along the shores, all transport went by sea. A decent coastal road system was decades in the future, and inland routes were nothing but horse trails. But every little town had something to make it special. Fish Rock had a farmer who exhibited 42 potatoes weighing 140 pounds. Point Arena had an asphalt leak in a bluff that was scooped up and used to pave the streets. Greenwood/Elk was proud of the fact that it kept 500 men working for 20 years in its sawmill. Manchester produced tons of butter.

Follow the Shoreline Highway for the first 35 miles of the Mendocino Coast, driving north. Some locations and place names remain, but many photographs are of communities that are gone forever.

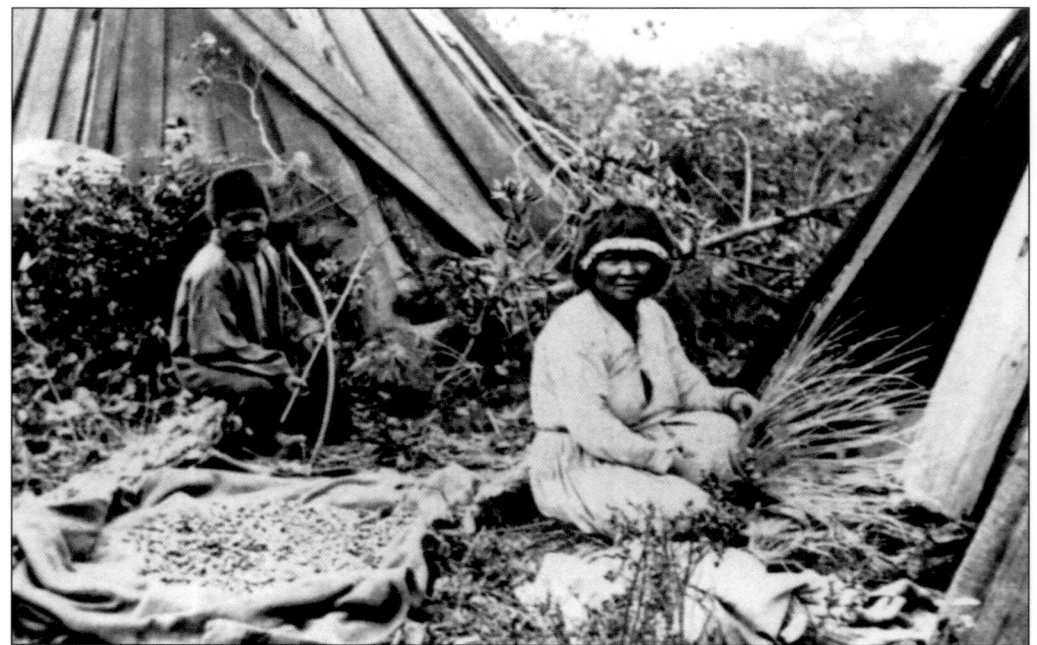

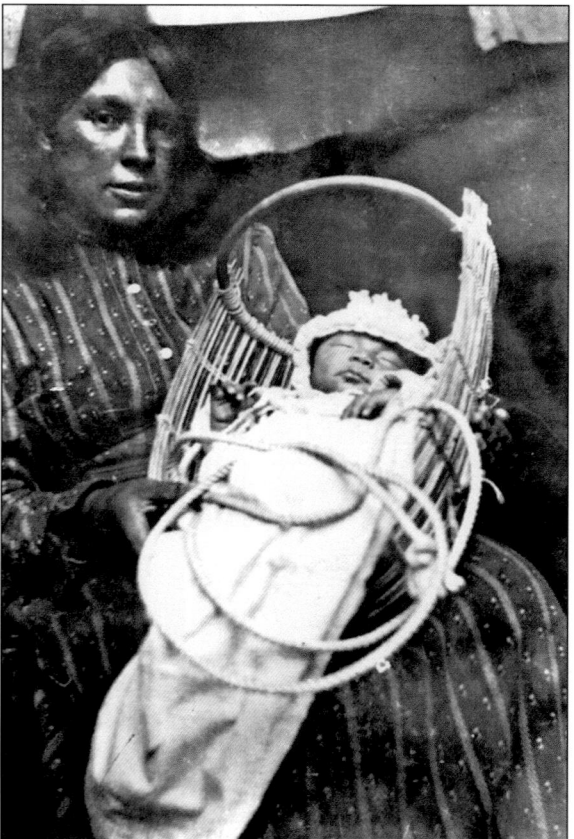

A Pomo woman works on a basket in front of a board shelter near Big River. Before European arrival, the shelter would have been made of slabs of redwood bark and wood. The boy shows his bow and arrow. Acorns, a major food source, are drying on a ground cloth before being ground into a meal.

While Pomo natives adopted Western dress, they retained their traditional baby baskets. The infants were tightly laced in, and a tumpline around the forehead allowed mothers to carry babies on their backs, leaving hands free for work. As infants grew bigger, larger baskets were made for them.

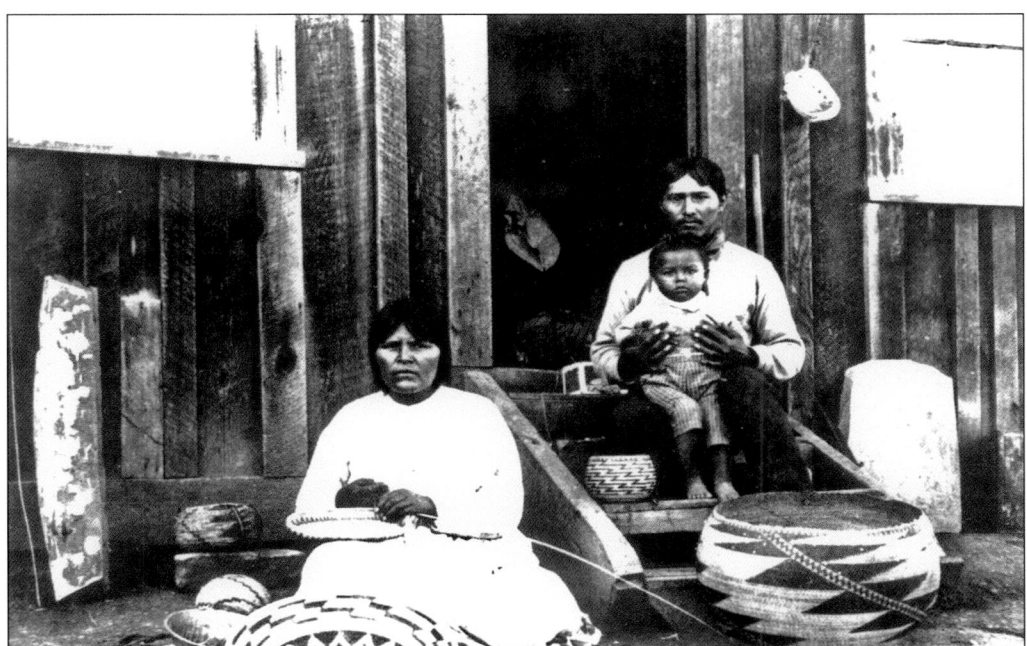

A basket maker sits with her family in front of their cabin with her handiwork on display. Pomo baskets could be as small as a fingertip or extra large for storage. They were so finely woven that they were waterproof. Cooking was done by putting heated rocks into the basket with food stuffs and water.

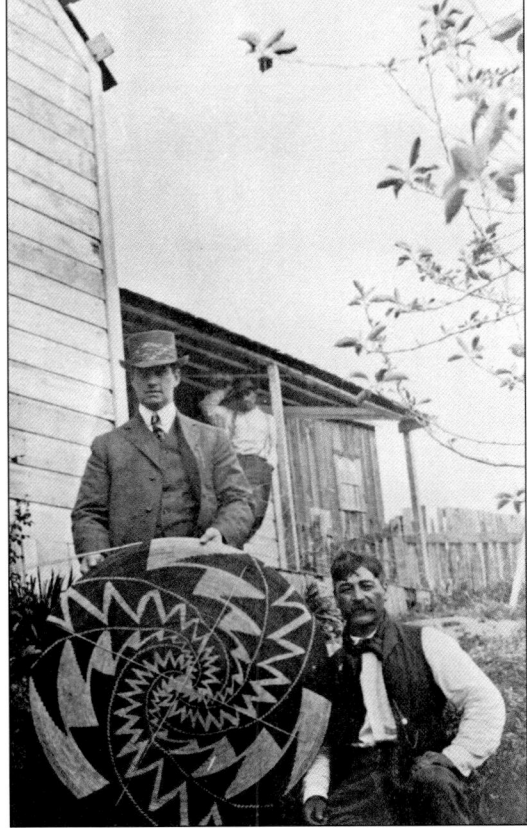

The intricacies and beauty of basket design can be seen in this unfinished basket in Point Arena about 1909. Baskets for the tourist trade were produced in larger sizes than those for traditional uses. Native women could earn their own money and support their families through basket sales.

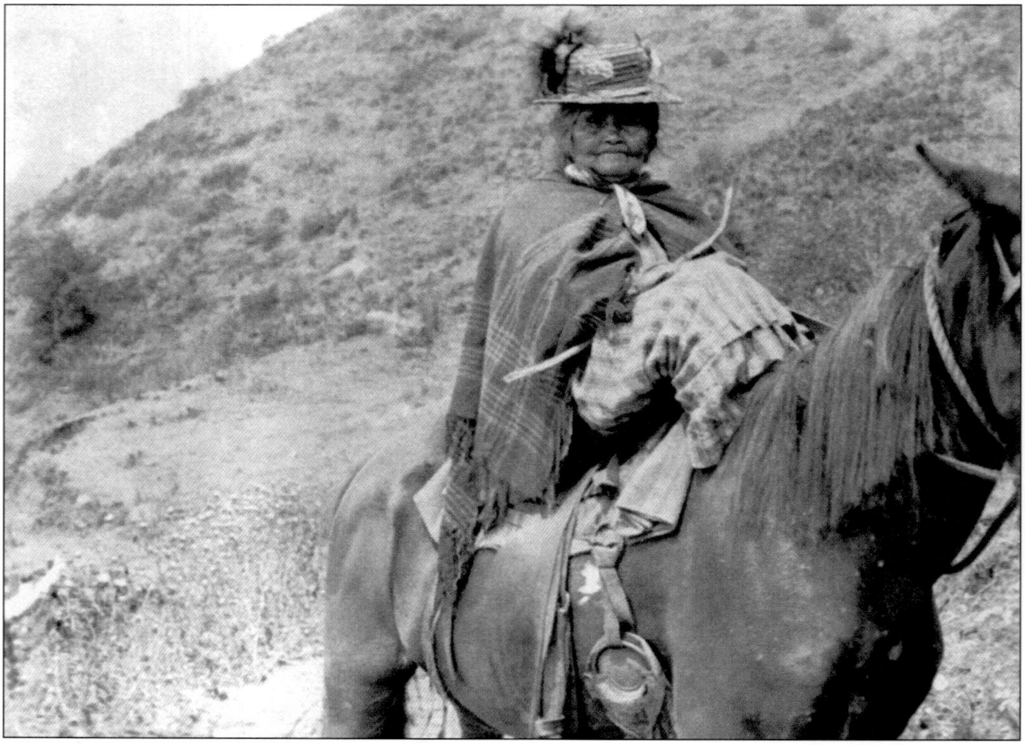

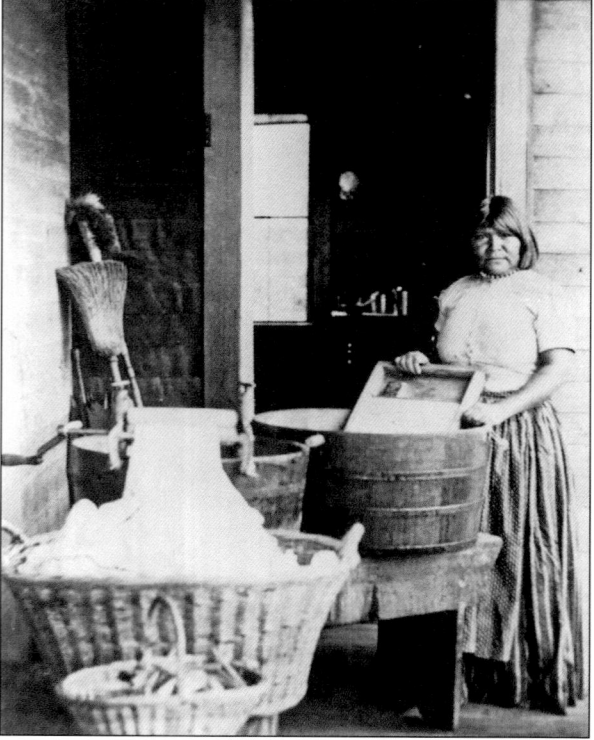

Susy Martin Turner was a Native American woman from the far north coast region of Usal. Riding side saddle, she is warmly dressed with a fashionable hat. Native American territory this far north along the coast was usually inhabited by the Coast Yuki tribe. Many early settlers married native women.

Native Americans quickly became the servants of the new settlers. Females became washer women and nannies for white children, and males worked menial jobs in sawmills and logging camps. Work as cooks usually fell into the hands of Chinese men. Native men on census records were often listed as "apprentice."

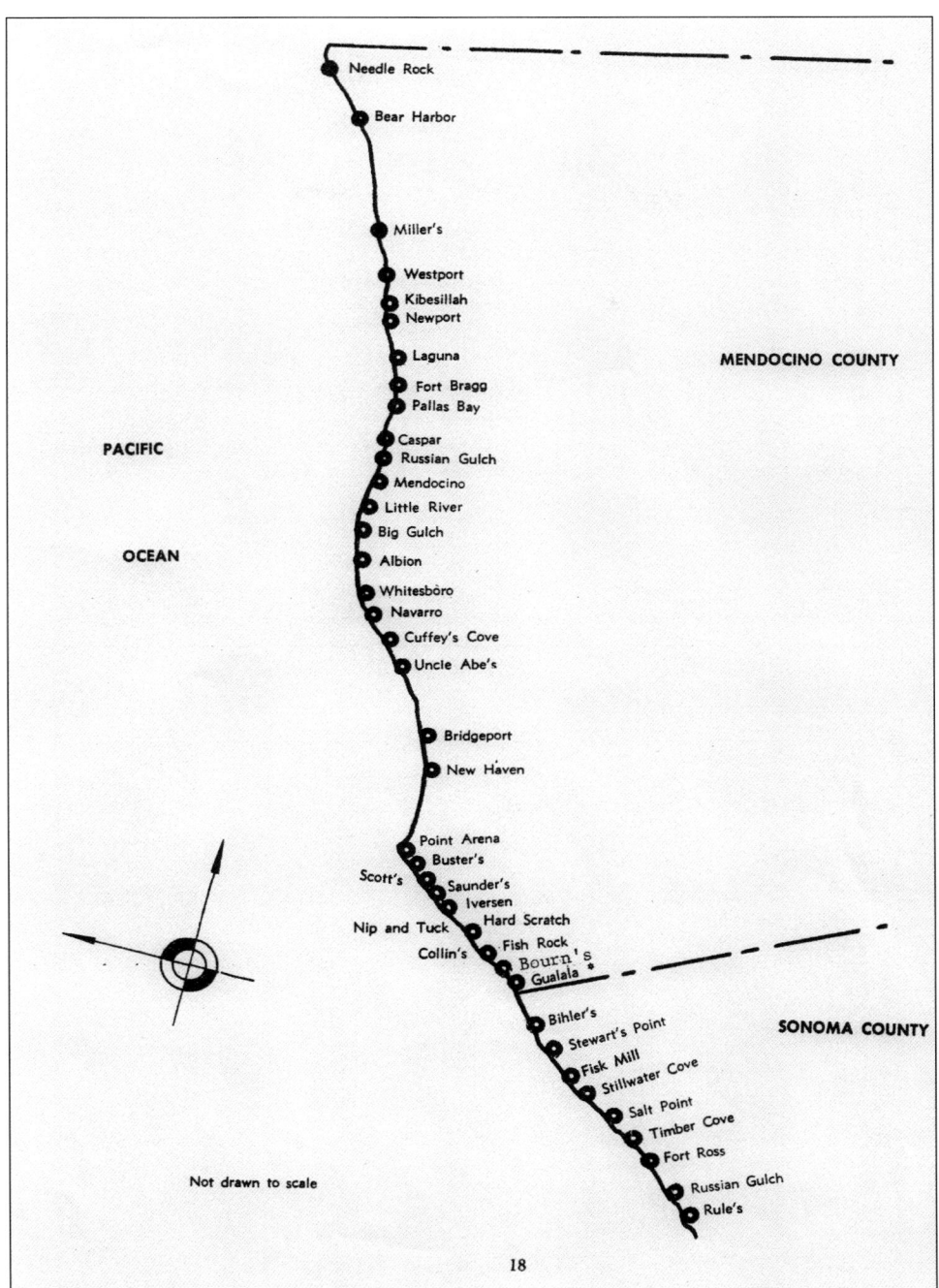

More than 80 towns, villages, and names of shipping points were attached to spots along coastal bluffs and riverbanks a century ago. Some places survived and prospered, and some folded up and vanished off the map. Some, like Kibesillah (Flat Rock), had native origins. Others, like Ten Mile River, let travelers know how far it was from the Noyo River to the next big river. The narrative of this book takes the reader from Gualala on the south to Needle Rock on the north of this map.

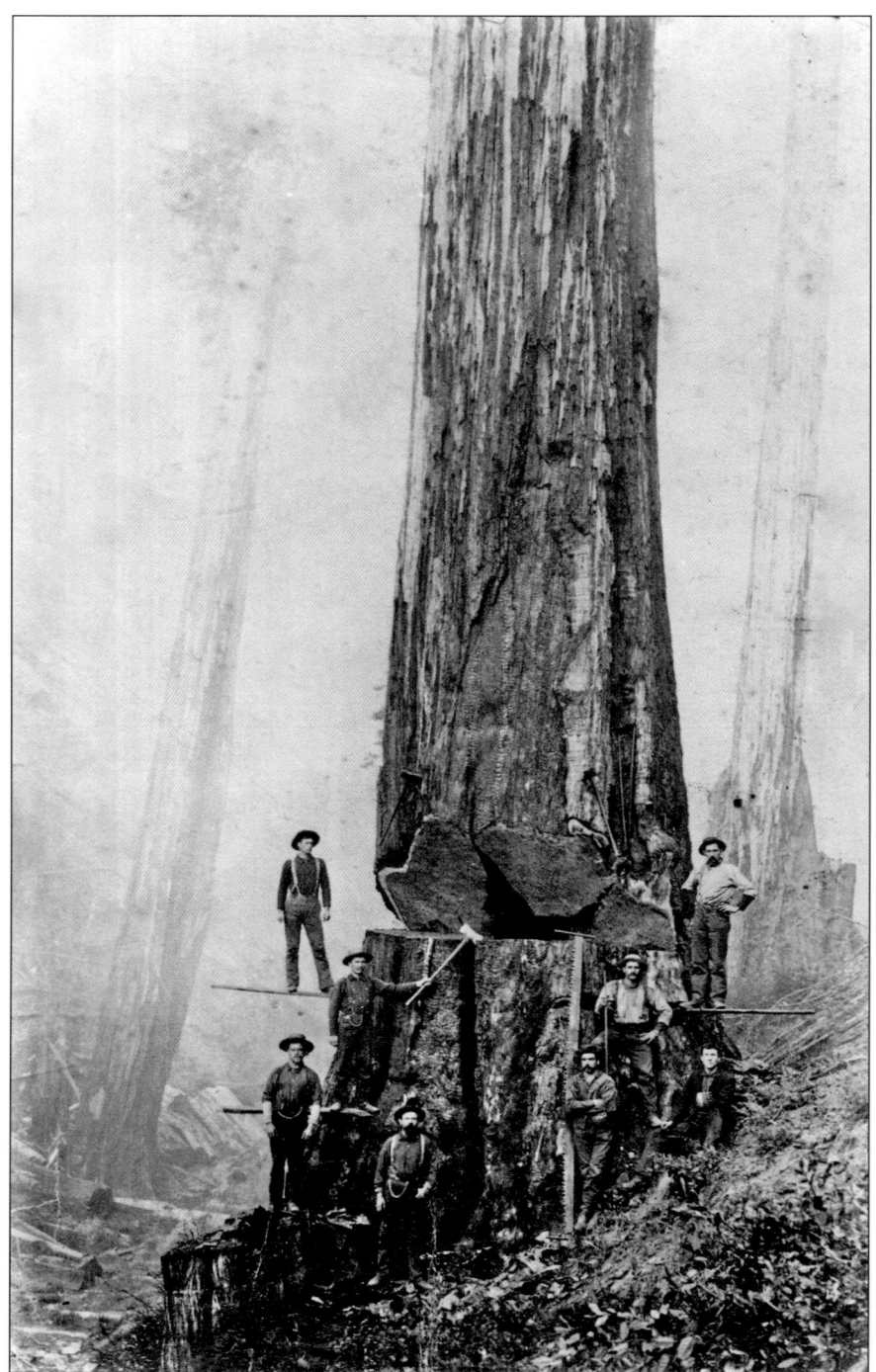
Taking down a big redwood took days of hard labor from a crew of men. These trees could not be cut at ground level because they were too big to move. Spring board holes notched into the tree supported fallers above the butt flare and allowed them to cut the tree into a manageable length. Spring board holes are visible in many old, moss-covered stumps today.

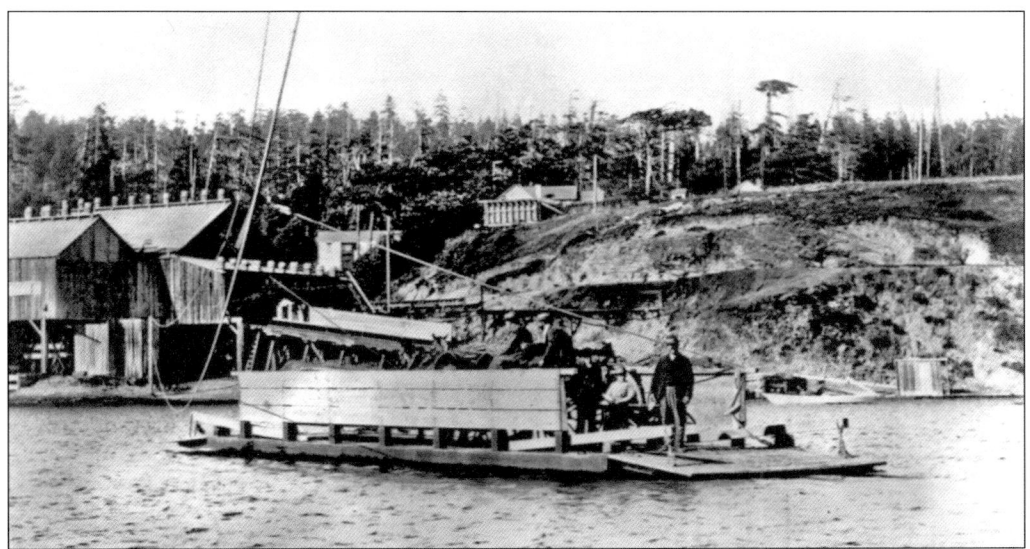

Entry into Mendocino County from the south necessitated the use of a ferry. It cost 75¢ for a horse-and-buggy to ride the ferry, and a foot passenger cost 25¢. Until a bridge was built, travelers paid the ferry toll or swam. In this 1890 view, sawmill buildings can be seen in the background. Note the water barrels on the roof of the mill. This was an early form of fire protection.

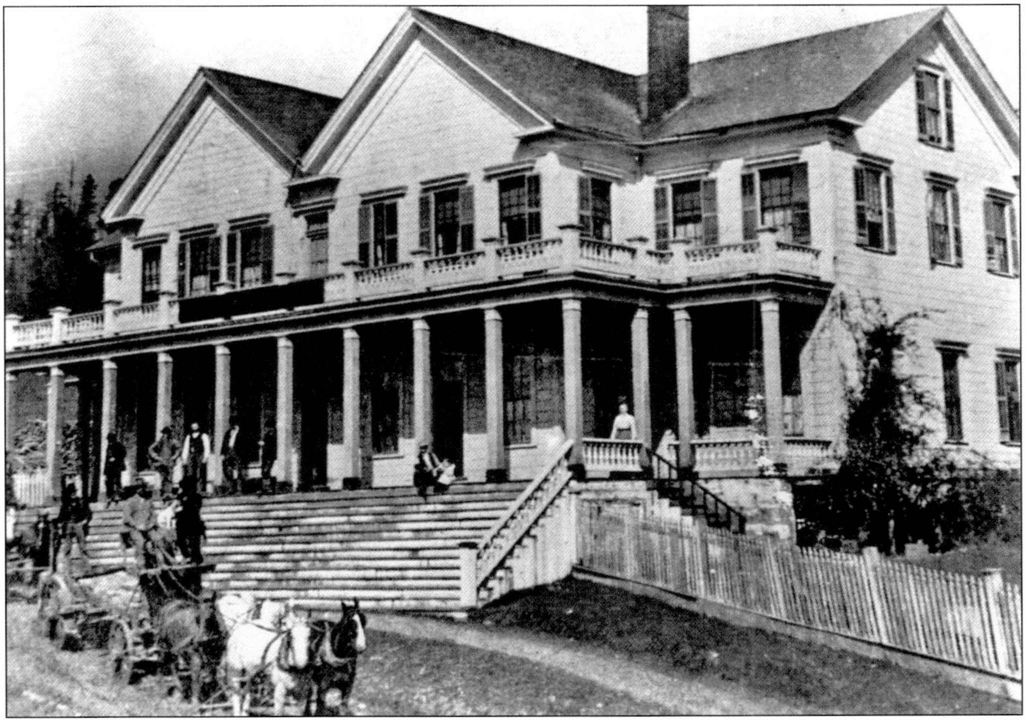

Opened in 1872, the Gualala House was the pride of the town and had the only saloon for 50 years. Coastal visitors and traveling salesmen stayed here, and mill workers boarded here. Jack London enjoyed steelhead fishing in Gualala. The hotel burned down in 1903, but the safe on the second floor with $18,000 in it was shoved out of a window and saved.

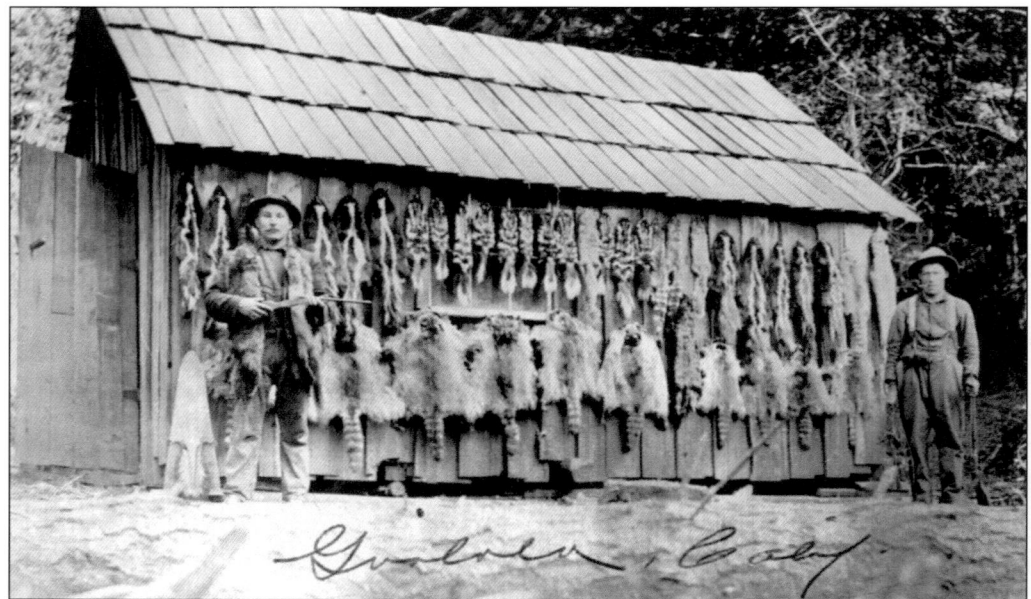

In addition to supplying venison and elk meat to cookhouses in the lumber camps and sawmills, hunters often ran trap lines to make additional income from furs. Here raccoons, civet cat (spotted skunk), and more cover a cabin wall. These Swedish hunters were proud of their catch in Gualala. Trapping on the Mendocino Coast continued through the Great Depression.

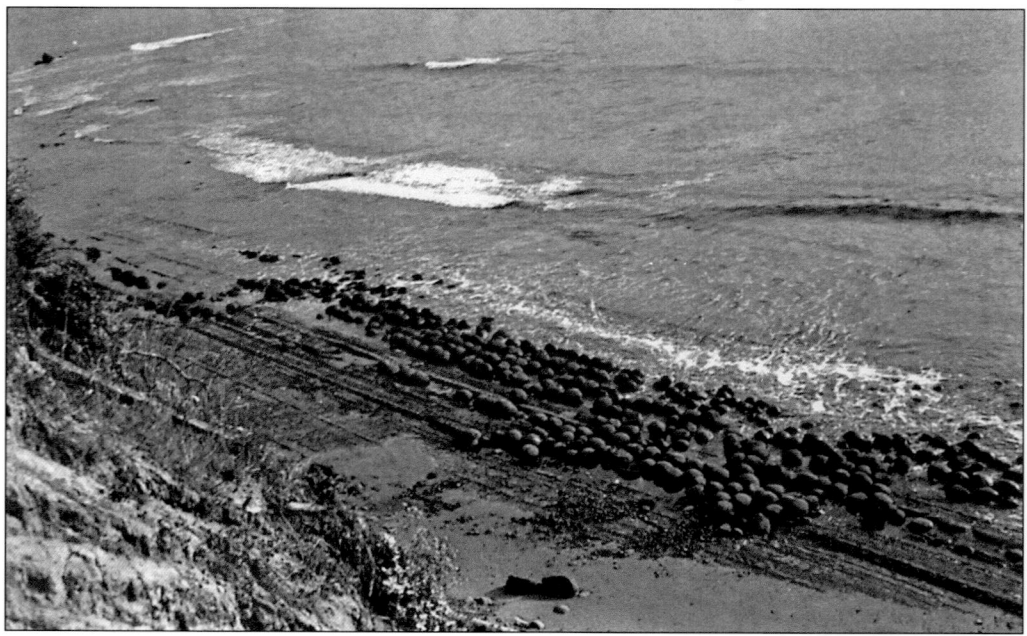

A small portion of state park land gives access to Schooner Gulch. There was an early shipbuilding venture here, and to the south is Bowling Ball Beach, so named because of the spherical sandstone rocks covering the area. Visitors should pay attention to the tides when accessing the area, as beach shoreline can disappear when high tides come in. The only parking in this area is on the west side of the Shoreline Highway, facing south.

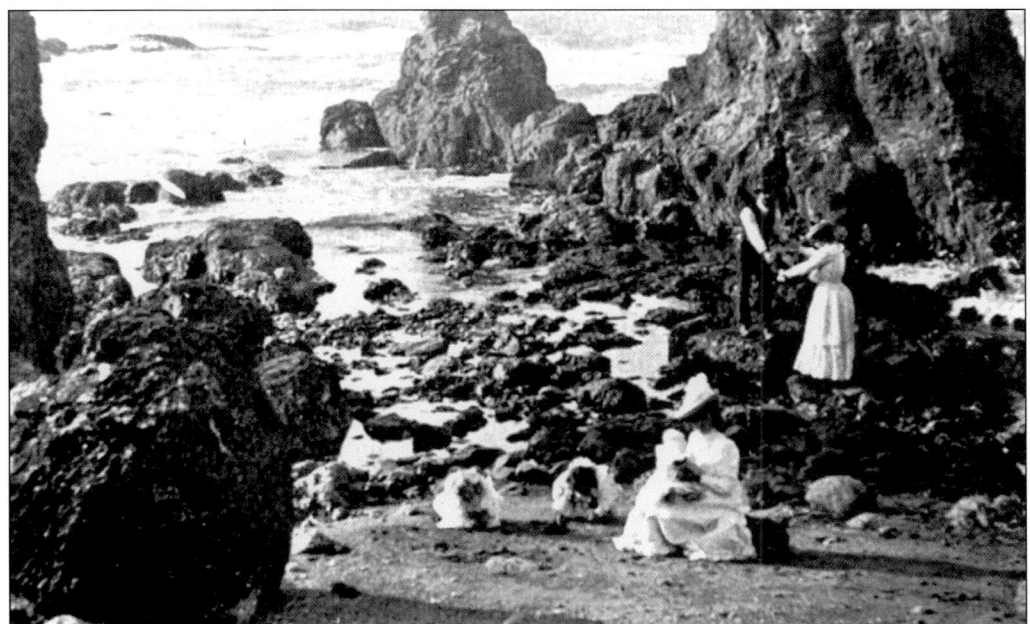

A photograph like this invites all sorts of questions. Why are the woman and girls dressed in white? Is this not rather fancy for a day on the beach? Is it a special occasion? What are the little girls looking at? Is the lady holding a baby? Will the people on the rocks slip? Perhaps they were stopping at the beach on the way home from a celebration or wedding.

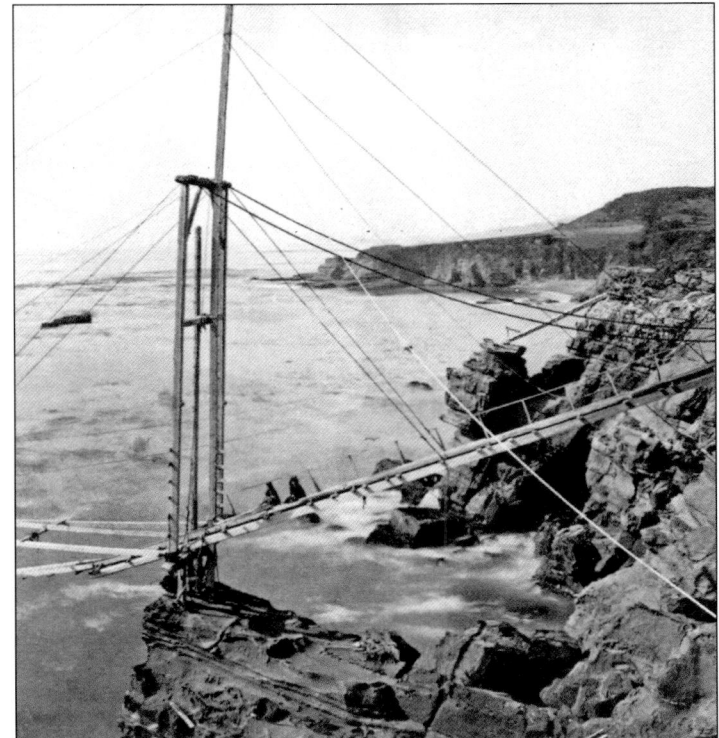

In this 1870 image by M. M. Hazetine, his daughters Althea and Effie are sitting on the loading chute at Robinson's Landing, north of Gualala. Chutes like these allowed cargo to be slid from the landing point on the bluff to the shops deck below. Winter storms often destroyed the fragile structures, which then had to be rebuilt.

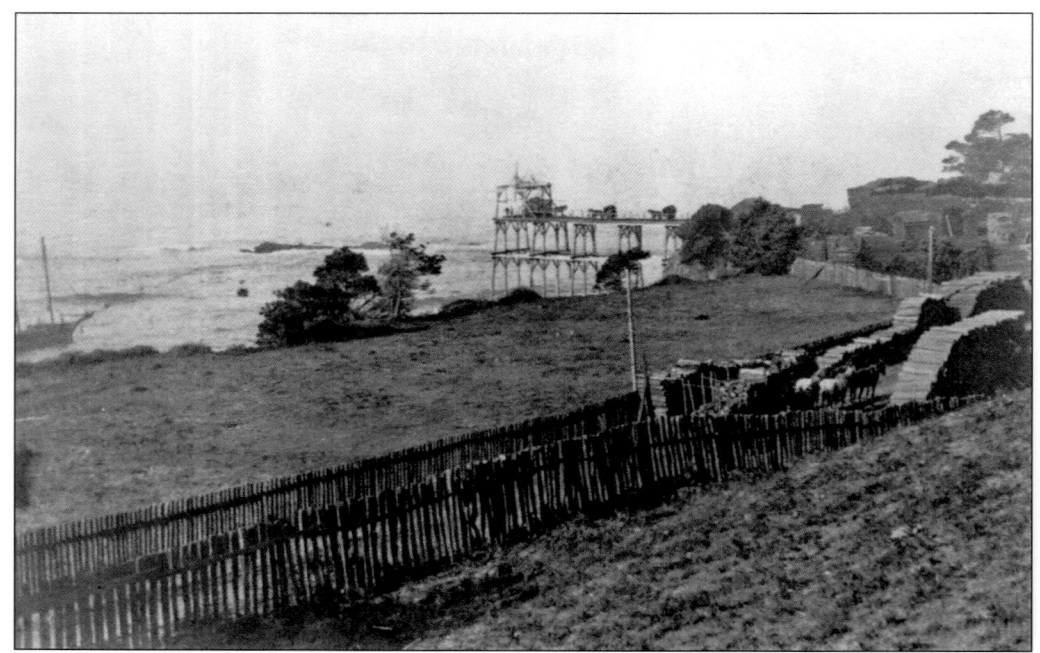

Bourne's Landing, or Haven's Anchorage, became the distribution point for goods coming into the Gualala area because it was a more protected anchorage than Robinson's. Trains and wagons brought goods to the shore for shipment. Tracks for the railroad were 68 inches apart so that two draft horses could walk side by side to pull a loaded car. Operations here lasted into the 1930s.

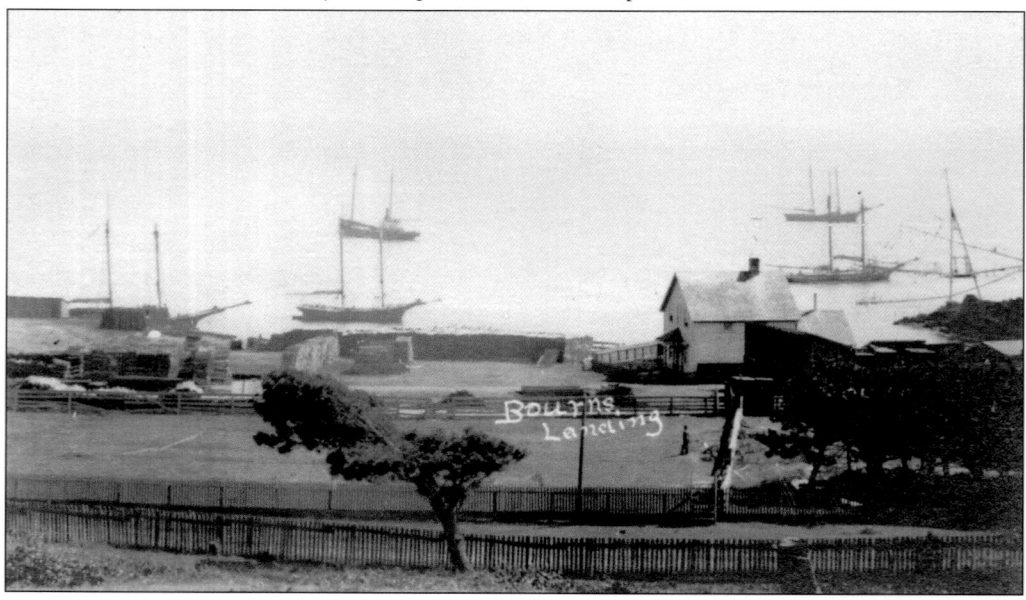

In 1870, the St. Ore's brothers developed a wire chute that stretched from shore to ship, lowering finished goods bundled in a sling. This was faster than an apron chute, which sent boards down one at a time. The brothers built a wharf, and in this c. 1897 photograph, loaded wagons wait their turns. Today St. Orre's Restaurant (spelling has changed) with its onion dome, a Russian architectural element, sits along this stretch of highway.

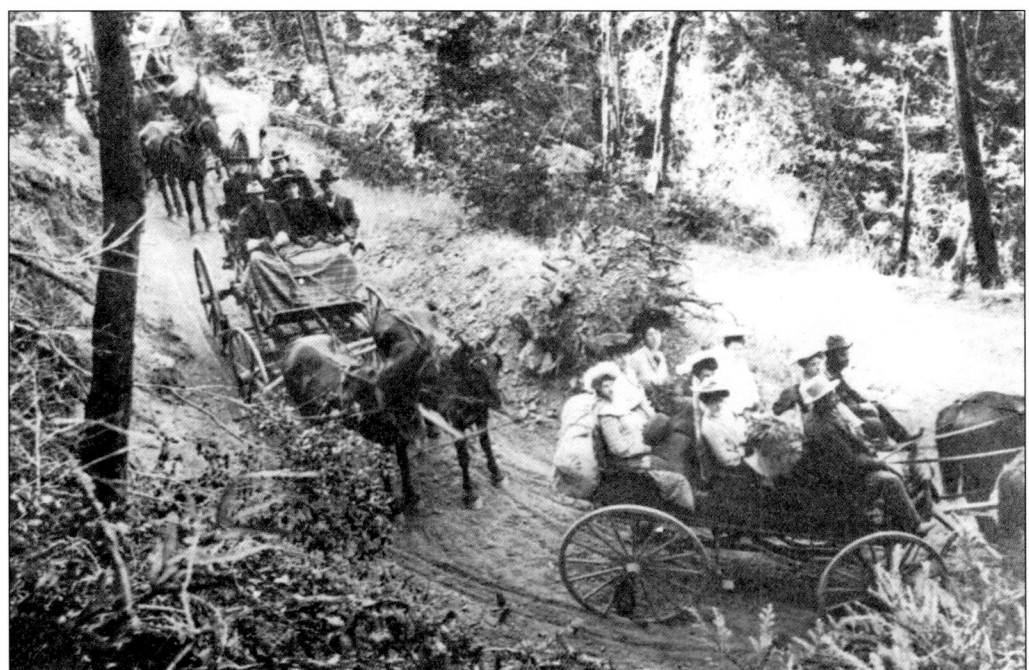

Stages took visitors seven miles up the Garcia River to Point Arena Hot Springs, which opened in 1904. A rustic hotel with dining, dancing, and swimming pool, it included six 112-degree mineral springs. Twelve dollars a week paid for room, board, and amusements—including hunting, fishing, croquet, billiards, a bowling alley, and a darkroom for photographers.

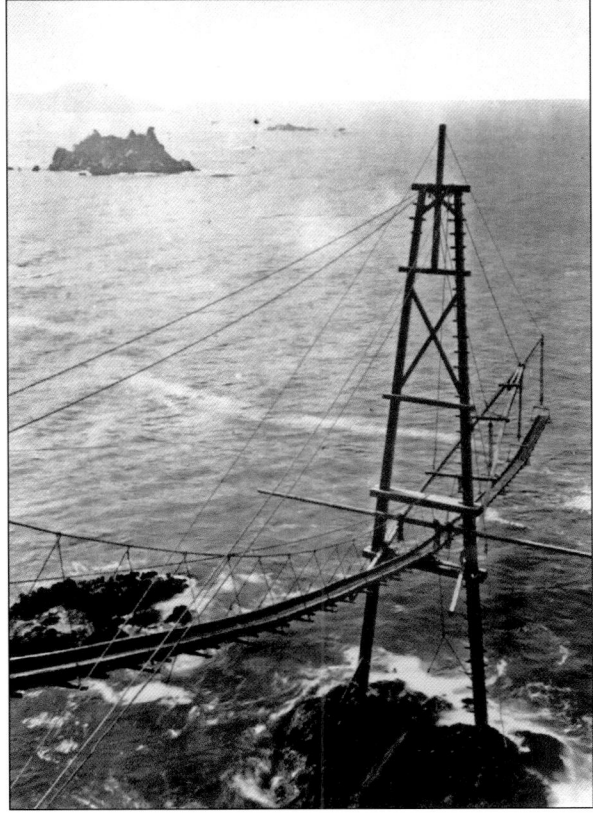

Nip and Tuck was the name of the next apron chute shipping point north of Collins. Names like this one and that of the area called Rough and Ready might describe the tight spots coastal schooners had to fit into to get a load of lumber. Perched on a 75-foot-high bluff, Nip and Tuck had been abandoned by 1885.

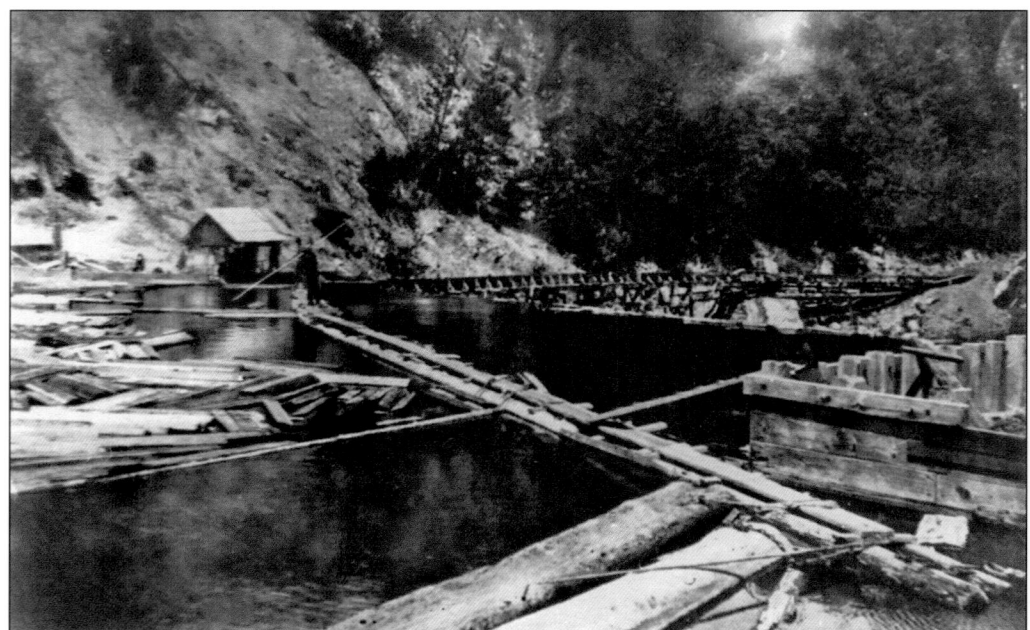

On the Garcia River, ties and boards were started on a longer ride down the flume. The flume chute appears as a ladder-like structure toward the back of the photograph. Men on a catwalk would pole the ties to the intake. This flume in 1889 ran at night because upriver winds from the northwest slowed movement during the day.

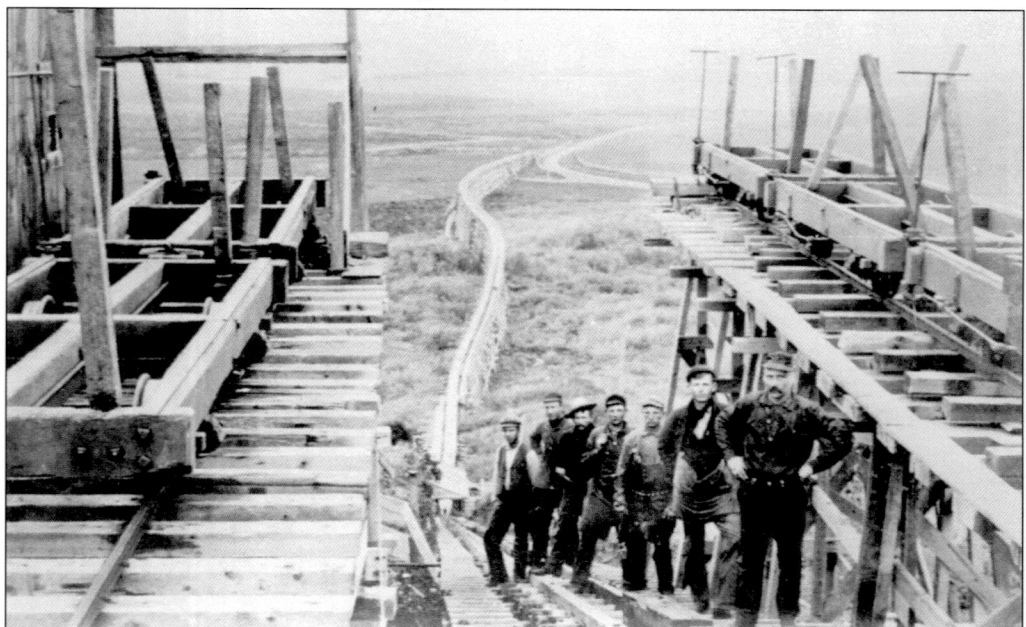

In 1897, the hoisting crew at Rollerville stands on the lifting rollers. From the starting point seven miles up the Garcia River, it took four hours for the ties to travel down river. Five thousand ties a day passed along the flume, which was 30 inches wide. The flume was abandoned and torn down about 1915.

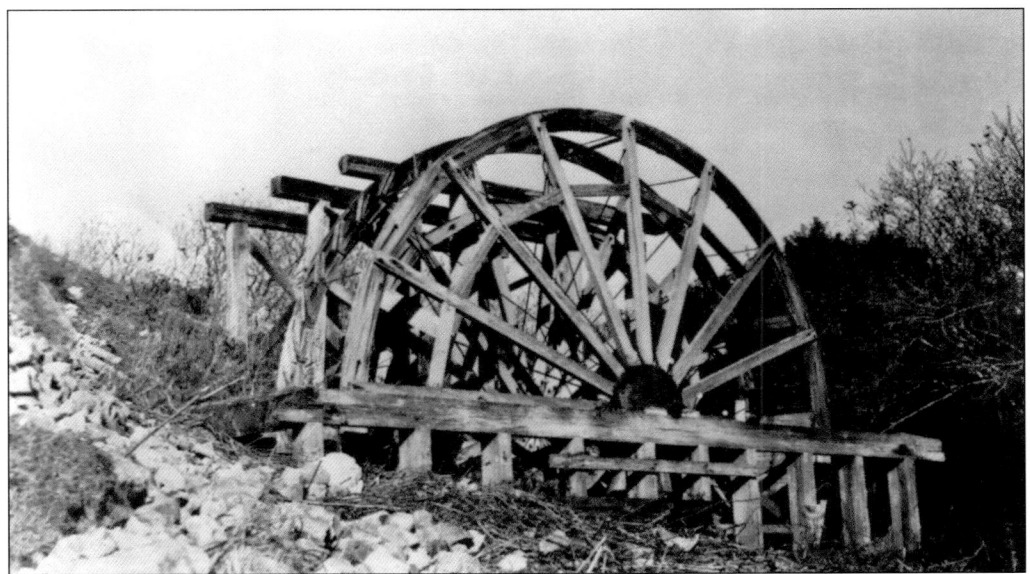

An overshot waterwheel provided power to the hoisting works, where lumber encountered traverse lifting rollers set at three-foot intervals. The cog gears on these rollers, which were covered in short spikes, matched cog gears on an iron shaft within the flume powered by this waterwheel. The power of water coming down the river flume forced the lumber onto the spiked rollers, and that lumber traveled uphill at a 45 degree angle from roller to roller 300 feet to the top. There a tramway, and later a railroad, hauled the lumber to the port. This photograph shows the remains of the wheel about 1930.

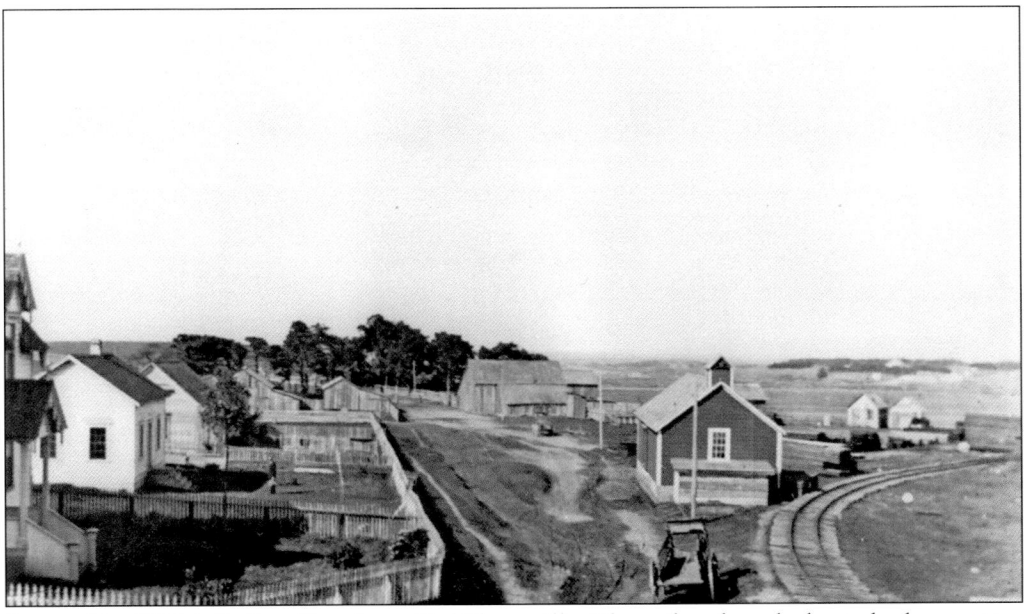

Pictured in 1906 is Rollerville, also called Flumeville. The railroad tracks hosted a locomotive so small it was nicknamed "the Coffee Pot." All the lumber from the Garcia River flume passed through town toward shipping points. Today this is the turnoff westward to the Point Arena Lighthouse from Shoreline Highway.

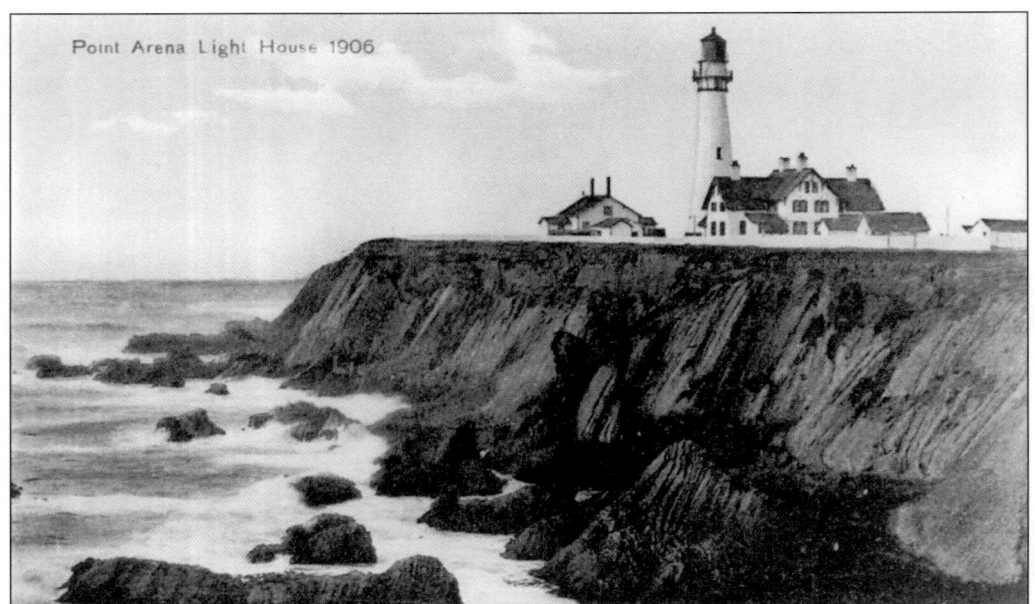

Punta de Arenas (Sandy Point) was always a dangerous spot for coastal shipping, so a 156-foot-tall lighthouse was built in 1870. A kiln was built on site, and 500,000 bricks were made for the tower. Built for $120,000, it burned lard oil originally for a light visible 19 miles to sea. A steam fog whistle sounded during dense fog.

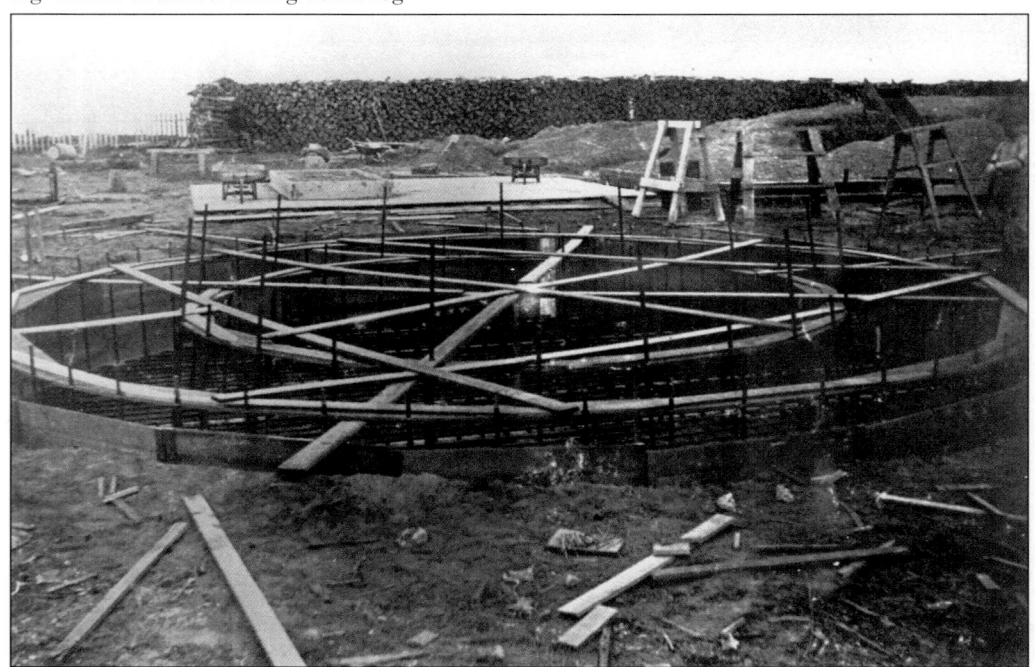

The 1906 earthquake cracked the brick lighthouse tower, and it was torn down and rebuilt of concrete laced with steel by 1908. The 1939 lighthouse keeper's homes are now available as vacation rentals. In the winter, the Garcia Riverflats to the north host visiting tundra whistling swans with seven-foot wingspans.

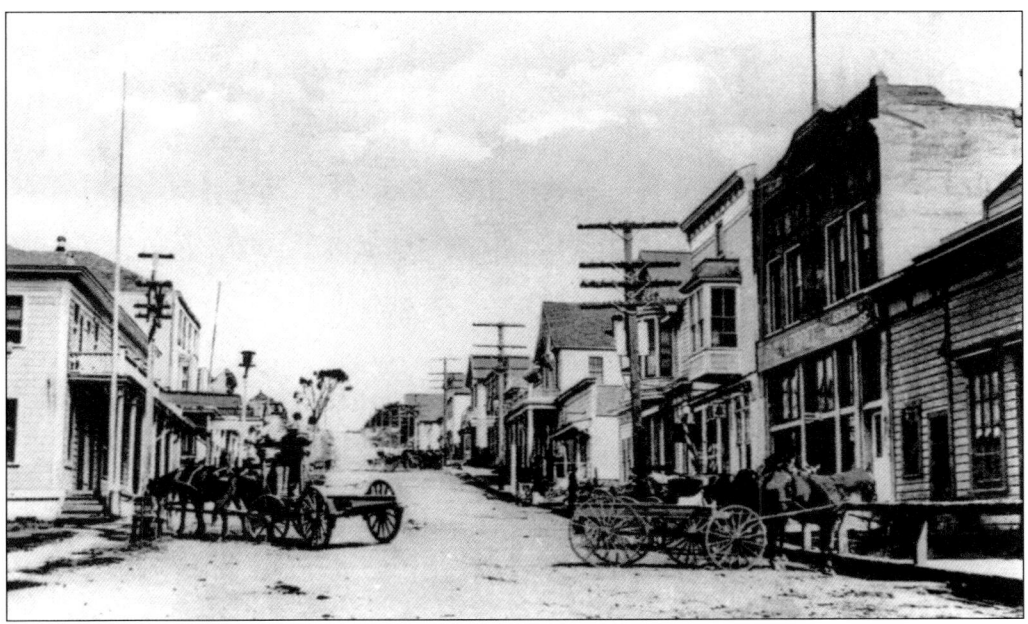

More than a century ago, Point Arena was a bustling business center. The Point Arena harbor and wharf made it a popular shipping point for wood products brought in from surrounding areas. Arena Cove had a whaling station, and today the cove offers some of the best surfing on the coast.

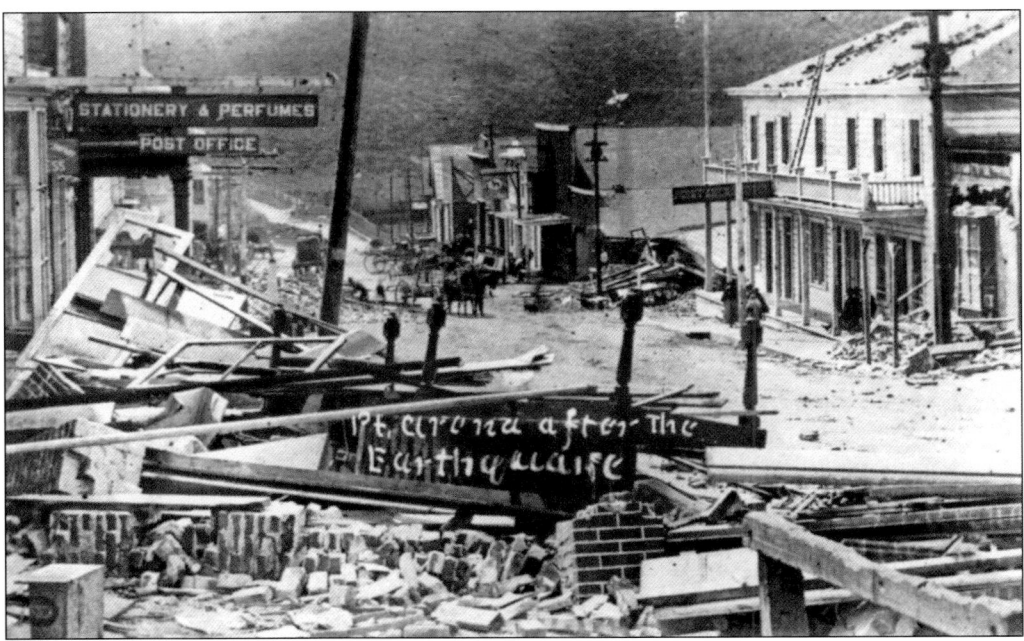

The few downtown buildings that survived the 1906 earthquake were again damaged when a devastating fire swept the town in 1927. The town, founded in 1859, had a tannery, paper mill, and a big lumber mill up the Garcia River to support it. It remains one of the smallest incorporated cities in the state of California.

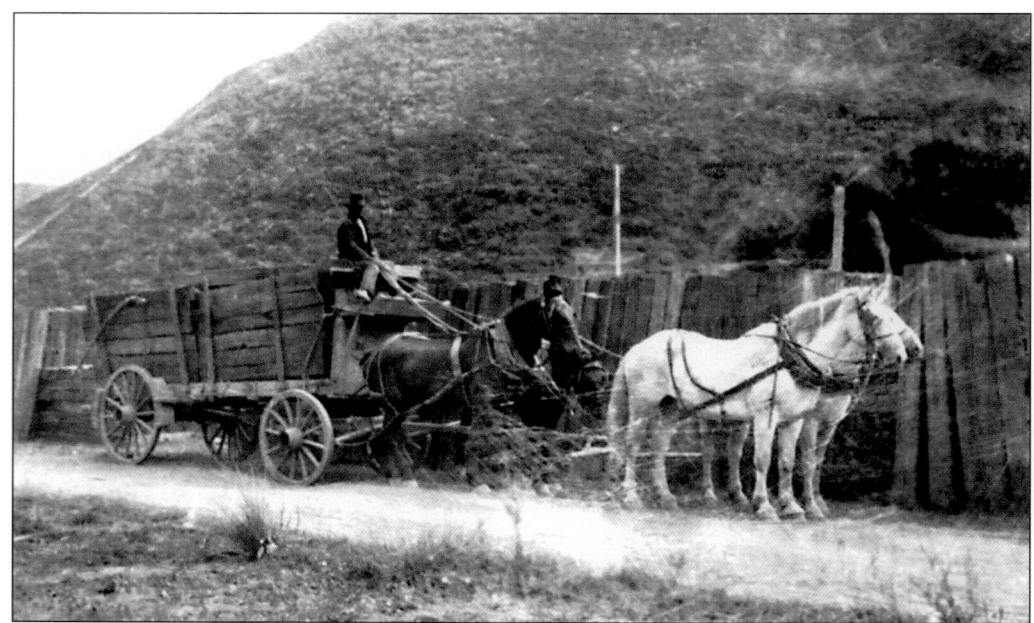

A railroad tie wagon on the coast road that would one day become the Shoreline Highway headed to the New Haven landing near Manchester. South of town, the 1911 Manchester School awaits restoration along the west side of the road. Brush Creek was the site of the 1868 Eagle Paper Mill, which was short-lived due to a lack of raw materials.

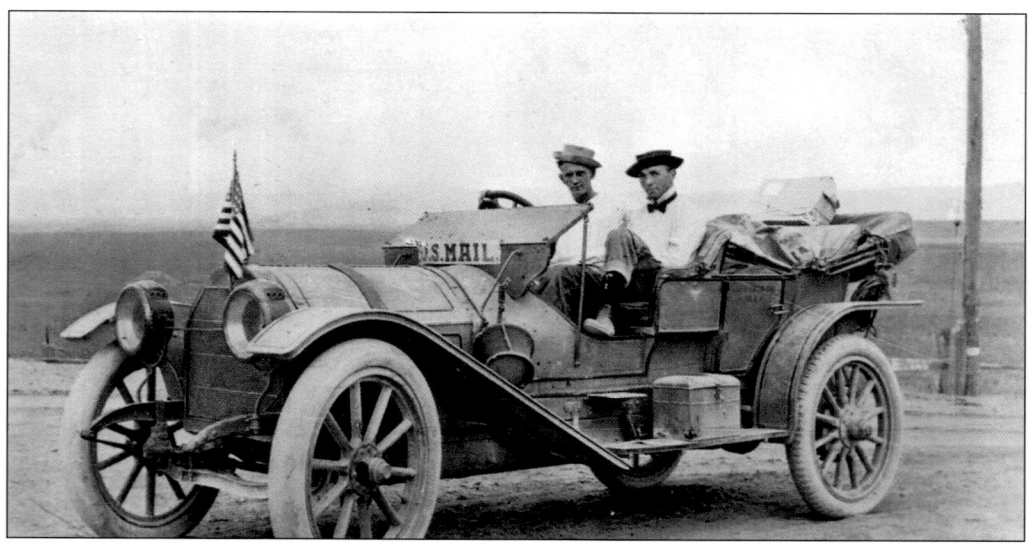

Flying a flag and sporting a United States Mail sign to signify its importance, a car stops along the Shoreline Highway. Mail delivery by car was a speedy improvement over horse-drawn stage lines.

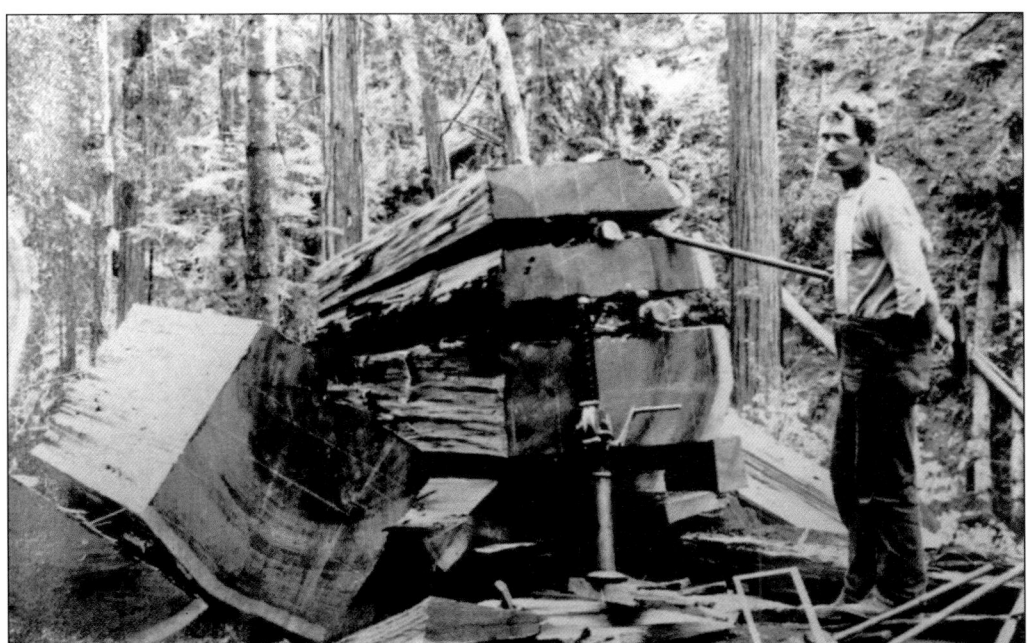

The slow, tedious, backbreaking process of splitting railroad ties can be seen in this photograph taken near Manchester. Jackscrews and gluts (wooden wedges) aid this individual in 1909. For a tie 8 feet long and 6-by-8 inches, a "tiewacker" would receive less than 50¢. On an especially good day, a man might earn $8 splitting ties.

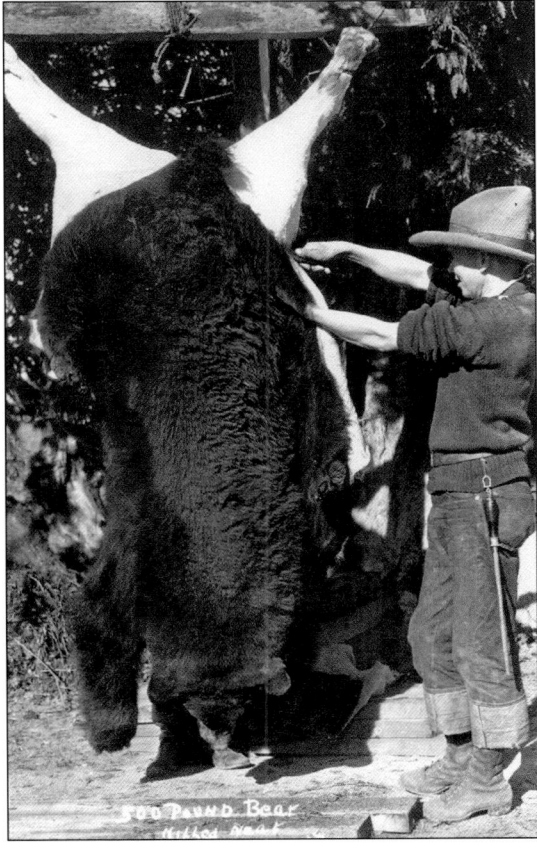

When the Manchester area was first settled, it was famous for its grizzly bear population down along Alder Creek. The skin of this bear will mostly likely be tanned in local tanneries to provide warmth over a bed in a cold, drafty cabin in the winter. The bear meat was eaten in cookhouses, and melted bear fat grease was rubbed into leather boots for water proofing. Manchester is also famous for butter production.

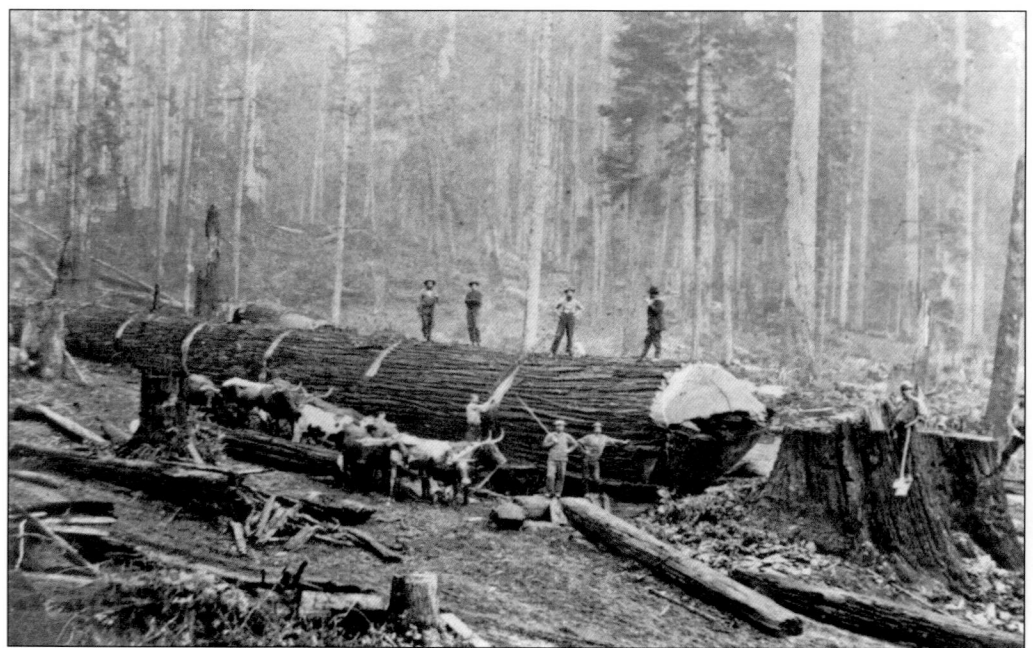

Almost all aspects of early redwood logging can be seen in this photograph. The chopper with his ax stands by the stump. The buckers are dividing the 12-foot-thick log into movable, 20-foot sections. The ox or bull team awaits, and the bull puncher is ready to drive the team with a goad stick when they take off down the trail.

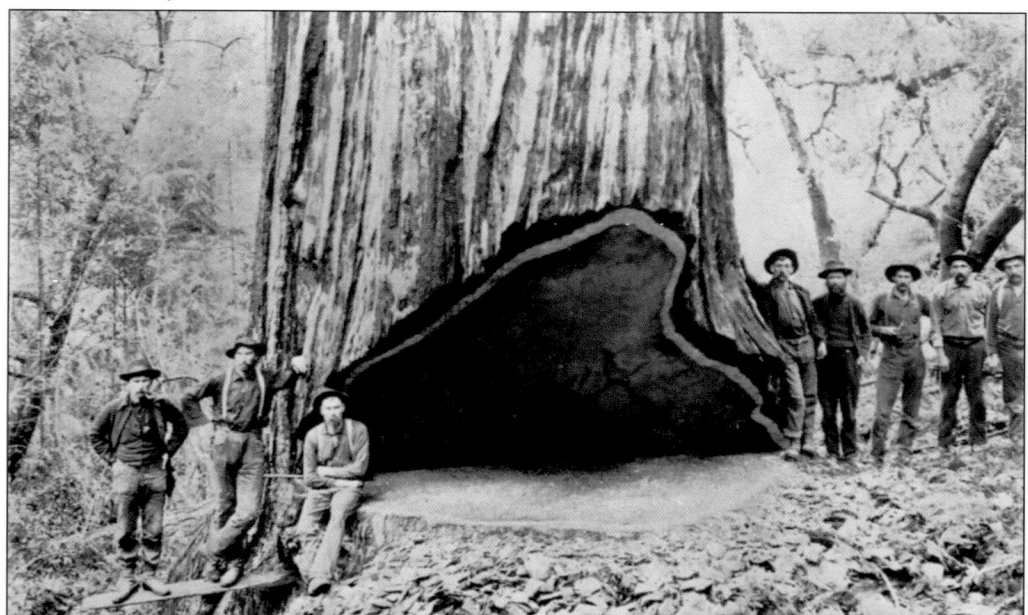

Loggers stand next to a cut in a redwood with an 18-foot diameter on Alder Creek prior to 1911. There was a three-foot-wide, narrow gauge railroad 17 miles up Alder Creek, and logs were hauled to Greenwood for milling. Finns, Irish, Italians, Russians, and Chinese were part of the multiethnic woods crews on the North Coast.

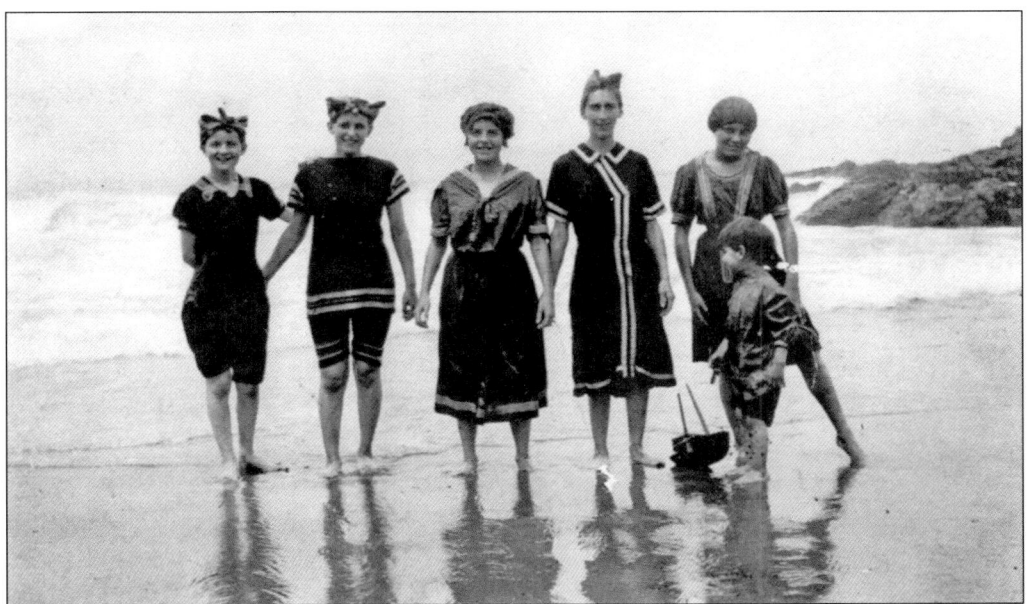

Bathing beauties of an earlier age cavort on a Mendocino Coast beach. Their bare lower limbs may have been scandalous to some old-timers. The Pacific Ocean is always cold, so the heavy bathing costumes of the era were probably welcome. Crab parties were popular: crabs were caught and brought to a pot of boiling water on a beach campfire for an instant dinner.

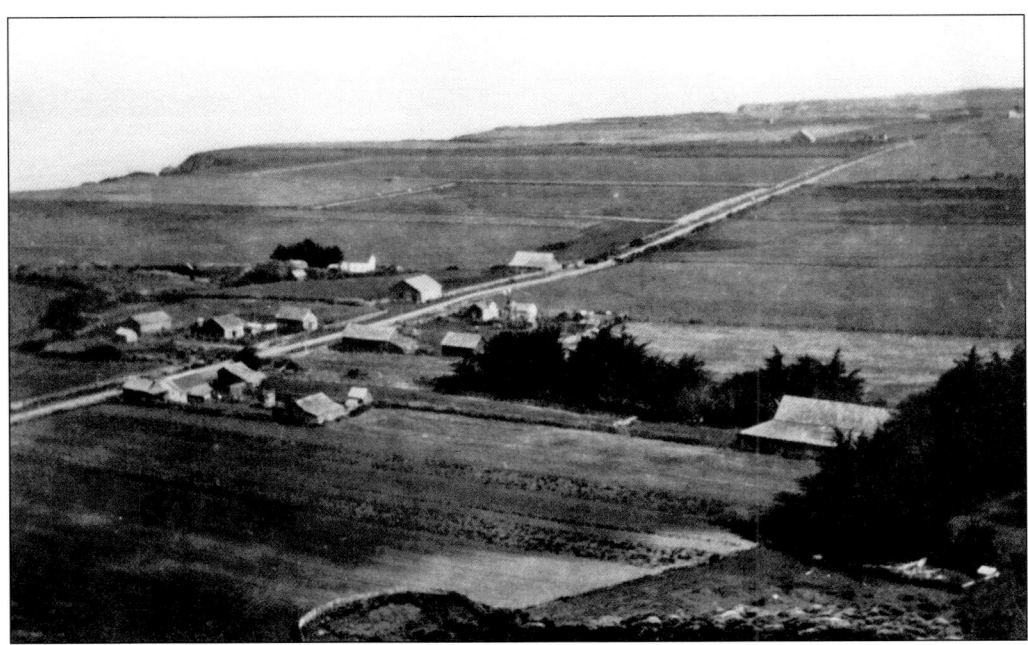

Bridgeport is even less populated today than it was in this early photograph. New Haven was the nearest landing, two miles south. There was a creamery, a school that lasted from 1860 to 1900, and a mill up Switzer Gulch with 70 employees. The rich loam soil—10 to 15 feet deep—produced two-pound onions, 35-pound cabbages, and 100-pound beets.

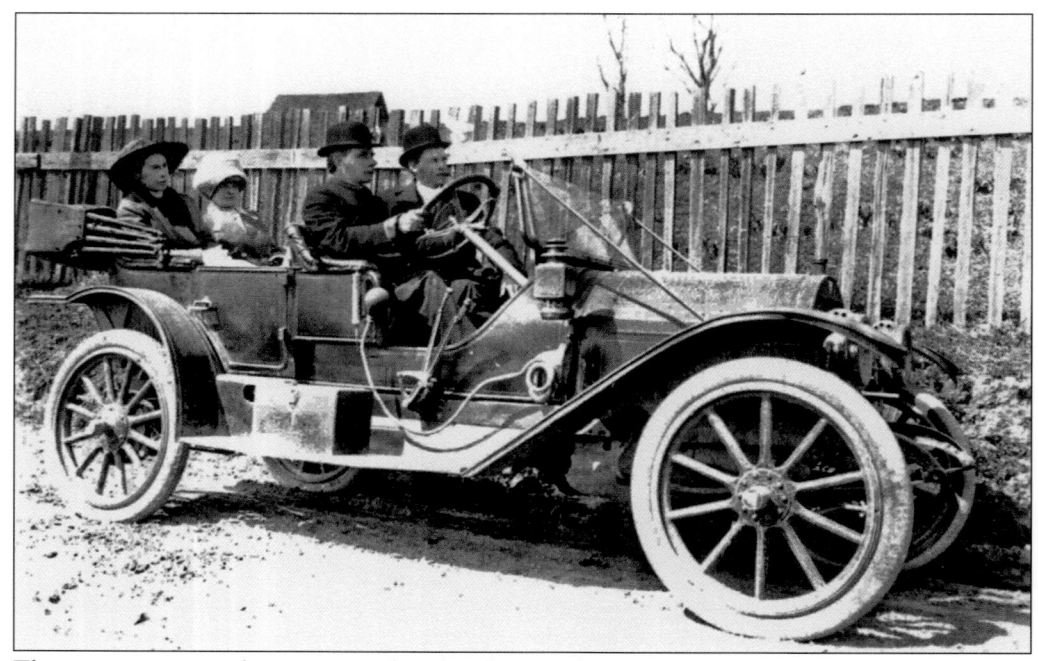

These motorists out for a spin on the Shoreline Highway appear very serious. It could be they were just cold from moving along at such a brisk rate. Fences here kept livestock off the road, but animals in the road were a constant problem for early drivers. A blast on the horn by the driver's hand might clear the roadway.

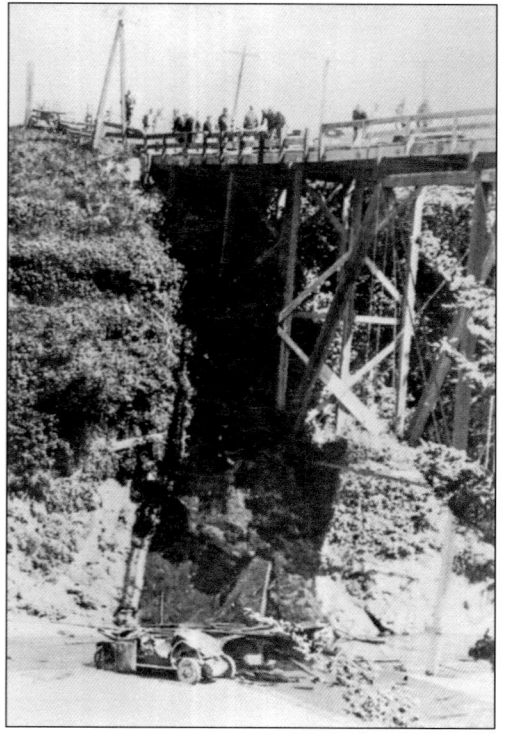

The spot on the Shoreline Highway is unidentified but it could be any one of the hundreds of creek crossings. A moment's inattention to driving was as dangerous then as it is now. And accidents attract as many onlookers now as they did then. It's hard to tell if the car went off the cliff or over the rail. (Courtesy author's collection.)

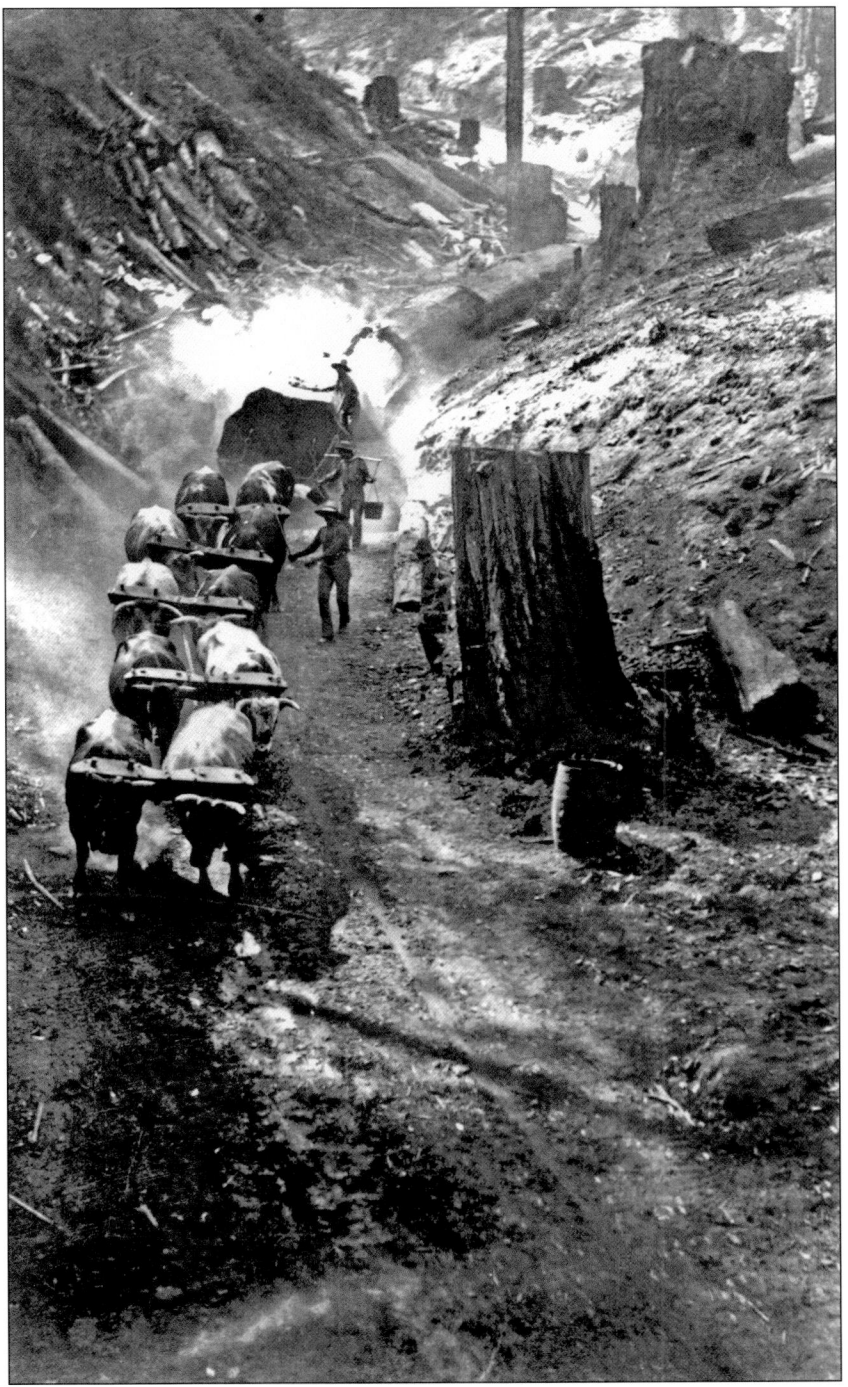

As oxen pulled their loads down skid roads, the bull puncher is visible driving the oxen onward, and water boys, or "slingers," with buckets are wetting the road to slick it up so the load slides along easier. Chinese were often used for water boys. Use of oxen teams ceased around 1915 when steam-powered equipment took over.

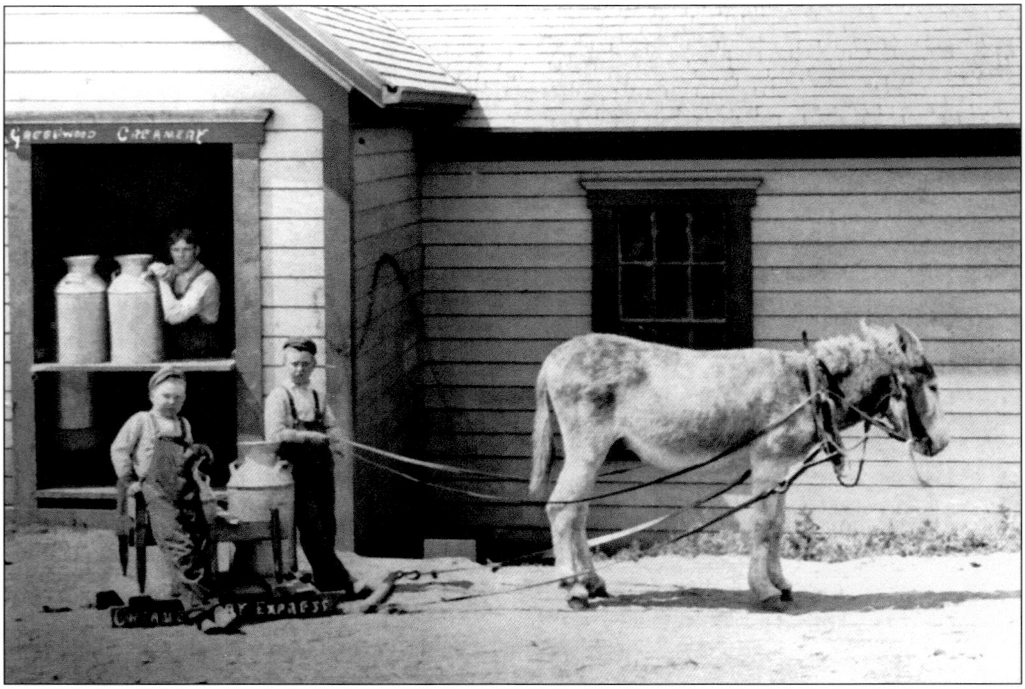

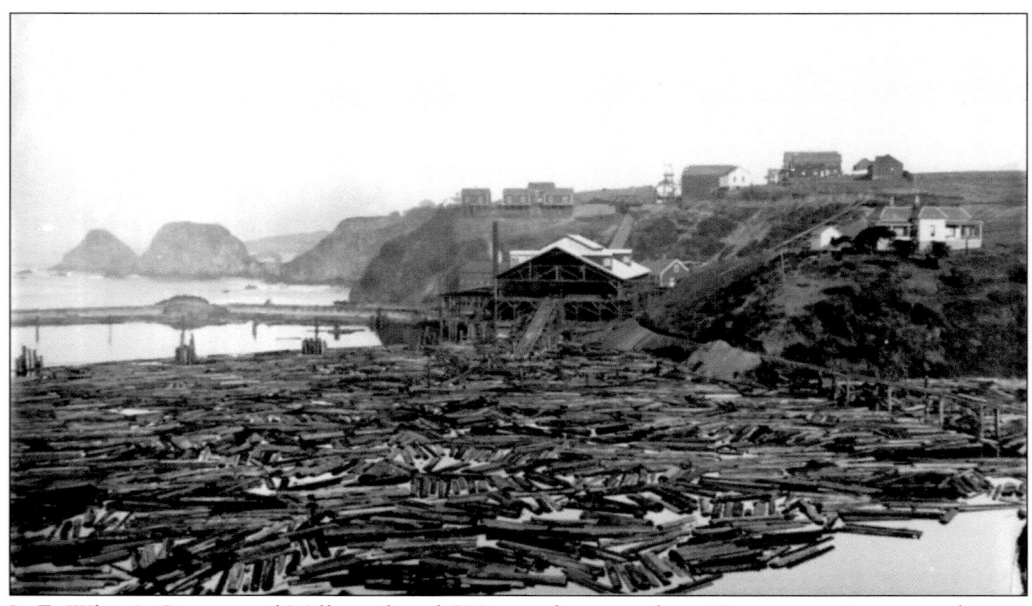

Creameries like this one in Greenwood/Elk produced butter for export to San Francisco or locally to cookhouses at sawmills and logging camps. Fresh milk and cream were always preferable to "canned cow." A local dairy with 56 cows produced 400 pounds of butter a week. North Coast butter sold for 32¢ a pound in San Francisco in 1894.

L. E. White's Greenwood Mill employed 500 men for more than 25 years starting around 1900. A fleet of four ships hauled lumber to San Francisco, and $5 bought a passenger a 12 to 16 hour voyage to the big city.

Before oxen could drag or "skid" logs through the woods, a roadbed called a skid road had to be prepared. There were always plenty of raw materials to work with. Small logs filled in the spaces between bigger ones. A steam donkey engine in the background to the left of the tree helped move the heavy stuff in 1897.

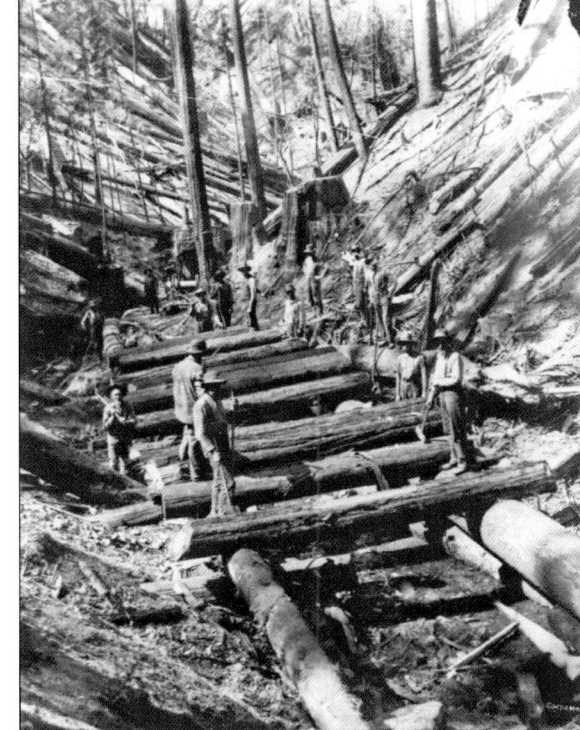

A finished skid road eased log transport. Water or grease was applied to the road ahead of the load. Boiled-down mutton tallow, bear fat, and seal oil were all used, if available. Horses or oxen could be used for teams. Oxen were stronger but horses were considered more intelligent.

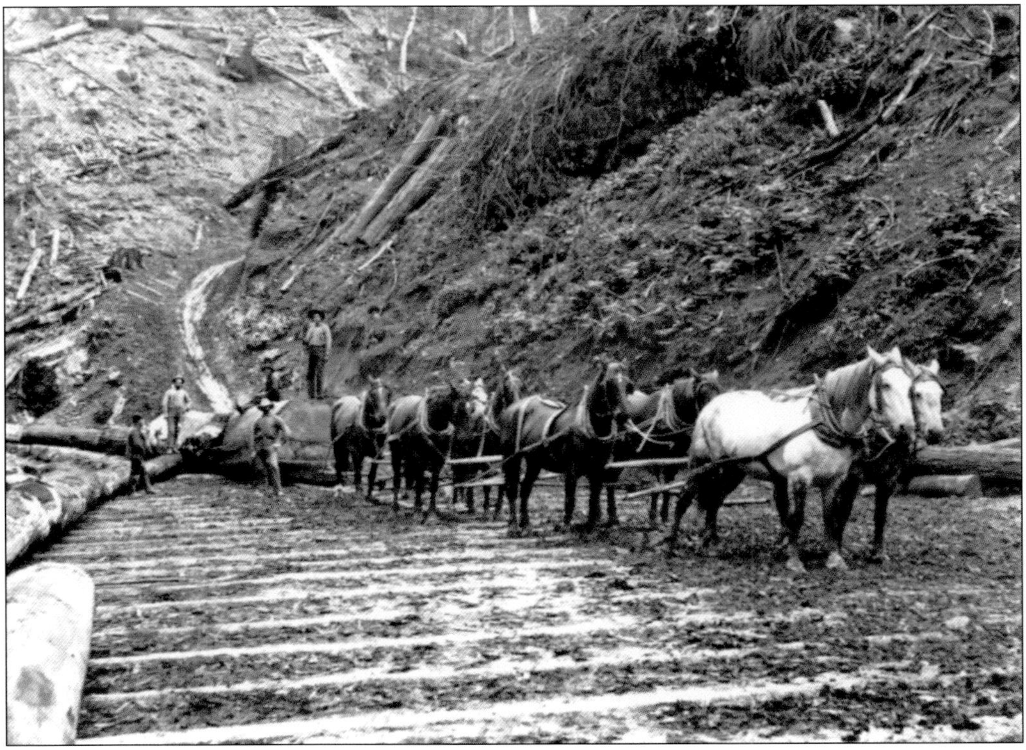

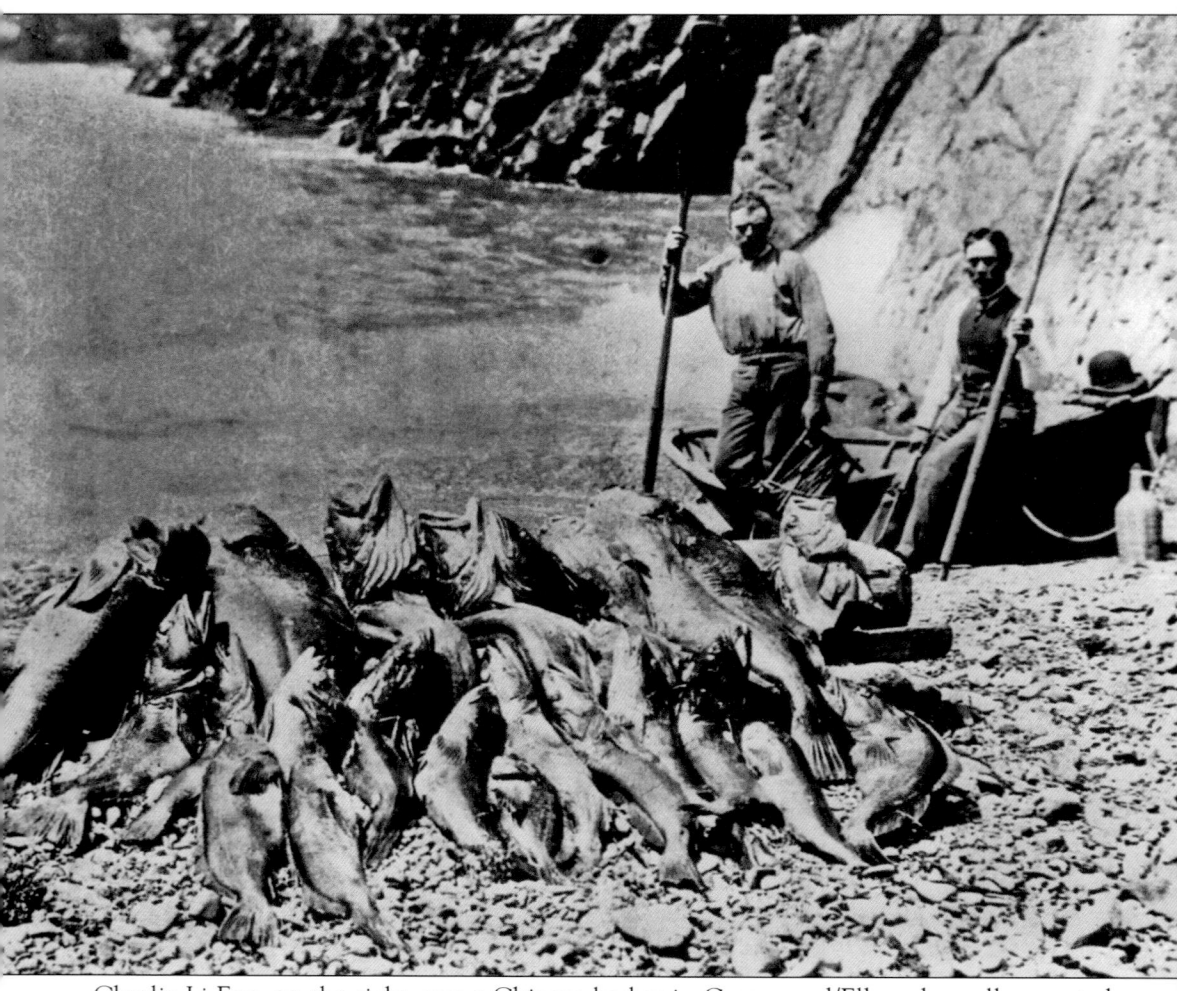

Charlie Li Foo, on the right, was a Chinese barber in Greenwood/Elk and a well-respected businessman. Earlier in life, he lost a leg in a logging accident. Here he is with an afternoon catch of Lingcod and bottom fish, which were most likely offered for dinner in the cookhouse that night. Li Foo died in 1898.

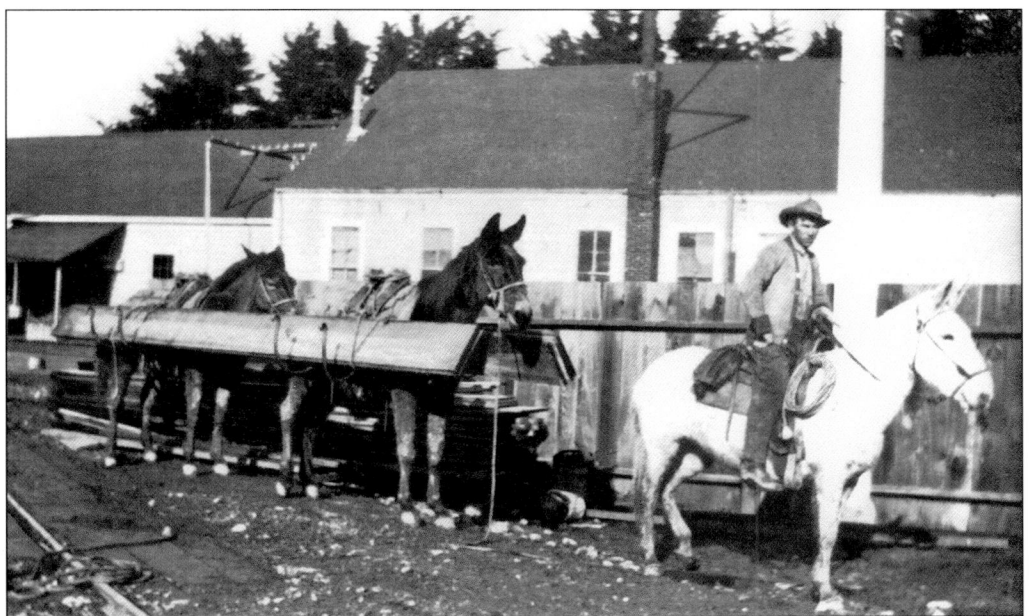

Tex McHenry was a packer for the L. E. White Lumber Company. Lumber companies would sell logged-over lands as home sites to employees, especially to those with families and children, and they'd then provide building materials at reduced prices. Note the strong bark hooks used to hold the boards to the pack frames.

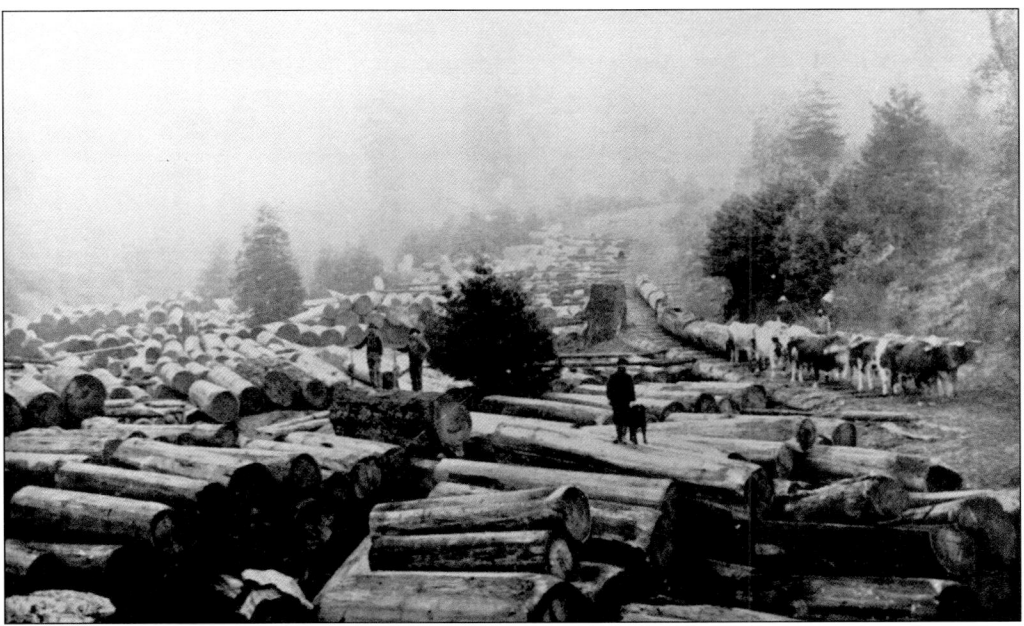

Loggers planned to let Mother Nature do the hard work here by moving the logs in flowing stream water to a sawmill downstream. Temporary dams across the stream or river would hold the logs as the water level rose when the fall rains came. When the dams were removed, the force of the water would carry the logs for miles.

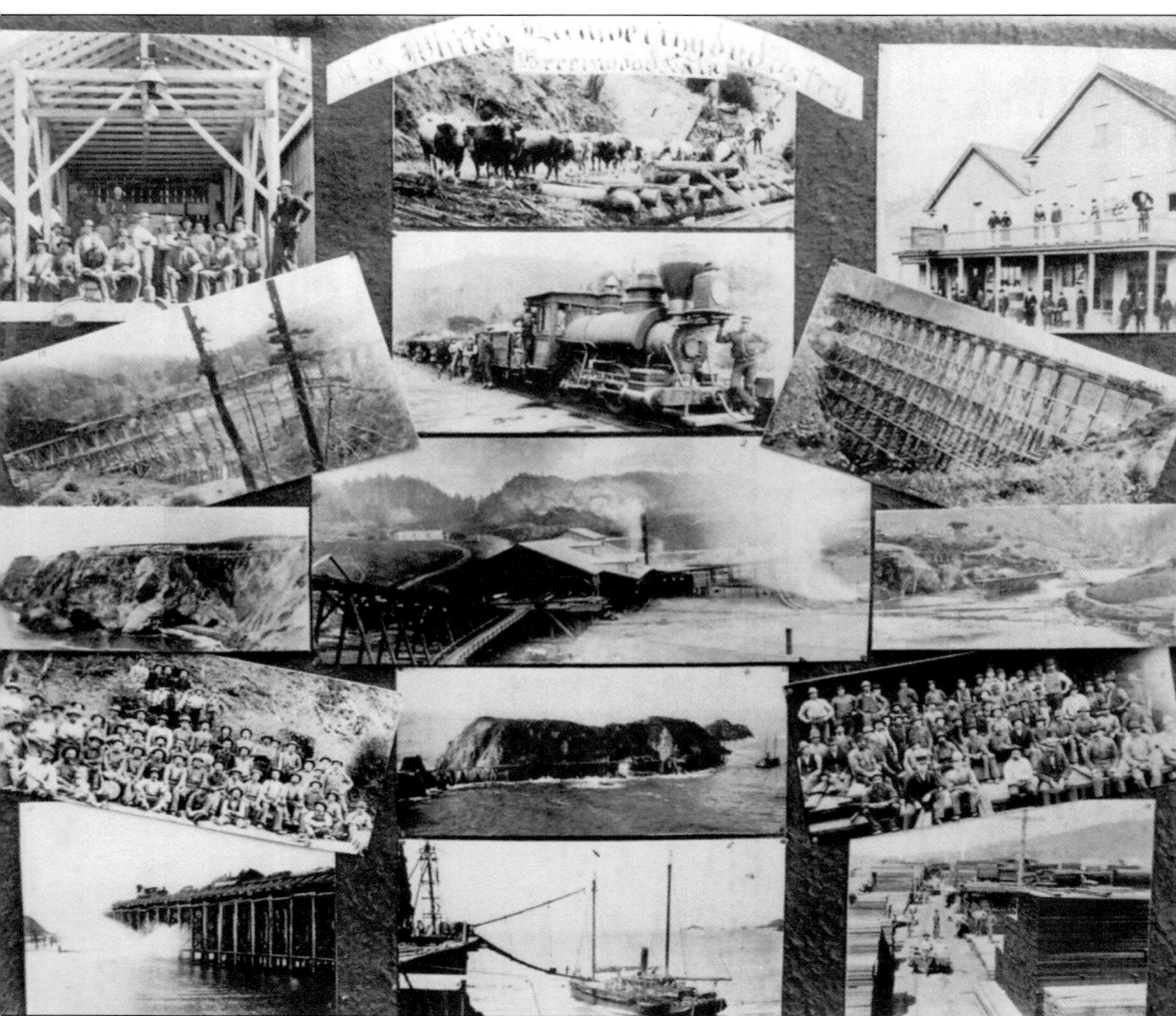

A 1910 advertising picture board for the L. E. White Lumber Company in Greenwood/Elk allowed traveling salesmen to explain to prospective clients where the lumber came from. Photographs showed oxen logging, high trestles, railroad operations, the sawmill, the shipping point and wharf, the work crews, and the town hotel. An ingenious trestle wrapped around the rocks in Greenwood Cove to get finished lumber products out to departing ships.

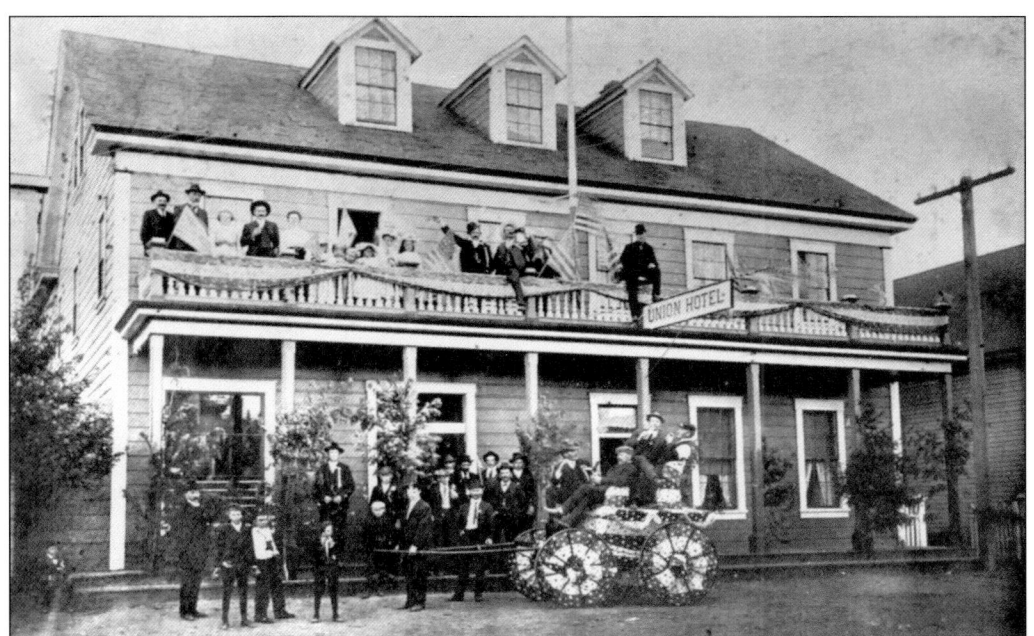

The Union Hotel in Greenwood/Elk is all decked out for the Fourth of July with bunting, flags, and a decorated wagon with humans for power. From 1890 to 1930, there were 12 saloon/hotels in town. Five were Swedish, five were Italian-American, and the Europa Hotel catered to Finns, Danes, and Germans.

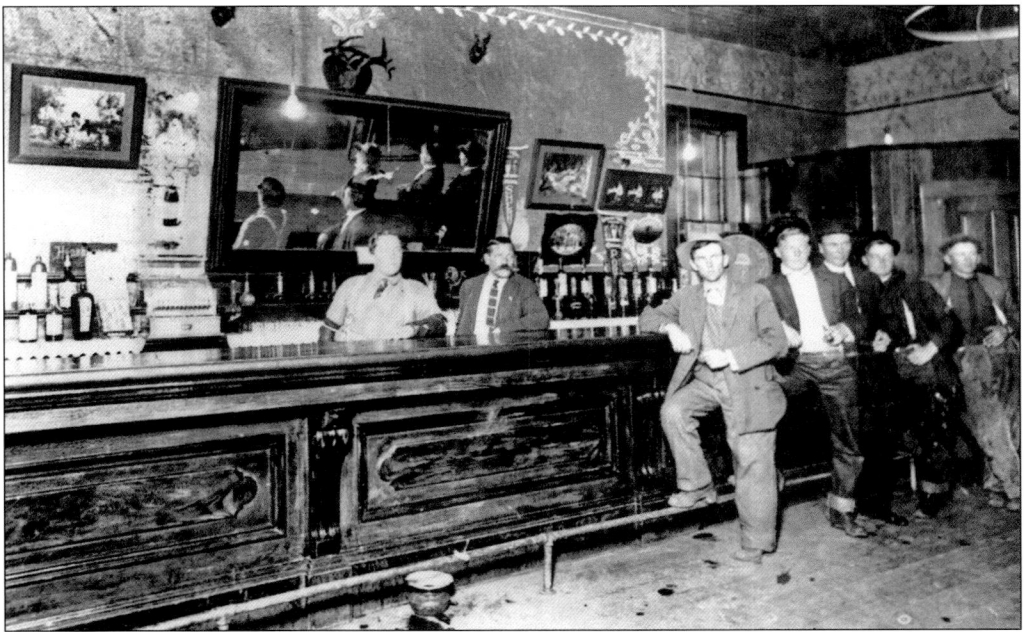

What more could a drinking logger want? There were liquor, companionship, trophy horns over the mirror, art, and a spittoon on the floor for used chewing tobacco. Many saloons also provided female companionship in rooms nearby for a price. Mostly saloons, like this one in the Union Hotel, kept a man warm and dry with a drink in his hand.

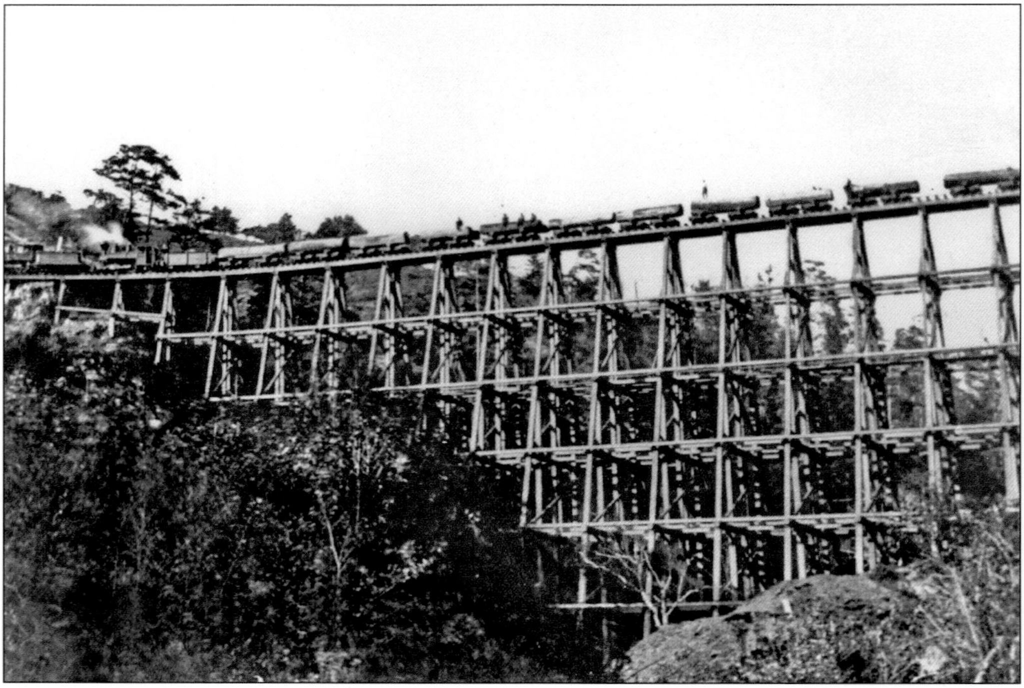

The North Fork branch of the Elk Creek Railroad had 101 bridges to cross on 19 miles of track. Two bridges were 100 feet high and 400 feet long. A steep four percent grade and little safety equipment caused more men to lose their lives on the rail line than on any other North Coast railway.

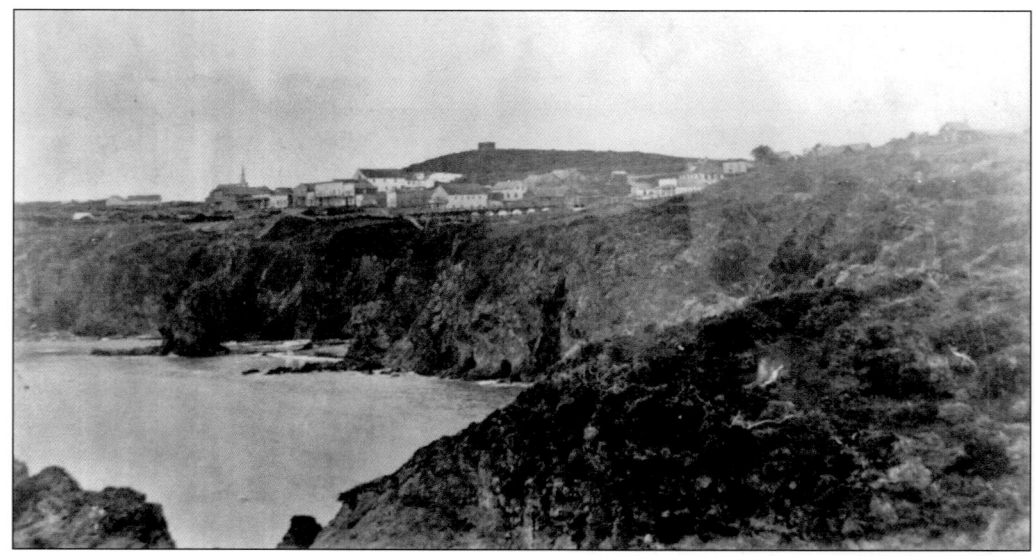

Today all that remains of Cuffey's Cove are cemeteries on the bluff along the Shoreline Highway at milepost 35.6. It was the first European settlement north of Fort Ross and was home to African American pioneer settler Nathaniel Smith. A visiting Australian whaling ship crew called him "cuffey," Australian slang for a black person. Cuffey's Cove became the place name of the town seen in this 1885 photograph.

Looking down the loading chute at Cuffey's Cove, one ship appears on the left border of the photograph, and another approaches this structure. Maneuvering into the tight spaces with offshore rocks was always a challenge to sailing captains. The locals joked that there was so little room, "a dog couldn't turn around," and the term dog hole was applied to many Mendocino County shipping points.

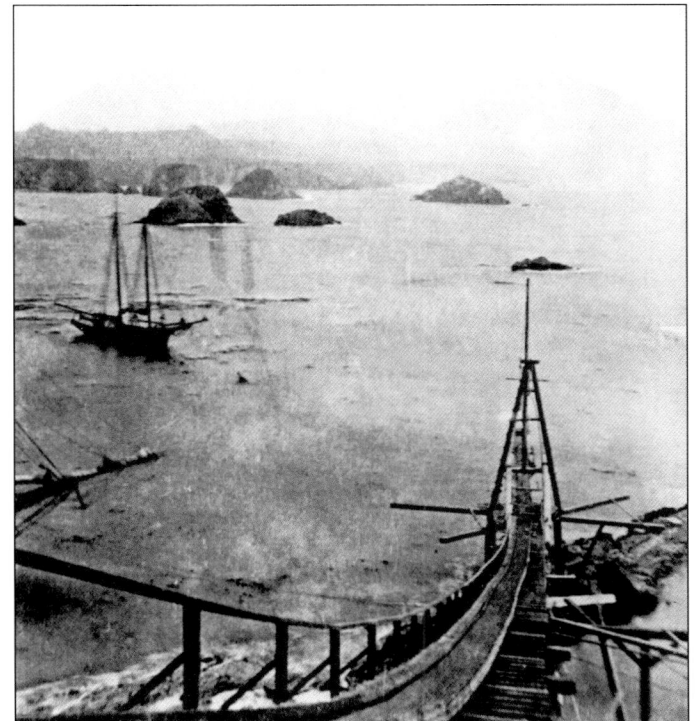

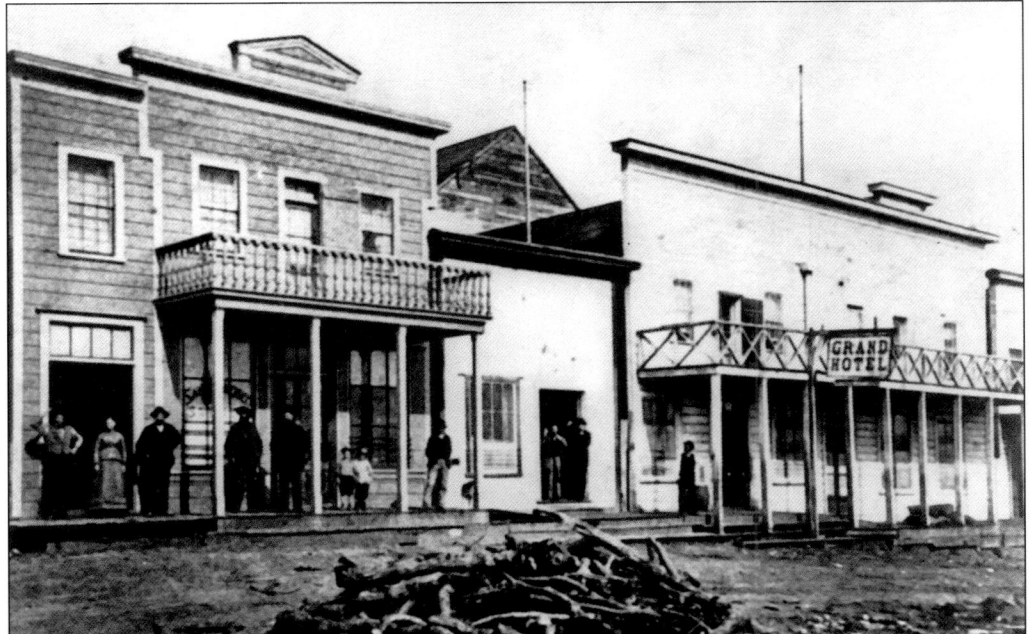

Cuffey Cove had homes, hotels, stores, saloons, and a church and was 20 years old when this photograph was taken. In 1868, three chutes helped load split timber products and red potatoes for shipment south. As often happened, Greenwood/Elk, just to the south, became bigger, and this town declined. Fires erased what remained.

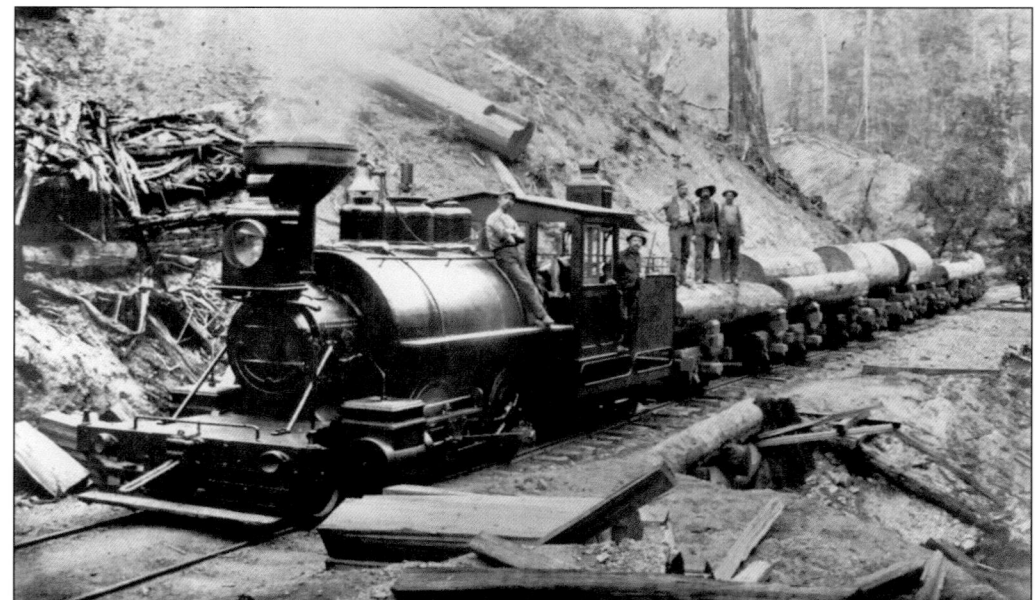

North of Greenwood/Elk, the mouth of the Navarro River was the next transportation point. Locomotive No. 2, also known as the H. B. Tichenor or "Old Molly," pulls a load into the Navarro Mill in 1880. When this mill closed, the Mendocino Lumber Company acquired the engine for their logging railroad. The last sawmill to function along the banks of the Navarro burned by 1902.

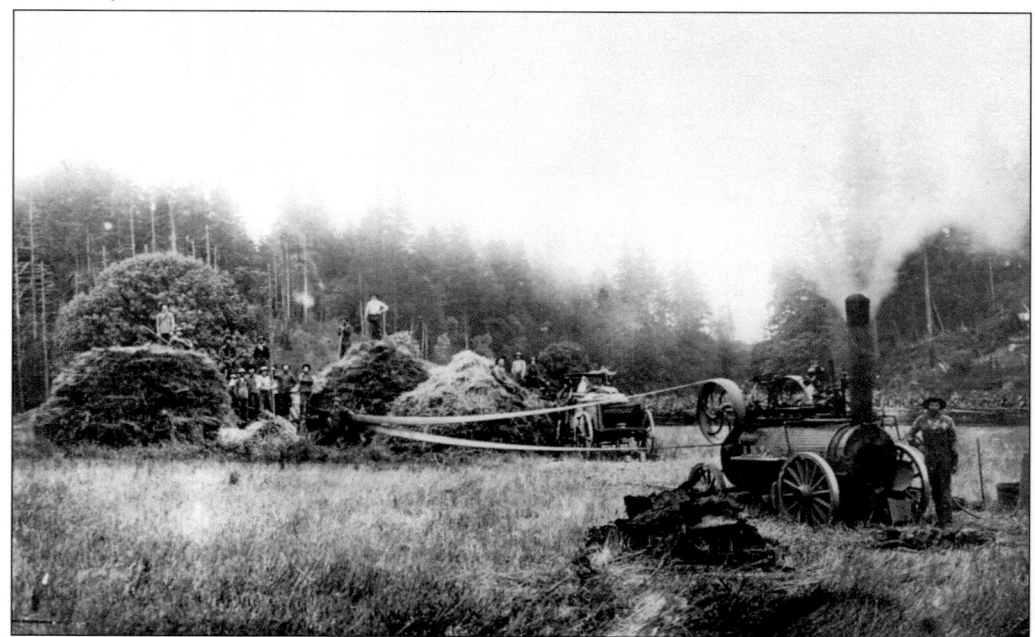

Before railroads became the motive power for logging, oxen teams did the job, and oxen needed hay for food. If a person did not like woods work, they could farm and grow food stuffs for logging camps, sawmill cookhouses, and hungry oxen. Steam equipment helped on the farmstead as it did in logging operations.

Two

MIDDLE COAST
14 MILES
NAVARRO RIVER TO LITTLE RIVER

From Cuffey's Cove north through Little River is not a distant journey but a lot of history is packed into this short stretch of coastline. Drop-offs of 200 feet border much of the west side of the highway until arriving at the Navarro River. It was not until the 1920s that an all-weather road, Highway 128, continued east from here. Just before the bridge on the north shore is an access road to the beach.

North of the Navarro Bridge, the Shoreline Highway traffic increases with the addition of the travelers coming to the coast from Anderson Valley. Navarro Ridge and Albion Ridge roads lead to hundreds of residences for everyone from rich retirees to back-to-the-land hippies and old-timers with families who hung onto the old home ranch for six generations.

Today's visitors cross the high bridge and can turn immediately east and wind down to Albion Flat. A century ago, this was a beehive of activity with a sawmill, railroad, and shipping wharf. It's all gone. The industry now is tourism. It's a lot quieter. But many lodging and dining establishments love to show photographs of what their area looked like back then. A particular bed-and-breakfast might have been the Wells Fargo stage coach stop 100 years ago. The mill owner's house from the 1880s now hosts cliff-side weddings. The old farm house hosts a restaurant whose owner had secret coves where he collected bucket loads of abalone back when that was still legal. The rumrunners during Prohibition sneaked in booze right past that vacation rental cottage.

Van Damme State Park offers trails through Fern Canyon and the Pygmy Forest for a break from driving and a chance to catch some fresh air. The park beach offers calm waters and tide-pooling and whale-watching opportunities from the bluff tops. Continuing north opposite Gordon Lane, a parking area allows a walk out to Chapman Point for a picture postcard view of Mendocino in the distance.

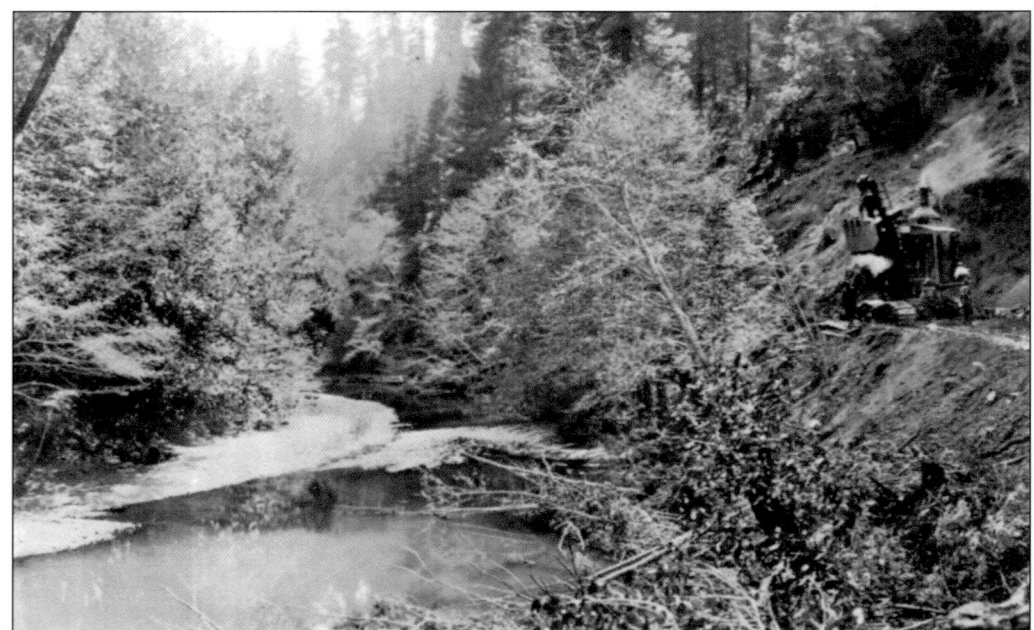

In 1922, a serious attempt was being made to produce an all-weather highway from Cloverdale to the Mendocino Coast. A steam shovel here carves a roadbed into the hillside over the Navarro River. Old abandoned railroad beds often provided a starting point. Log trucks were taking over from railroads and ocean shipping as the preferred method for moving lumber.

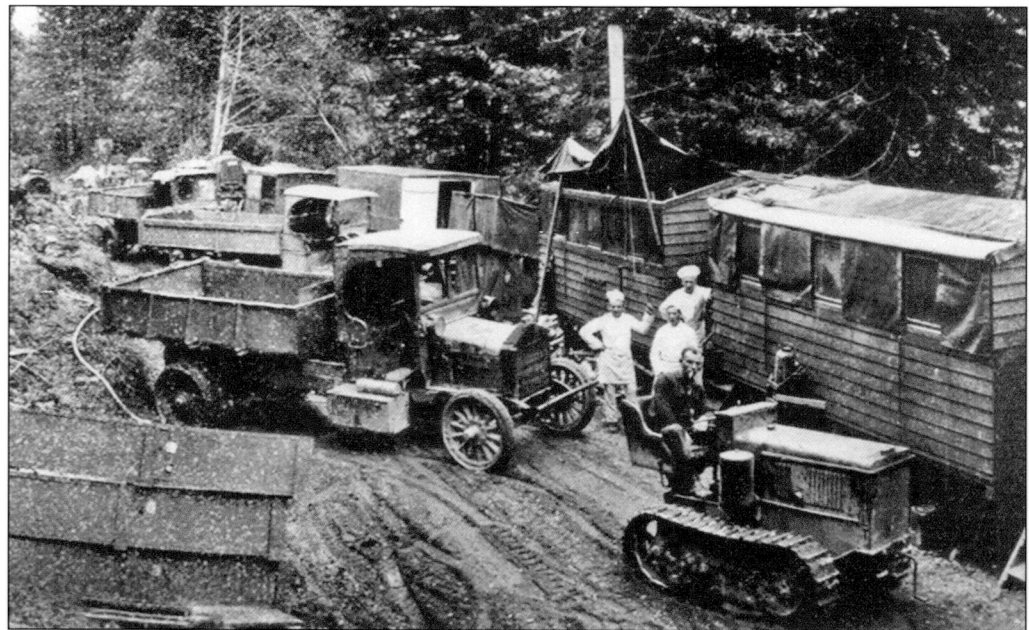

While Highway 128 was being built in the 1920s, there were portable camps that moved with the road construction to support workers. Decades before, this same method was used in railroad construction. Here cooks and a tractor driver take a break in front of a cookhouse next to waiting dump trucks.

When rail was still ruling transportation, a Shay locomotive moved loggers' dwelling cabins along the rail line toward a new camp on Albion Lumber Company timberlands. Once an area was logged out, the entire operation was moved into new timber. All logging camp structures were built to fit on a flat car.

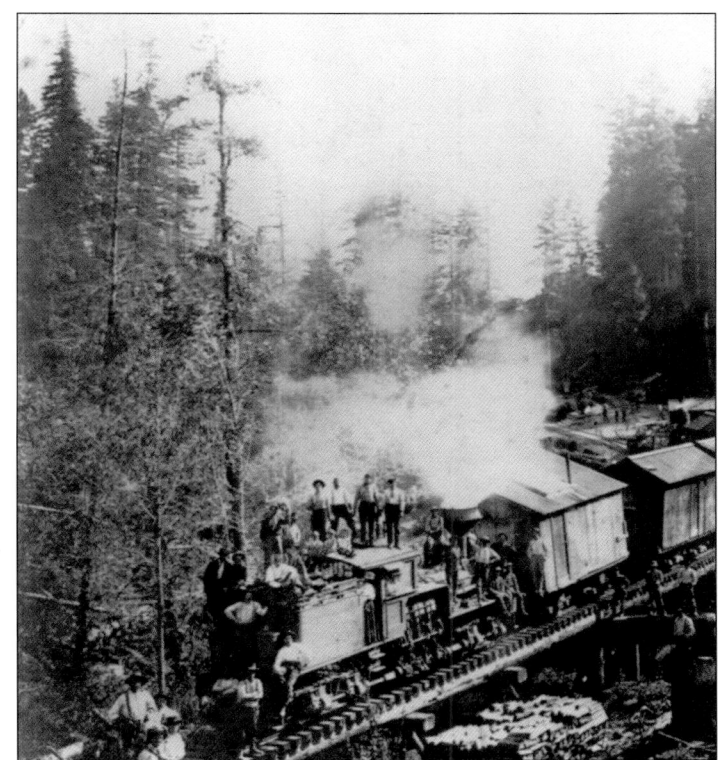

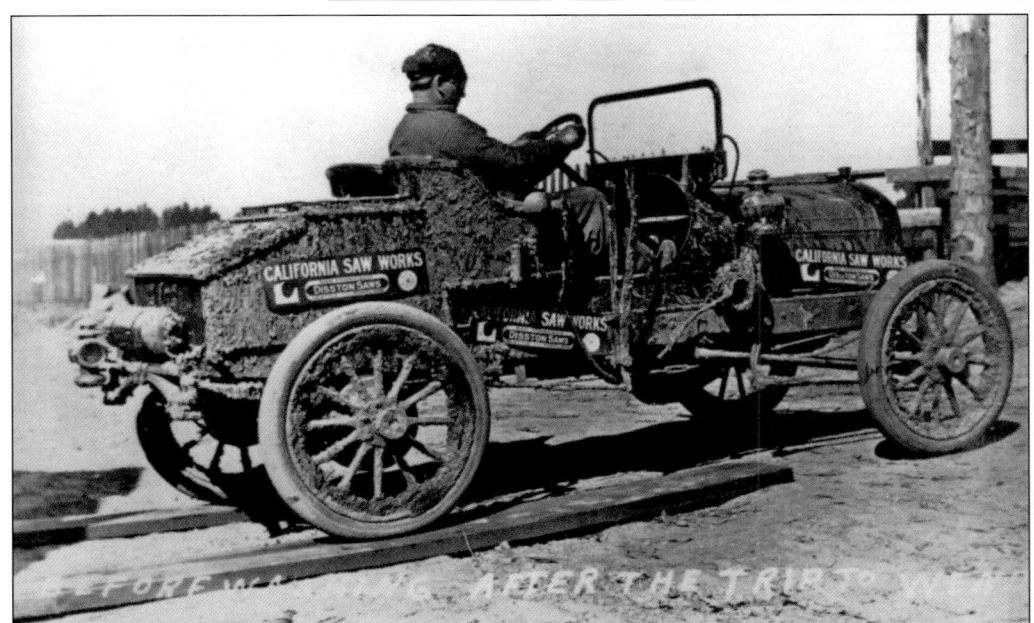

This California Saw Works car may have been mud-encrusted from traveling poor roads, but the salesman driving had carefully cleaned off the signage for the photographer. Every town had a big commercial hotel for salesmen visiting to sell industrial products to mills or merchandise to general stores.

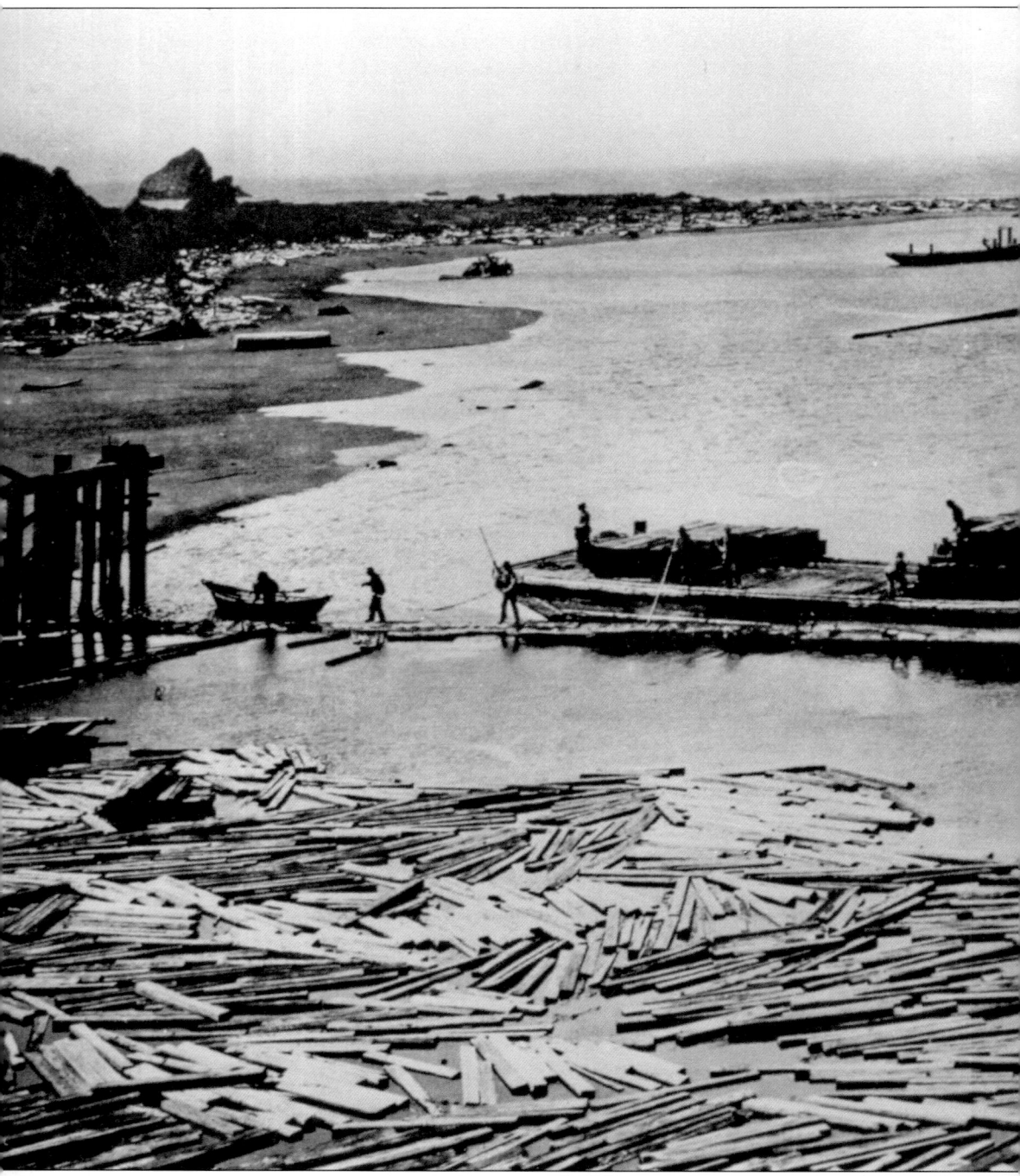

If there was no wharf, chute, or other alternative, wood products were loaded on a boat called a lighter, and the product was transported out to the steam schooner here waiting beyond the surf line at the mouth of the Navarro River. This method of loading was also used when the water was very shallow, though lumber schooners could often be more than 12 feet in depth. The workers walk along a boom designed to keep these ties from floating out to the Pacific. The ties were put

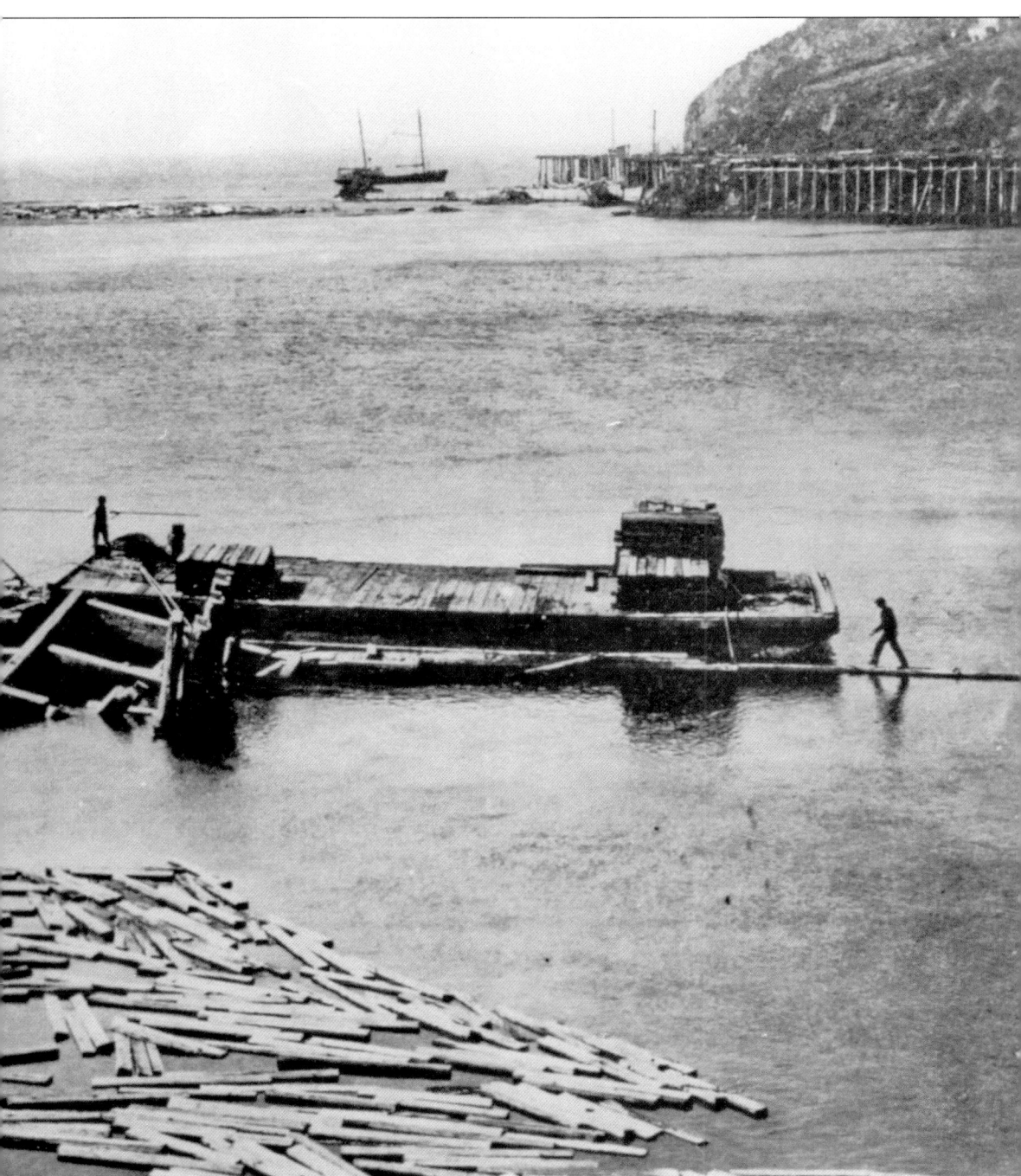

in the river 10 miles upstream and floated down to be collected at the river's mouth. If a boom broke, an entire season's work could wash out to sea. When that happened, gleeful farmers and ranchers would wait for the finished boards and ties to wash up on beaches. The materials would be collected and hauled back to land holding to be used as free wood for construction activities.

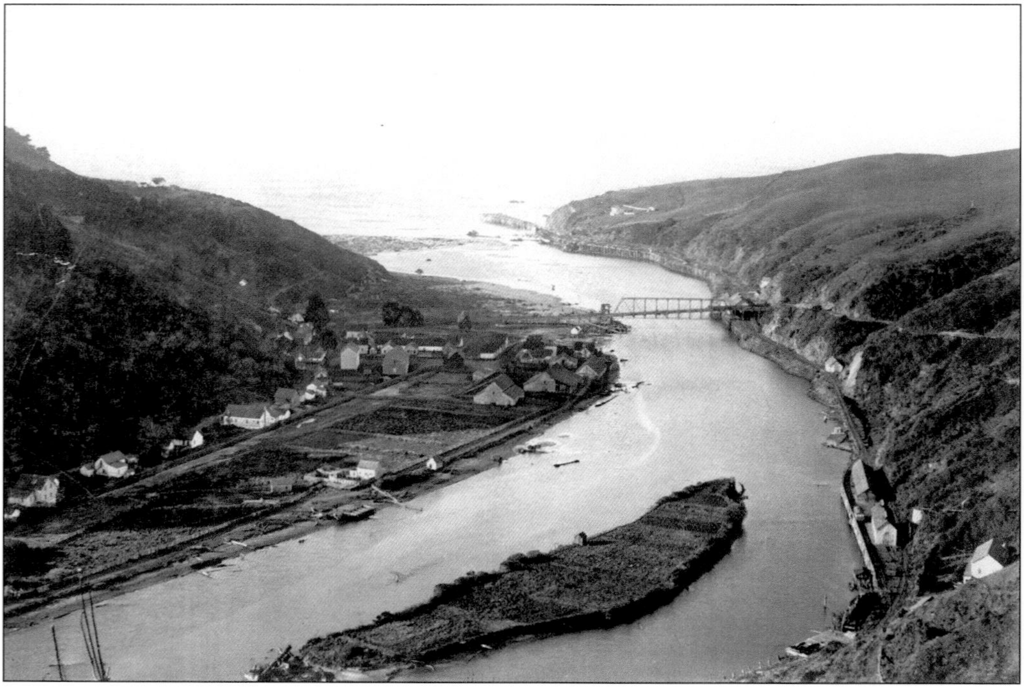

The bridge over the Navarro River had a tendency to change location around depending on the level of logging activity in the area. The left (south) bank had the sawmill in the 1890s, while the right (north) bank had the railroad and the wharf. The north bank road grade has changed little in a century. The island is smaller today after frequent floods. The first bridge was built here in 1869. The mill burned and closed, and the town vanished in the early 1900s. Today there is access to the beach just west of the south side of the bridge. The road here still floods frequently in heavy winter storms.

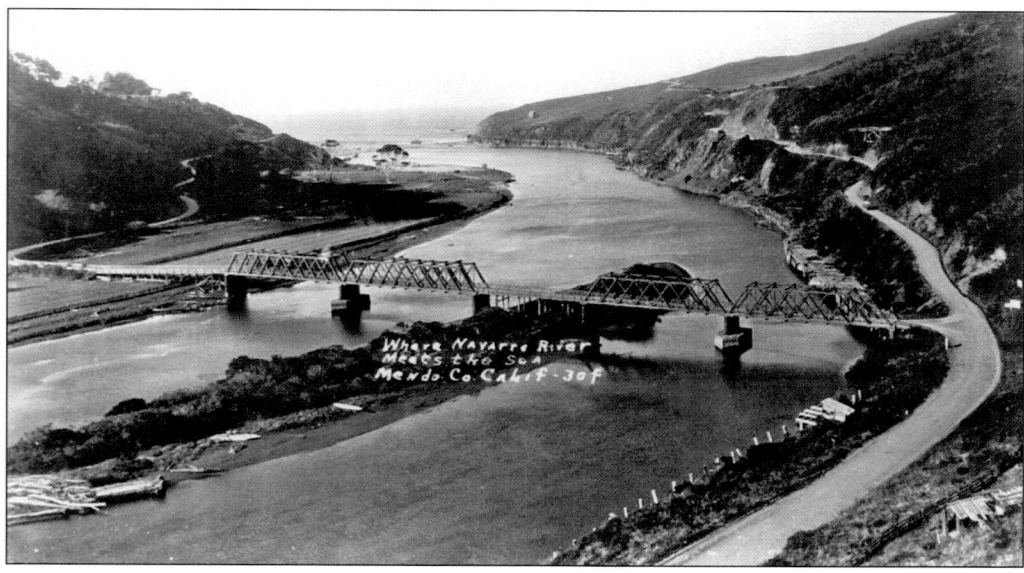

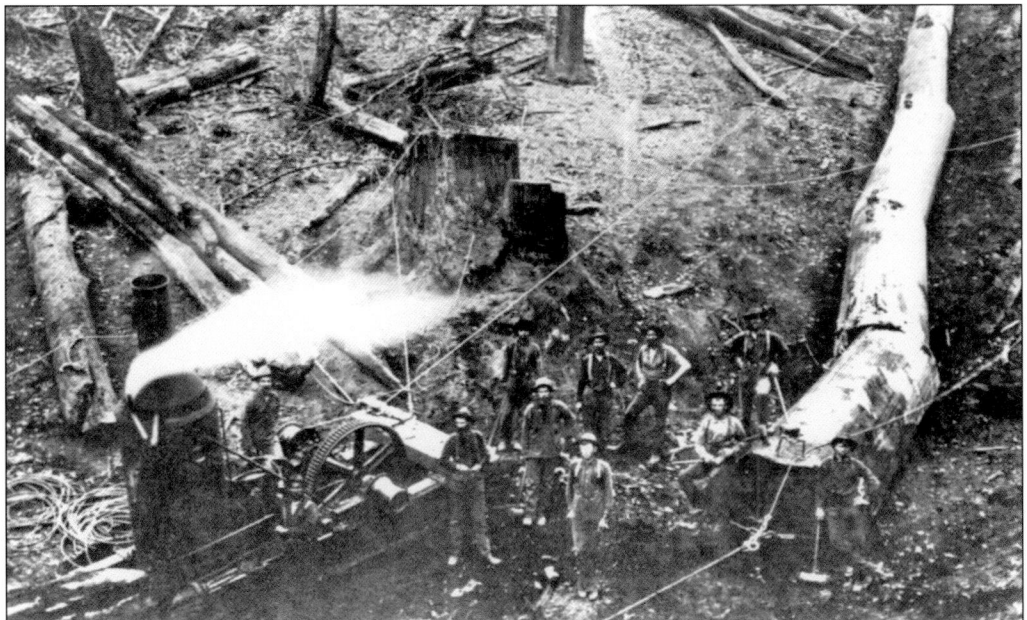

In the Albion Lumber Company woods, this crew had a steam skidder with a big bull gear to do the work a team of oxen did in the past. This mechanical contrivance didn't need to eat expensive hay; it consumed waste wood for power. It could be put on a sled and cable-tied to a tree in the direction the operator wanted it to go, and it would pull itself through the woods.

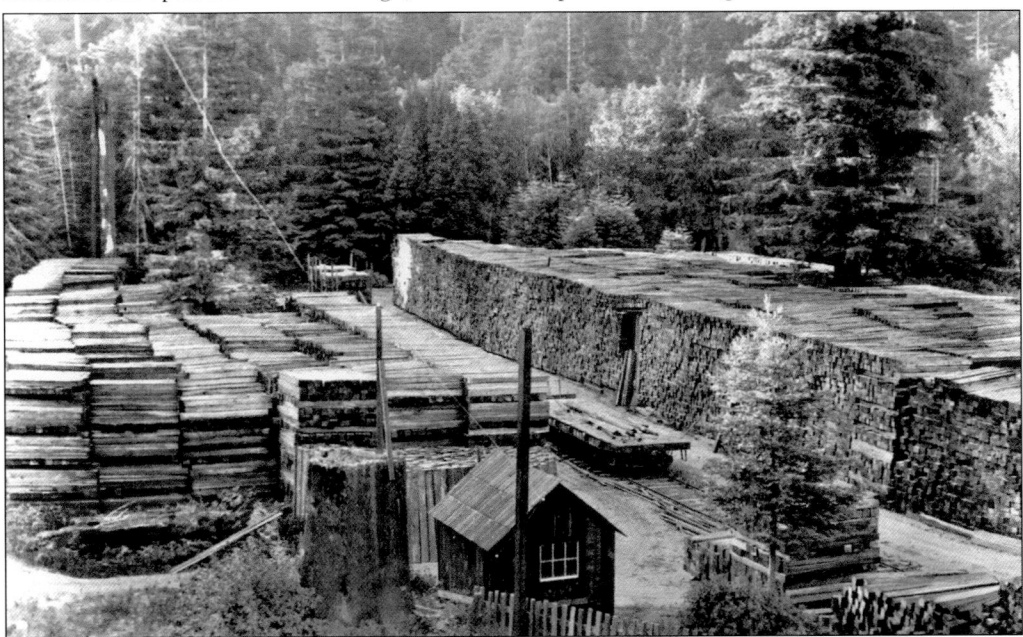

In the slow market of 1926, about 118,000 railroad ties lie stacked near the Navarro River awaiting a buyer. While railroad construction decreased in the United States in favor of highways, Mexico, Peru, and Australia still favored trains. Southern Pacific Railroad owned Albion timberlands, and sent railroad ties all over the Western Pacific area.

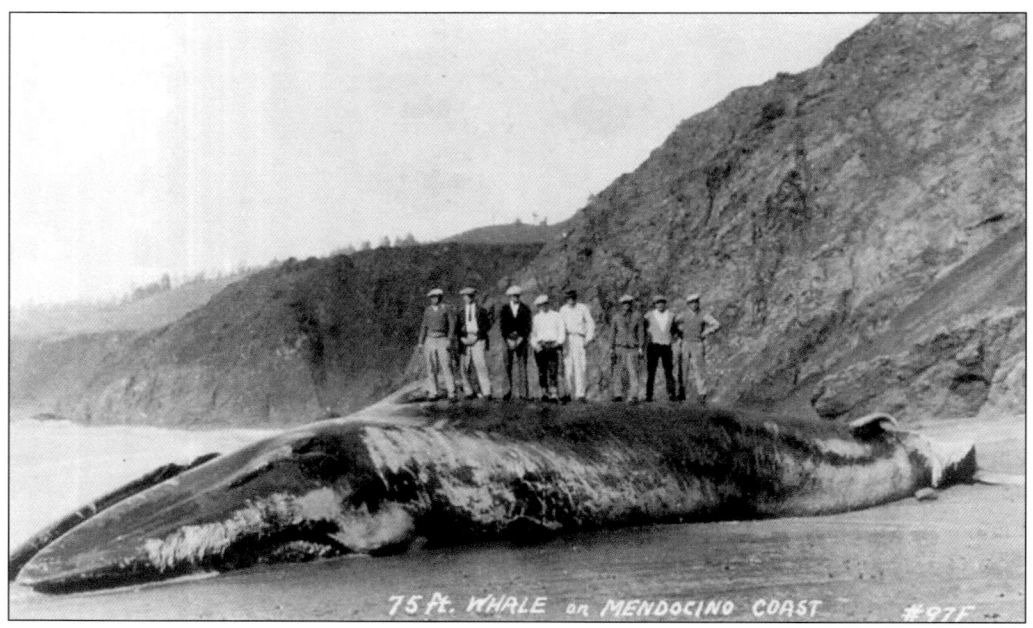

There's nothing like a dead whale on a Mendocino Coast beach to attract onlookers. This one was still solid enough to stand on. In earlier years, the native peoples would have welcomed such a meat source by drying and smoking it.

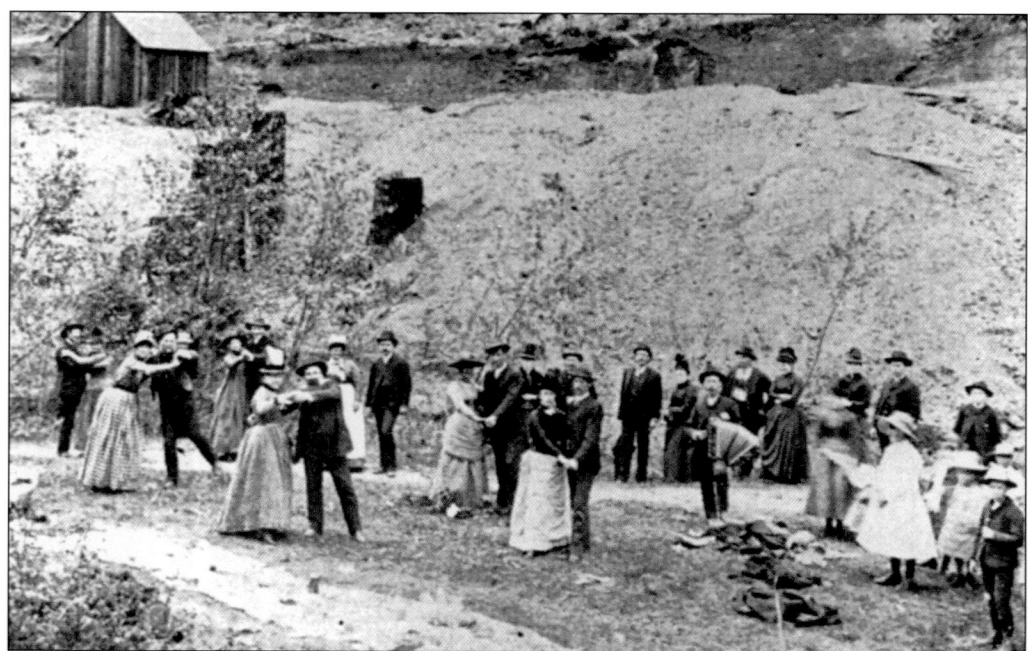

Dancers on the banks of Salmon Creek south of Albion enjoy the music of an accordion player as they pose for the photographer. This was an era during which everyone—men, women, and children—wore hats. The 1880s party was at Pullen's Mill, eight miles up Salmon Creek.

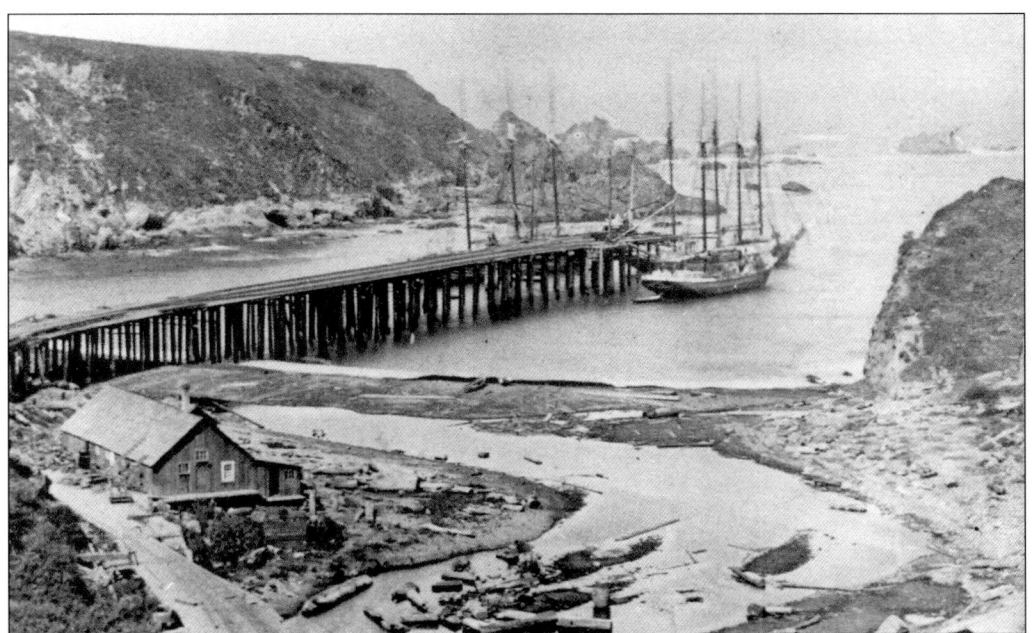

The wharf at Salmon Creek was capable of loading three lumber schooners at once. Getting in and out of the harbor was still tricky maneuvering. The railroad went from the sawmill and timberlands eight miles inland over a low bridge in the foreground and out to the wharf. Logs missed by the mill floated downstream to the ocean's edge.

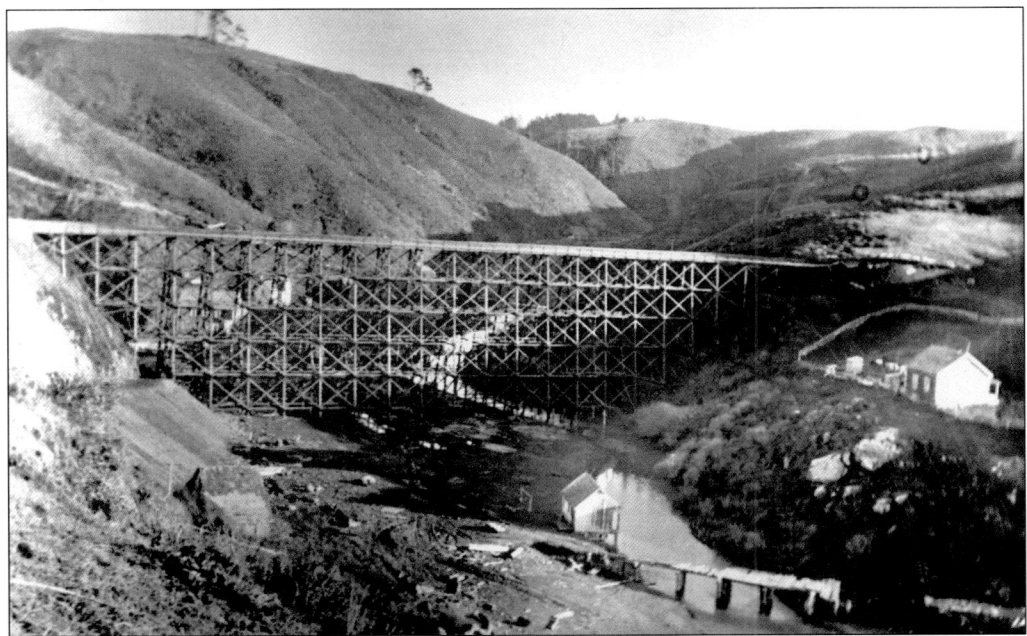

Bridges were replaced over Salmon Creek as modes of transportation changed. Some crossed at water level, and the 1950s bridge was 682 feet long on the bluff tops. The old railroad bridge is visible in the foreground. Today people drive on a newer high bridge without knowing all the activity that went on below years ago.

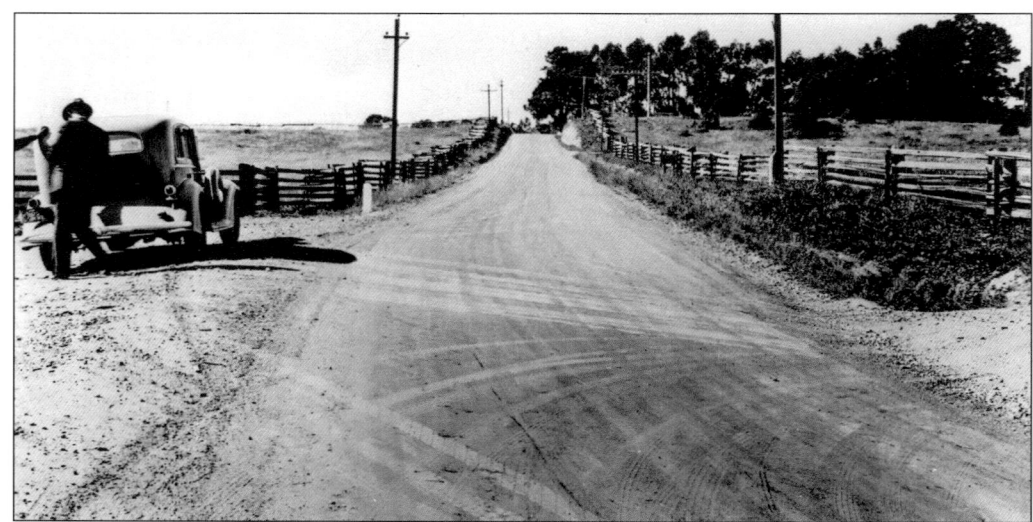

Many areas of the Shoreline Highway have not changed much over the decades. Car models change and eucalyptus trees flourish, but the road remains the same. The completion of the Golden Gate Bridge and creation of the Redwood Empire Association began to boost tourism in the 1930s, but it took another decade to get the road paved from Sonoma County to Fort Bragg.

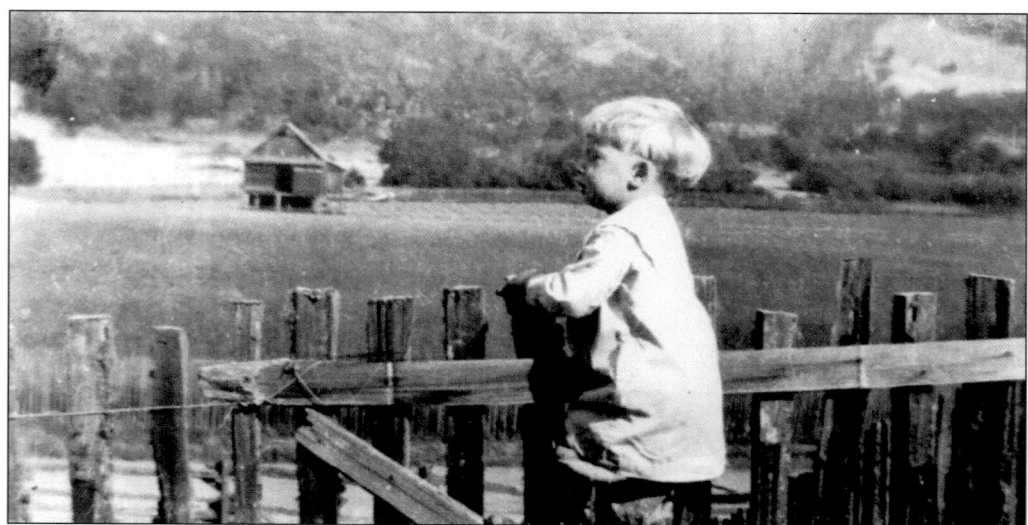

Horse teams pulling loads of lumber to shipping points had bells on their harness so oncoming teams on twisting roads could hear their approach. Children learned to recognize these distinct bell sounds and would rush out to greet the teamsters and wave as they passed by their homes.

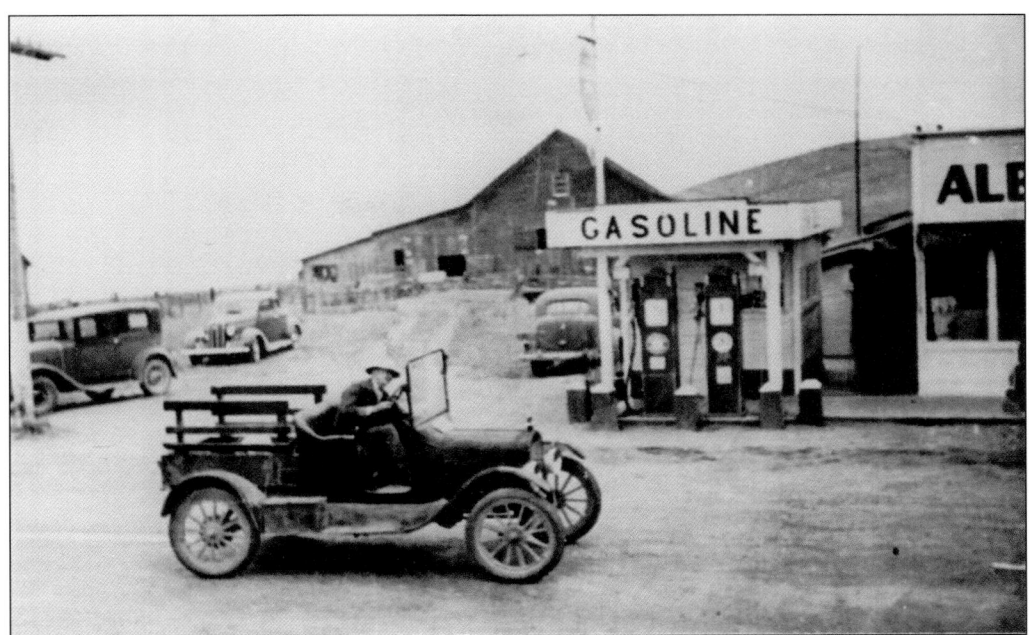

As the concept of the Shoreline Highway as a tourist route developed, service stations become more evident in the 1930s. Here a car adapted to function as a pickup truck passes by Albion. A 1936 Plymouth, 1930 Ford, and 1937 LaSalle are parked nearby. From here the highway crossed the Albion Bridge.

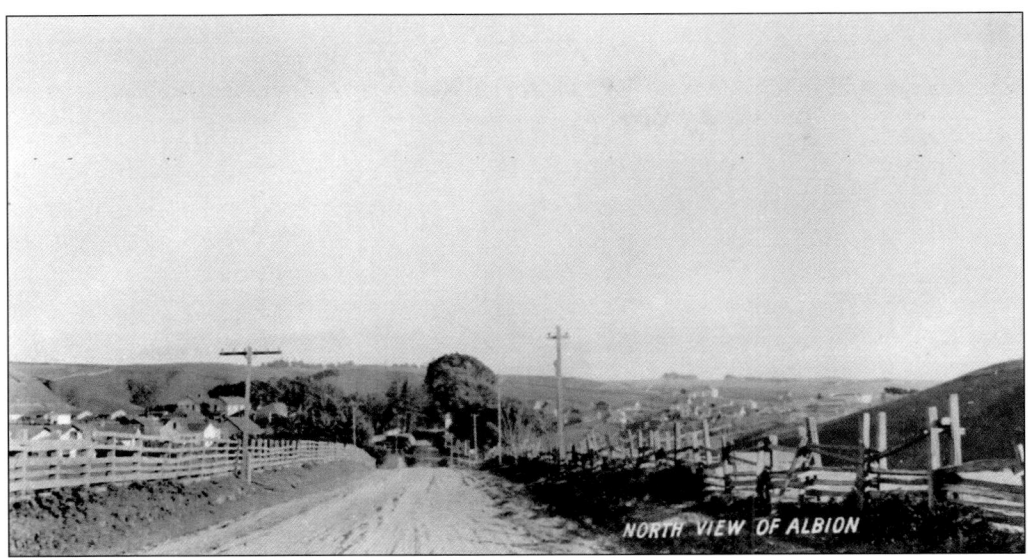

The date of many of the old Shoreline Highway photographs can be determined from the absence or presence of eucalyptus trees and their size. They were introduced into California by gold miners from Australia during the Gold Rush. They grew quickly and provided shade but proved to be useless as a timber crop.

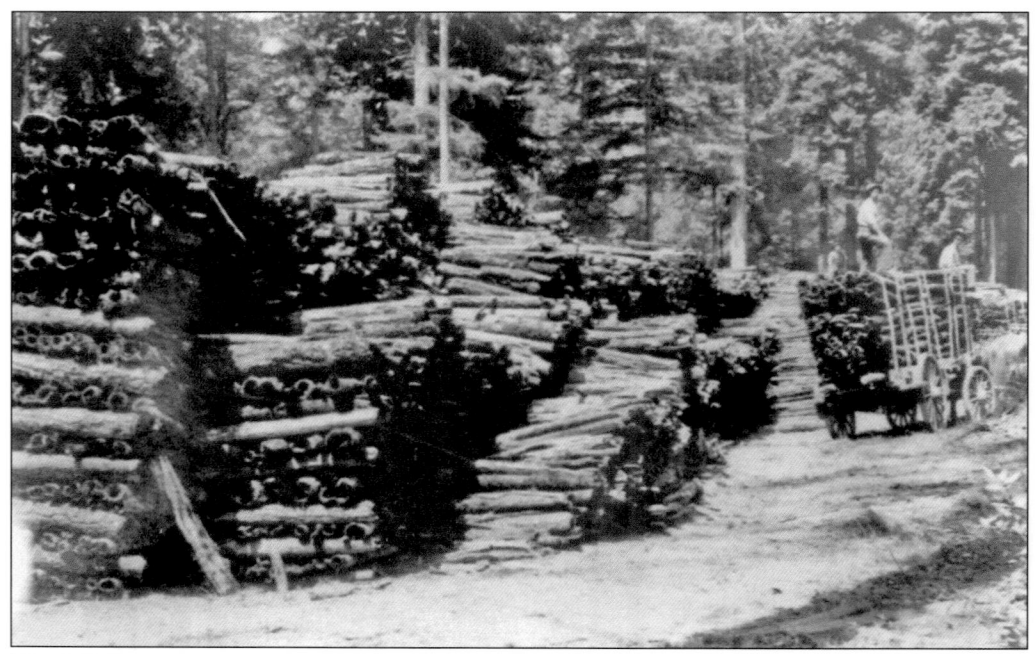

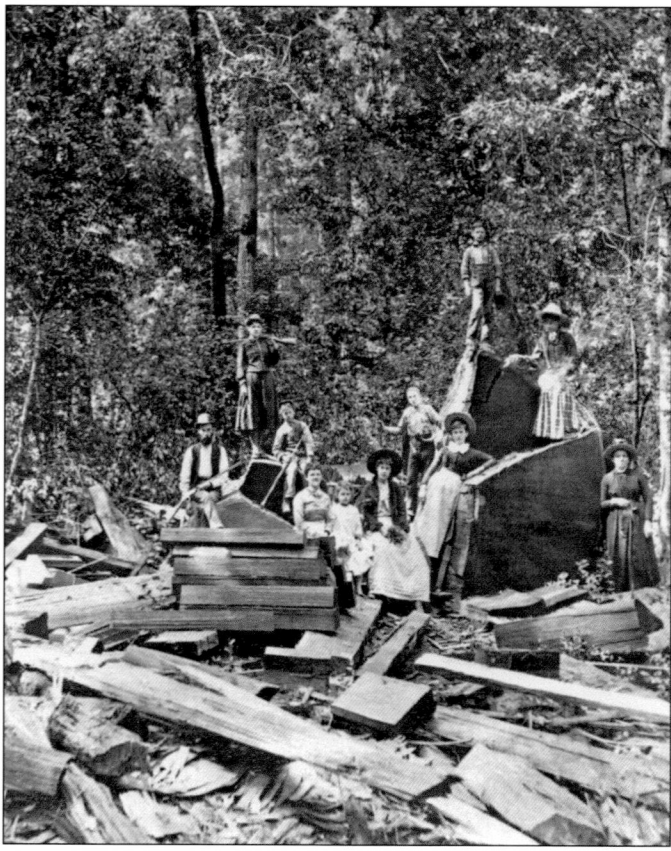

Collecting tan oak bark kept woodsmen as busy as they would be tie-making. A mill was not needed to cut the bark, and one man could handle a "curl," a 4-foot-long section of peeled tan oak bark that curls in on itself. The tannic acid in the bark was essential for leather tanning until synthetic chemicals were invented in the 1920s. Bark was often piled with ties to await a good market price for the product.

Photographers seemed to love to use their families in their photographs. Here photographer A. O. Carpenter is on the left. Her daughter Grace and her twin brother, Grant, hold guns in the center.

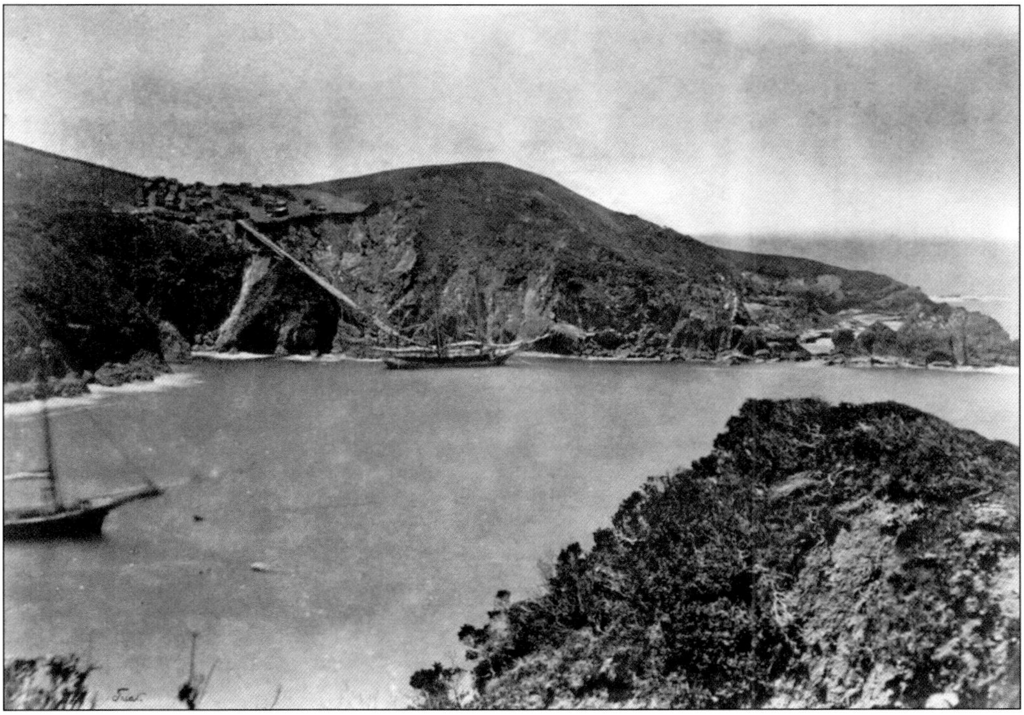

Even though there was a wharf in the Albion Harbor for Albion Lumber Company's use, Hadley's Chute operated on the south side of the harbor for smaller, independent wood product suppliers. This chute was in operation from 1870 to 1889. Tiny operations like this gave place names to more than 80 spots on the Mendocino Coast.

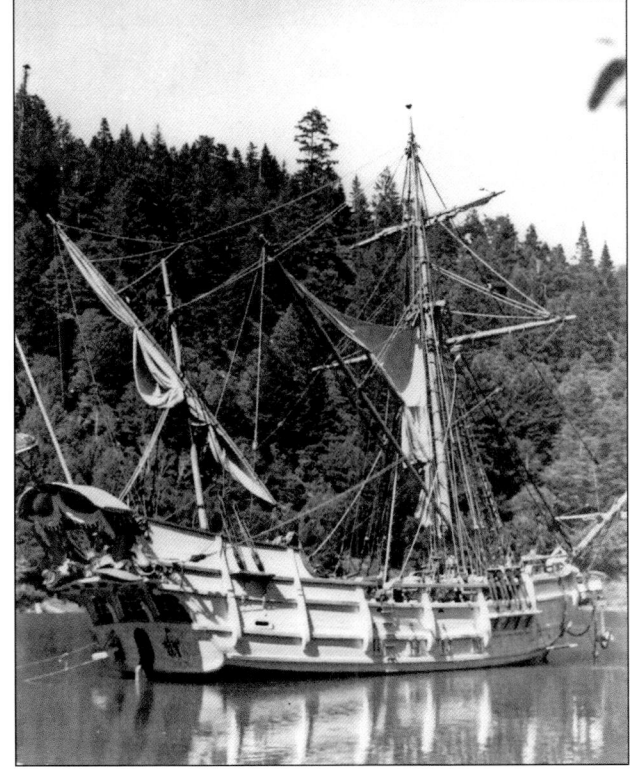

Hollywood has been filming on the Mendocino Coast for almost 100 years. The crew of *Frenchman's Creek,* which was filmed in 1943, towed a pirate ship on a barge from Southern California to a dock on the Albion River. Filmmakers launched it, used it in scenes for the movie footage, and abandoned it in the river. Vandals burned it after the movie production.

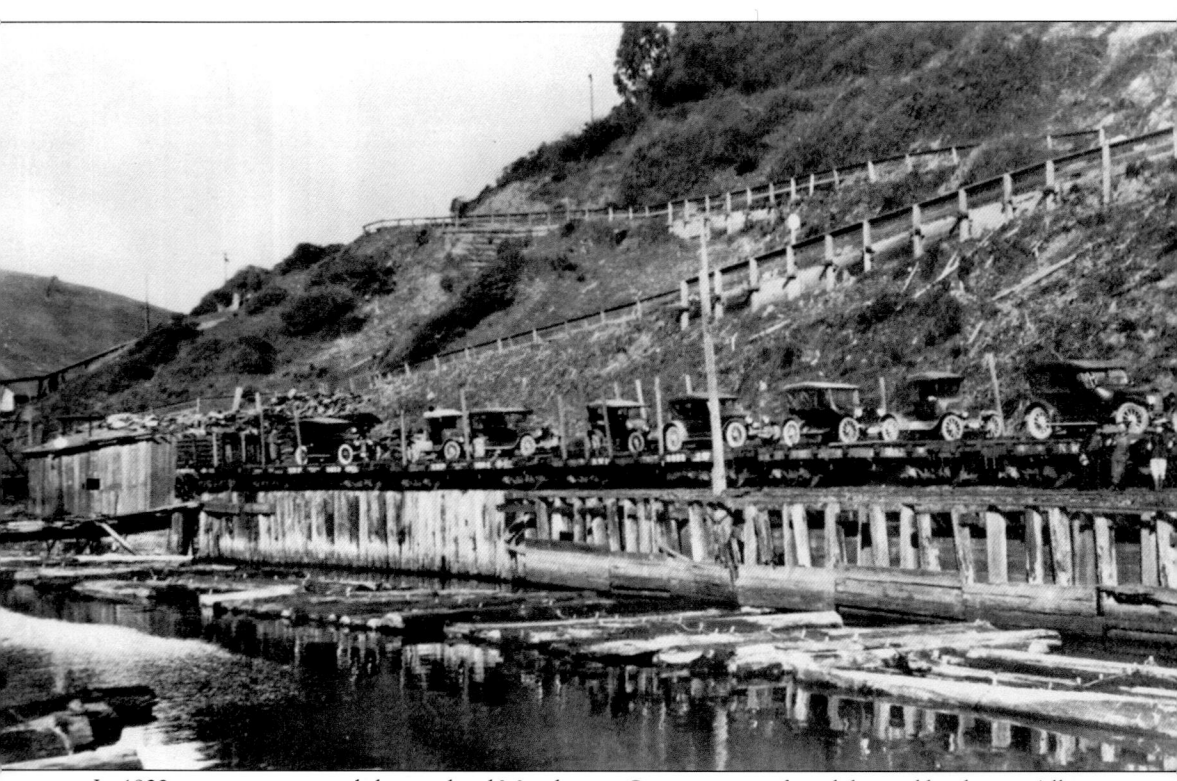

In 1922, to get an automobile to inland Mendocino County, it was first delivered by ship to Albion. Then it was put on the logging railroad and taken to the end of the rail line in Anderson Valley. From there, automobile dealers collected the cars and drove them on existing roads going east to their destinations in the interior of the county. This shipment included a Model T Roadster, 1920 Buick, 1922 Marmon, 1912 Dodge, 1916 Ford Roadster, and a 1920 Franklin. The twisty Shoreline Highway with its hairpin turns winds down the riverbank to the water-level bridge. In 1922, the lumber company had 25 miles of track into the timberlands east of town. The railroad ceased operations in 1930.

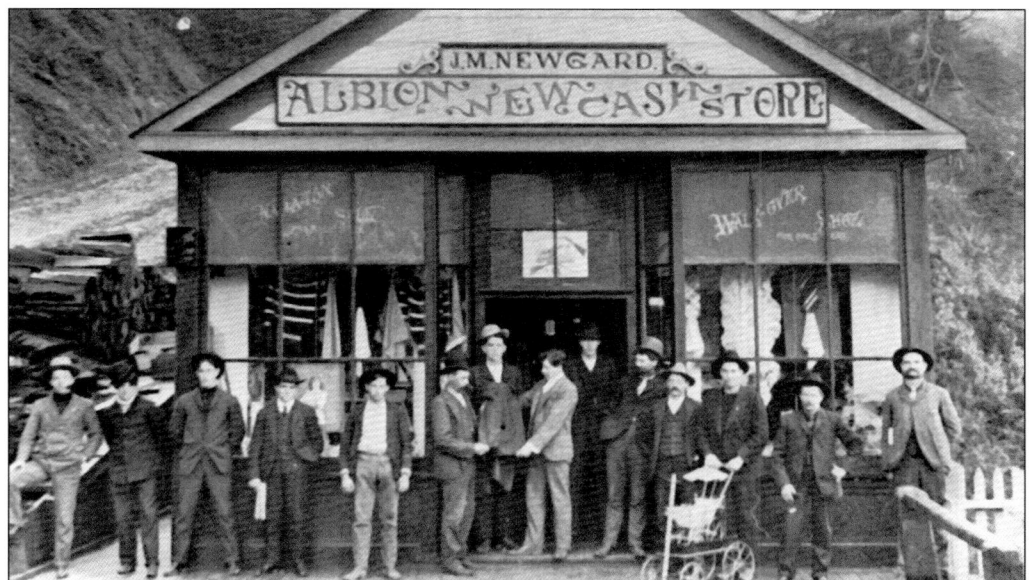

On the south bank of the Albion River at the bridge was Newgard's Albion New Cash Store. Here c. 1901 customers hold up clothing from the stock inside, and a man pushes a baby doll buggy for the publicity photograph. Stores like this specialized in a little bit of everything but kept large supplies of boots and pants to outfit working loggers and mill workers.

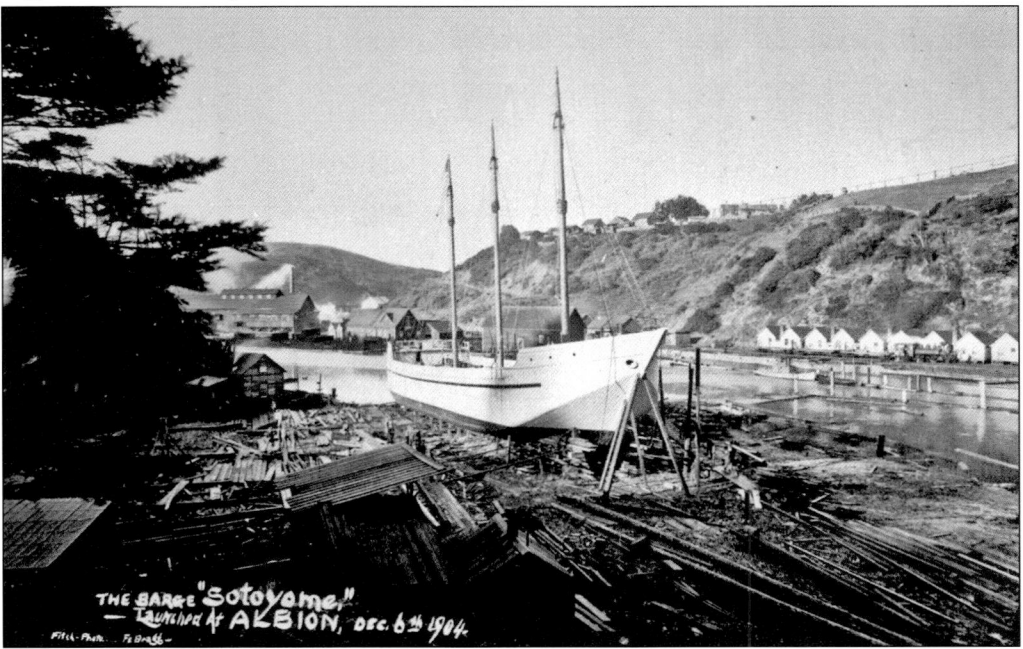

The *Sotoyome*, built on the Albion River, was so big that the shipway at Happy Valley had to be constructed on an oblique angle to have more access to water surface. At 130 feet, the hull was as long as the river was wide. Designed to carry immense loads of lumber, it was rigged with three masts and auxiliary engines. Unwieldy and slow, the *Sotoyome* had a 29-month career before burning near Eureka in 1907.

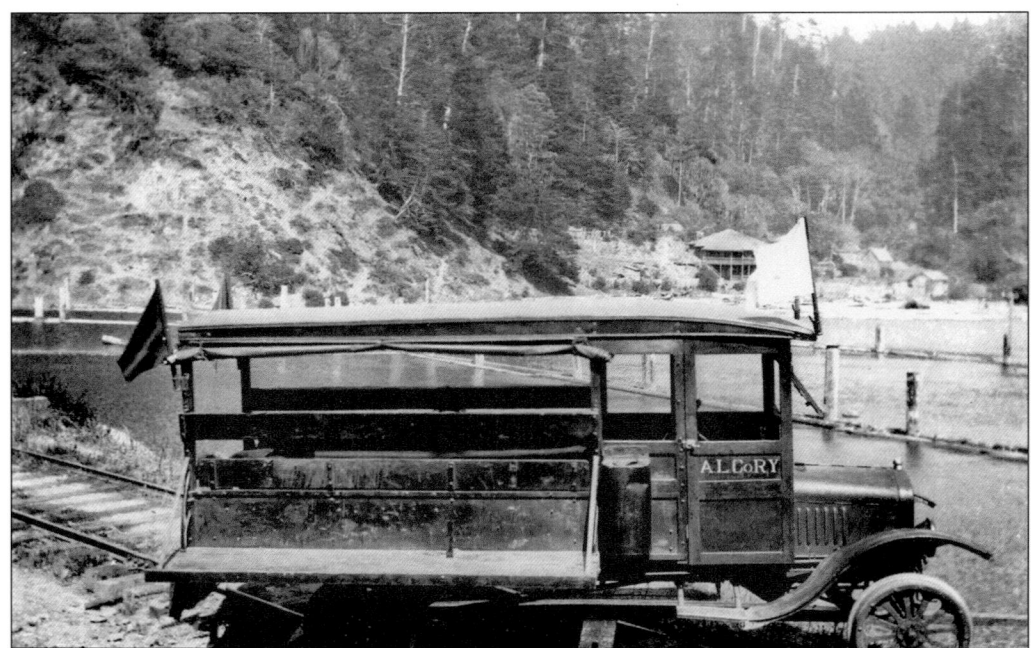

Albion Lumber Company's engine No. 7 was a freight jitney body on a Ford truck bed with flanged wheels and a stretcher that folded down from the side. After a logging accident, an injured logger could be transported into town quickly in this rig. Small work crews and visitors also could be transported easily, as a full-size locomotive, tender, and coach car were unnecessary to move a small number of people. The tiny turntable it sits on here was invented when the operators realized that driving backward from the end of the line presented problems.

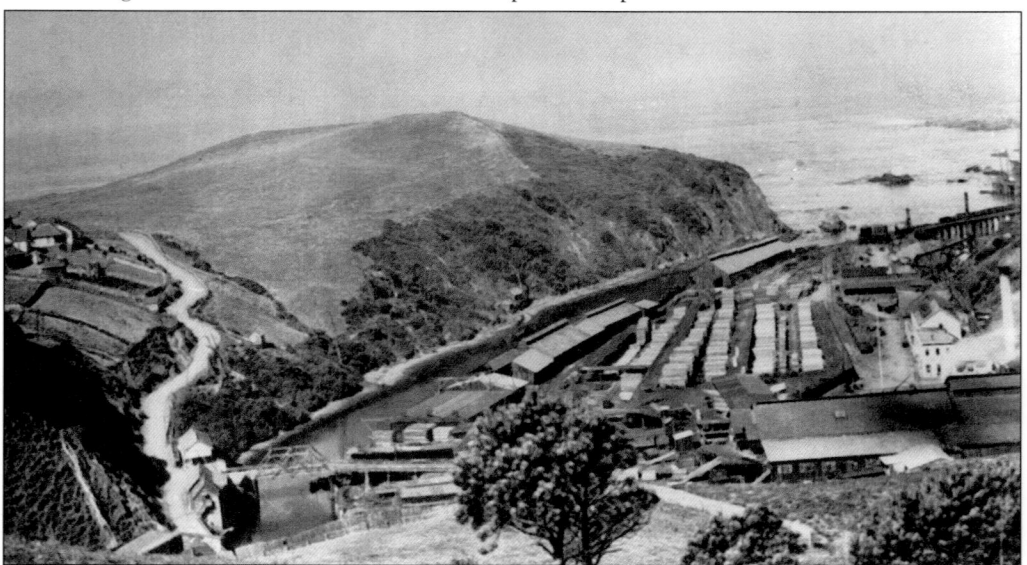

The grade of the Shoreline Highway was treacherous when unpaved and muddy as it approached the low Albion River Bridge. The mill here burned and was rebuilt time and time again. Today travelers can cross the high bridge going north, turn immediately east, and drive down the 14 percent grade to Albion Flat.

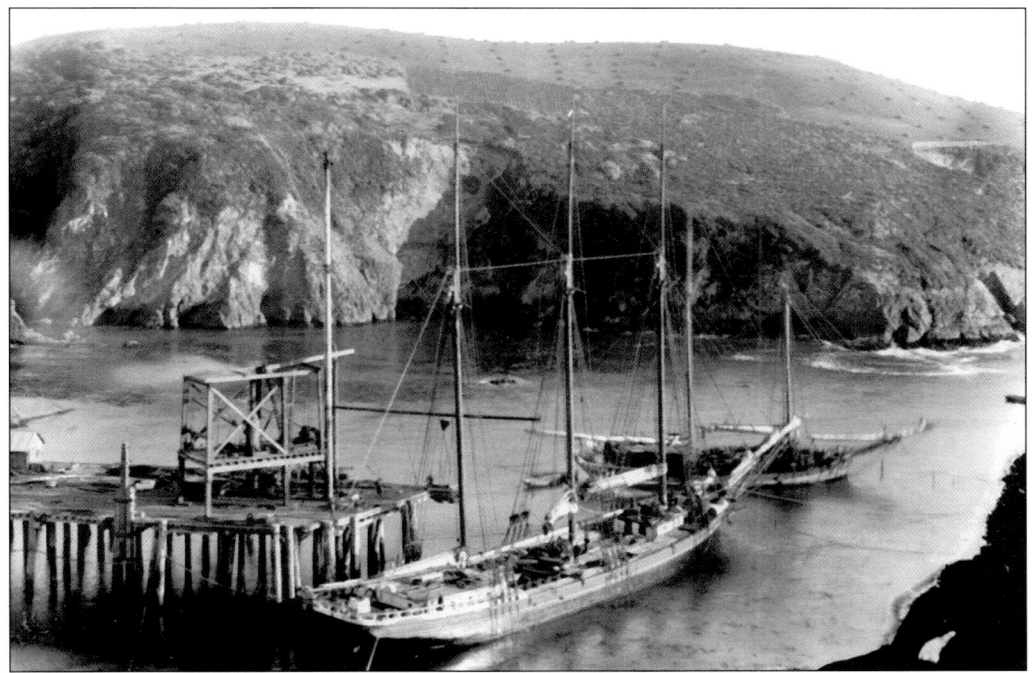

At the end of the Albion Wharf in 1897, the *Belauh* with a deck of railroad wheels is to be unloaded. The steam engine in wharf structure provided the motive power and strength to speed up operations. The *Amethyst* behind the *Belauh* is loaded with tan oak bark. Most schooners carried loads on the decks, as hulls were shallow to allow maneuverability in difficult mooring situations.

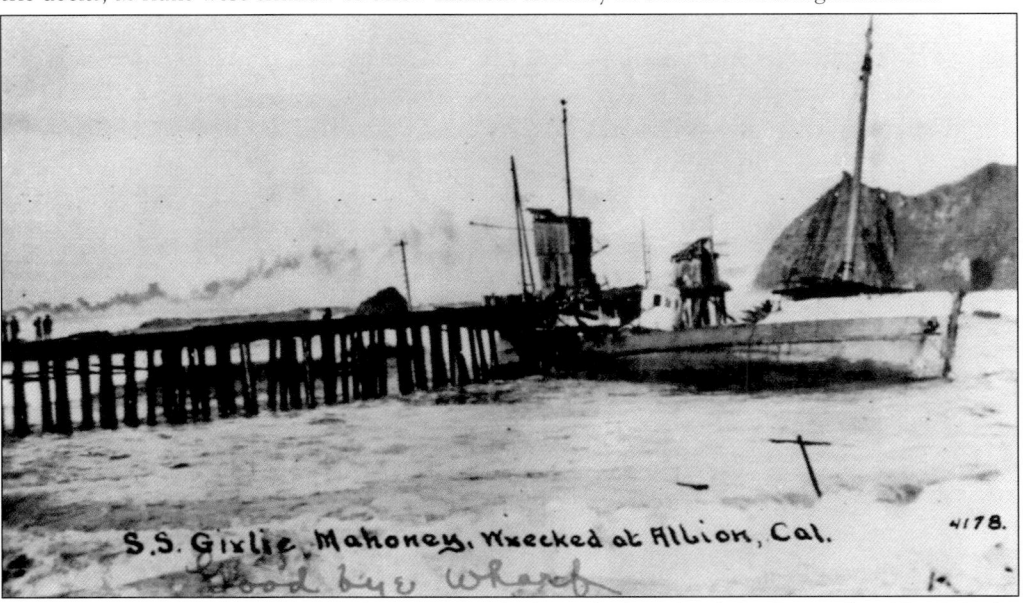

Ships are supposed to tie up at a wharf, not crash through the wharf. On December 23, 1919, the 15-year-old schooner *Girlie Mahoney* loaded with 361,000 feet of redwood lumber took out 150 feet of the Albion Wharf before landing on the beach a total loss. *Girlie Mahoney* had been built in Aberdeen, Washington, and was valued at $18,000.

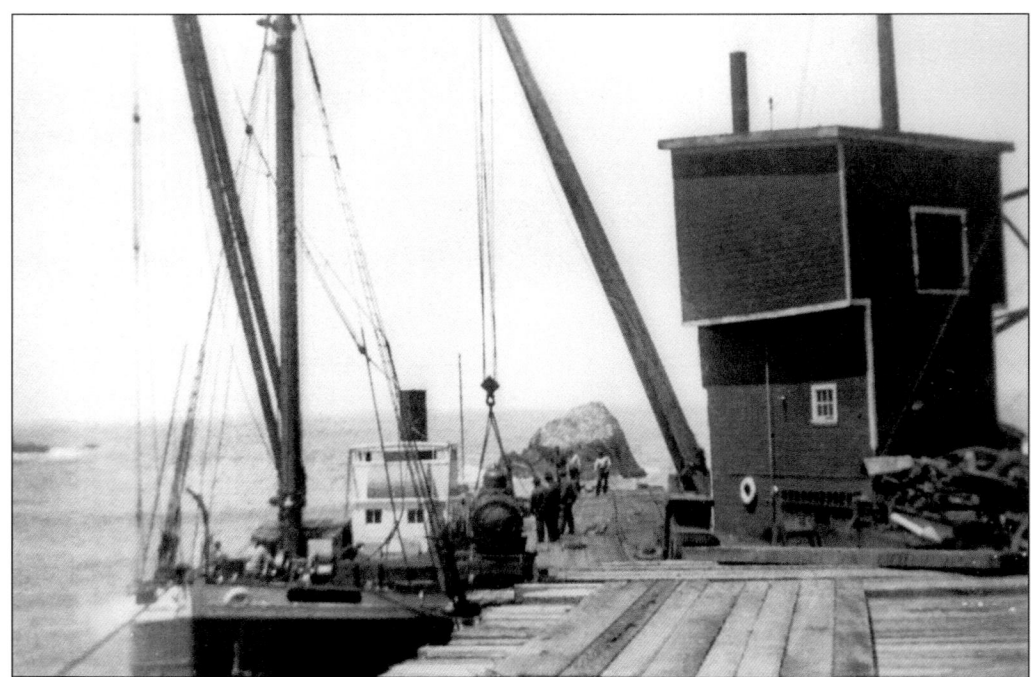

How is a railroad locomotive lifted off of a steam schooner and onto the Albion Wharf? Very, very carefully. Engines had been known to fall through their North Coast wharves if not treated carefully. This wood-burning locomotive No. 202 had been shipped to the Northwestern Pacific Railroad shops in Tiburon, down in San Francisco, for conversion to oil fuel consumption in 1923. The steam engine house on the end of the wharf had been enclosed by this time.

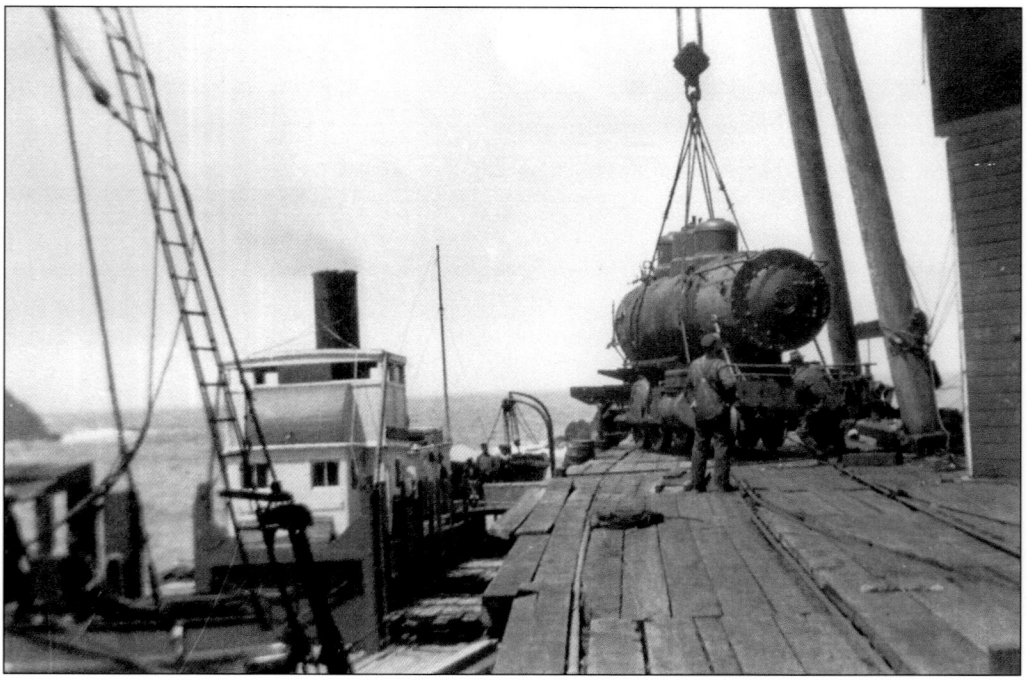

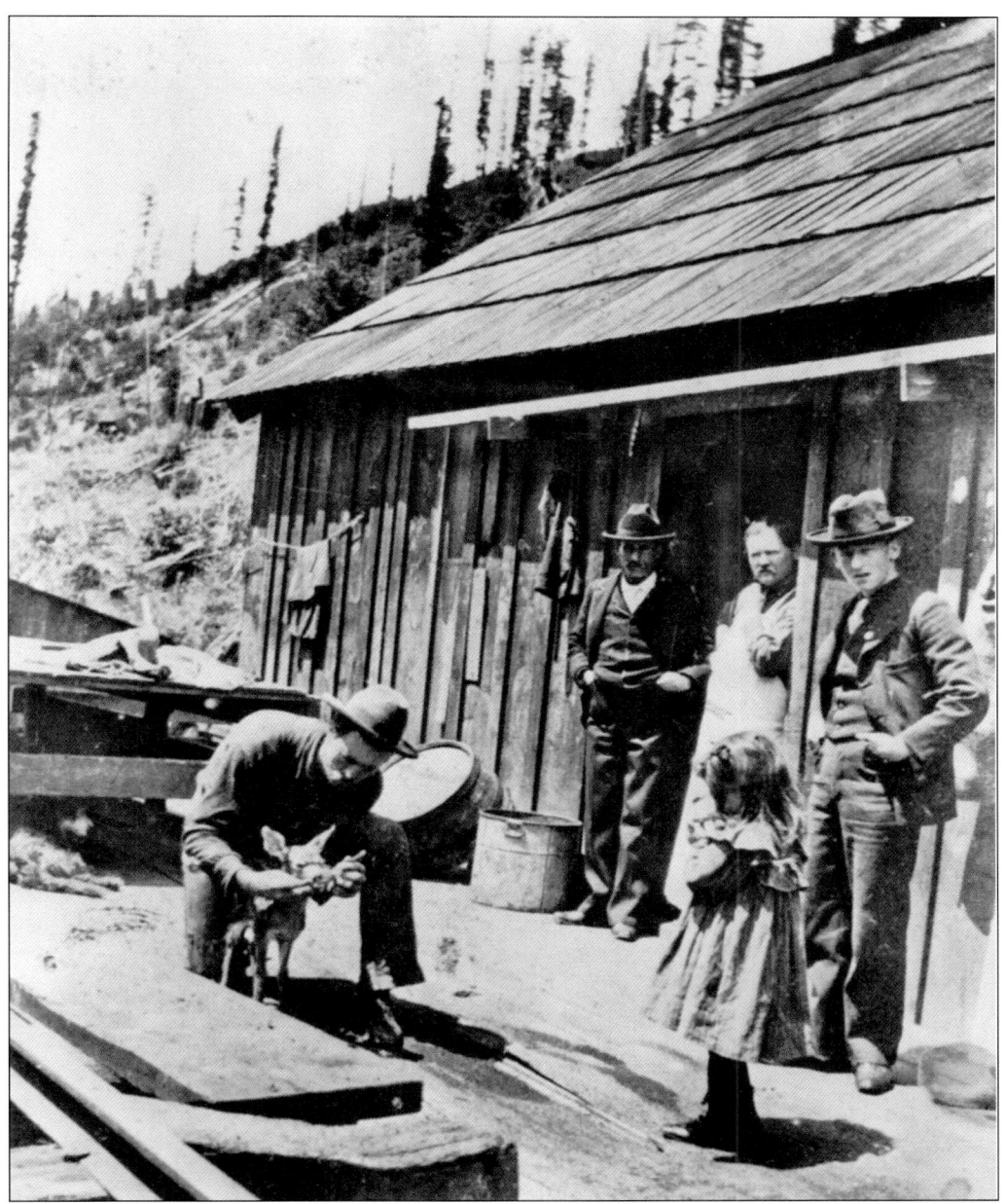

A logger spoon-feeds an abandoned fawn outside a cookhouse in a logging camp as a little girl, a cook, and others look on in awe. A wide variety of wildlife ended up being camp "pets." Ringtail cats (a raccoon-like creature) were popular pets in sleeping cabins because they caught mice. Raccoons became pets as did bear cubs and mountain lion cubs until they got too big.

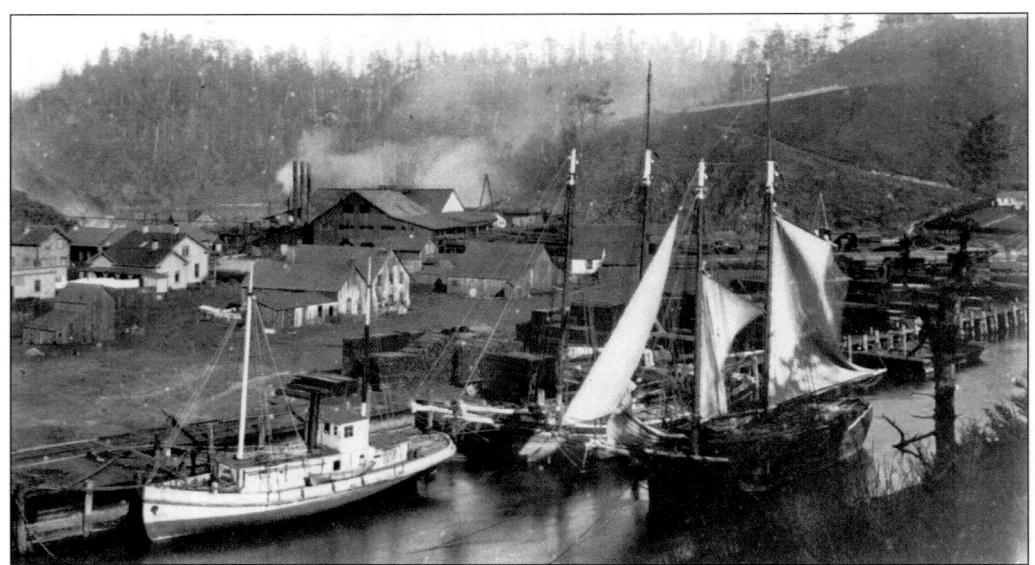

In this 1880 view, the tugboat *Maggie* and schooners *Albion* and the *Truckee* are all visible on the Albion River. This was the second big Albion Mill, which was built after a fire consumed the original structure. This mill burned in 1900 and was rebuilt yet again. The Southern Pacific Railroad bought the mill in 1907 for railroad construction lumber.

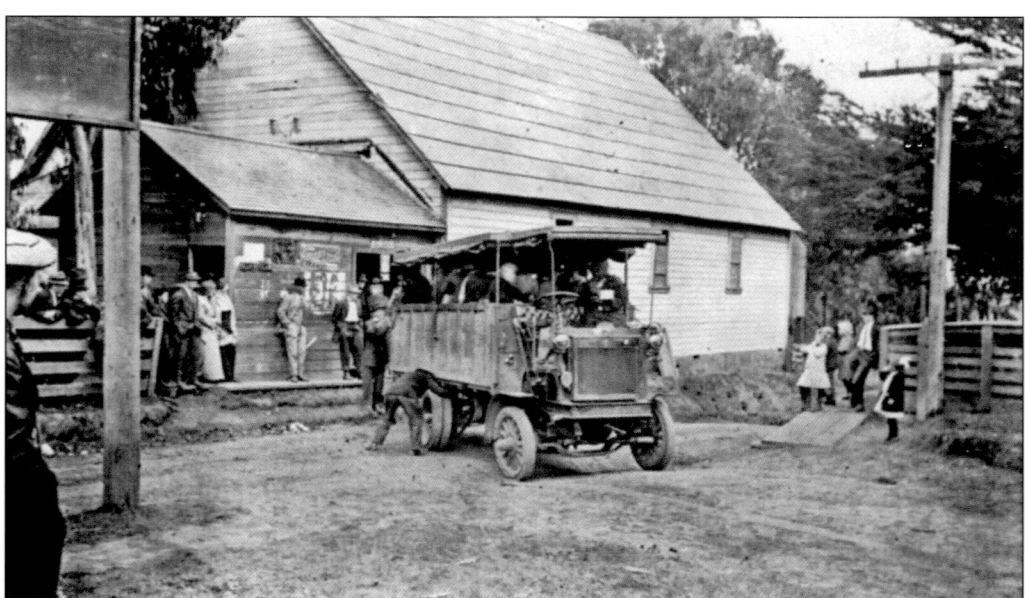

There's nothing like mechanical difficulties to attract a crowd. This 1906 auto stage, seen here near Albion, looks packed with passengers, and the driver appears to be oiling the chain.

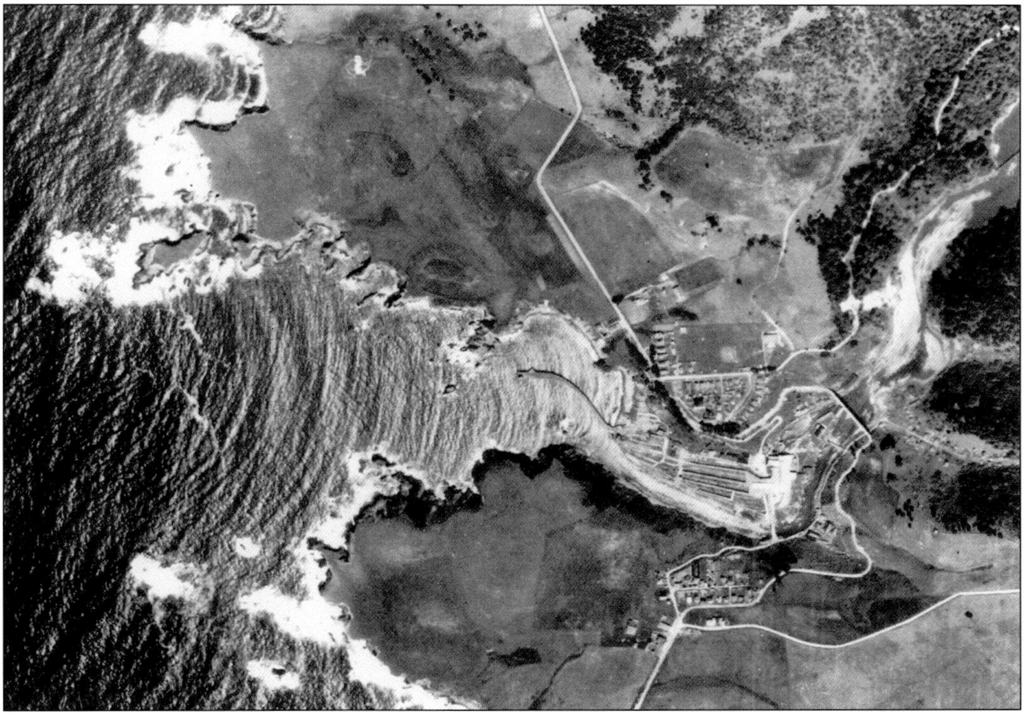

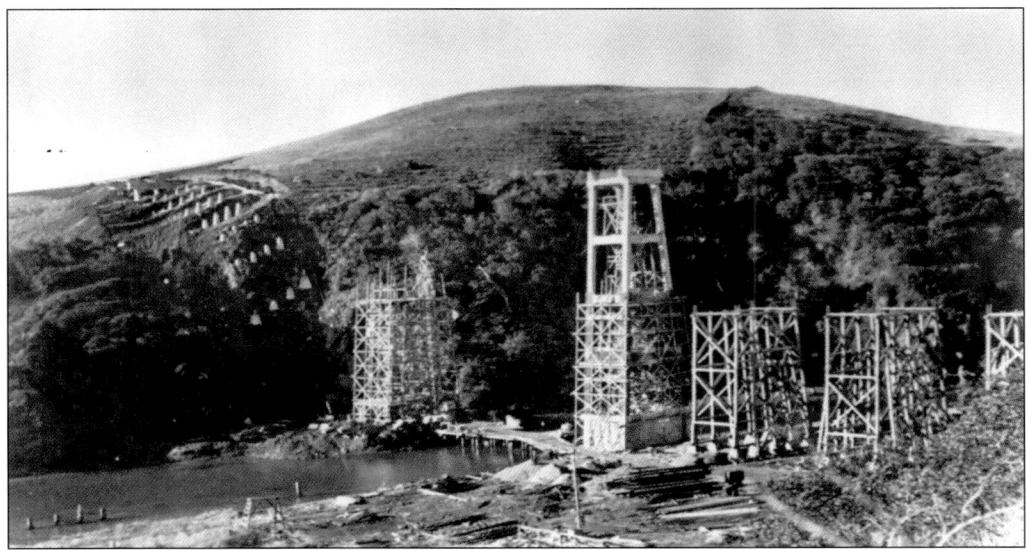

Pictured here is a view of Albion from above, possibly in the 1930s. The mill closed in the late 1920s, but the 1,200-foot-long wharf in the harbor is visible. The rich folks lived on the north (left) side of the river. The bridge is still at water level. Roads leave the Shoreline Highway for Albion Ridge and Comptche to the east.

The Albion Mill upriver was gone, and automobile traffic demanded high bridges over the harbors, not steep grades winding up and down to the river. Built in 1944 and still standing, this bridge is 122 feet above the water and is 468 feet long. The highway department considers it "functionally obsolete" but structurally sound.

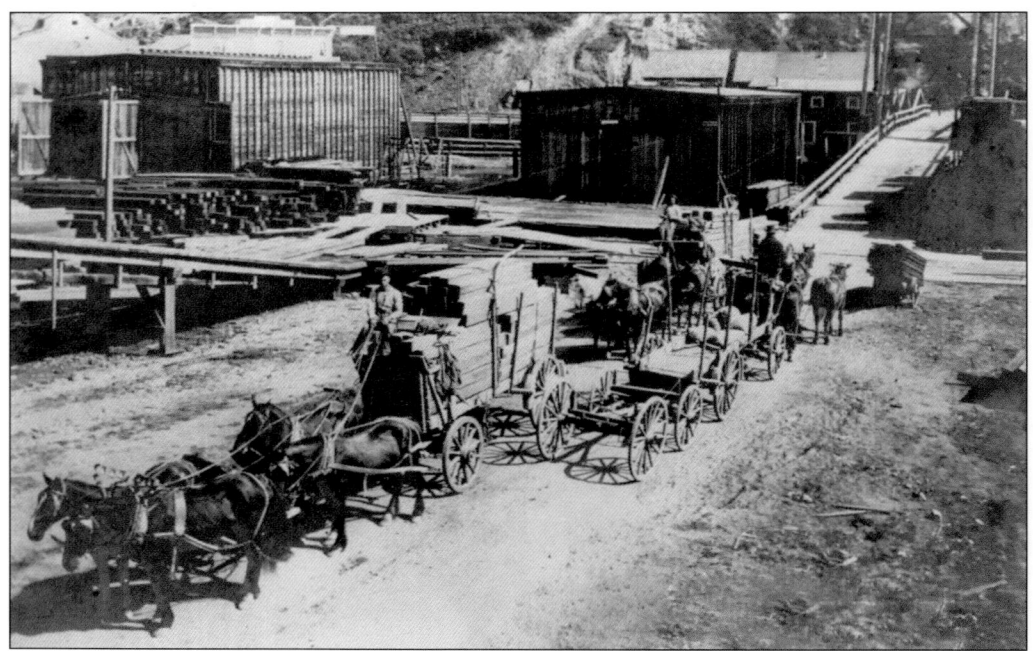

Wagons come and go over the Albion River Bridge around 1906. The wagon on the left weighed more than 1,900 pounds with a load of 117 railroad ties. The wagon behind it carried 137 ties. The empty wagon is headed back to the mill for another load.

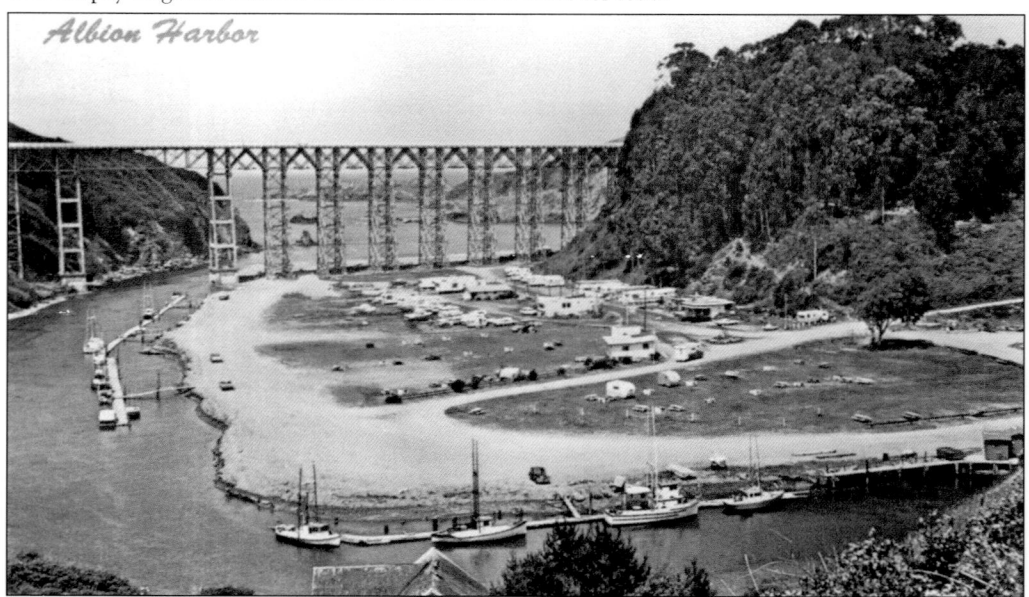

In 1965, the last vestige of industrial activity vanished at the Albion Mill site as timberland owner Masonite Corporation leased the property to Otto Miller. He created a fishing resort with a campground, docks and moorings, and a small restaurant. The scenic high bridge had replaced the water-level crossing upstream. Eucalyptus groves cover the north bank. Many North Coast mill sites are now campgrounds and state parks. Albion Flat has not changed much in the last 40 years.

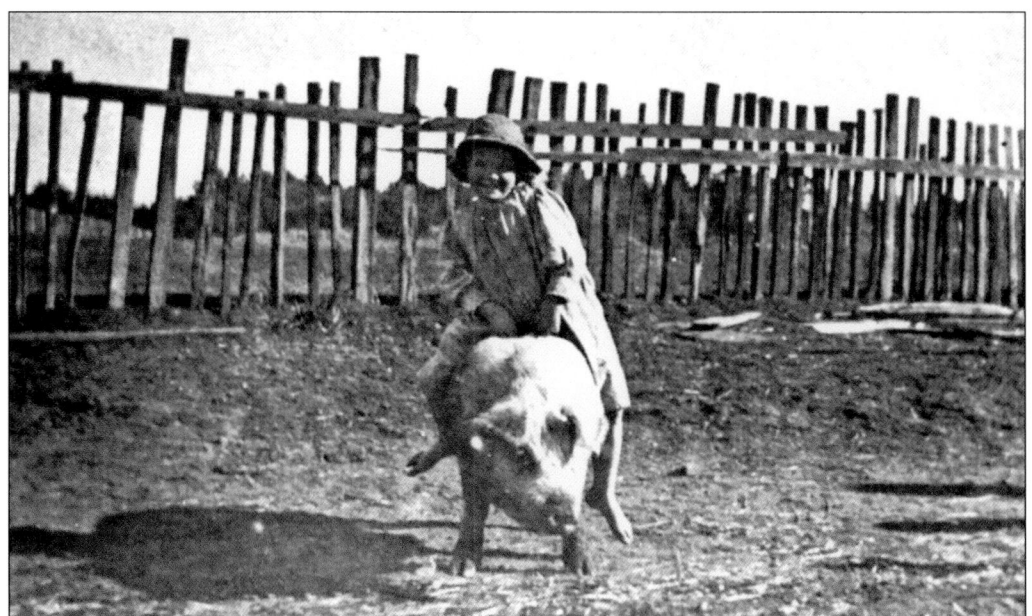

Kids along the coast found entertainment wherever it presented itself. No one said, "You cannot ride on a pig." If the pig (or the sheep or goat or calf) was willing to put up with the imposition, the ride was up for grabs. There were dozens of tiny schools educating children that came and went as fast as the shipping points and logging camps.

In the Little River woods around 1870, a team of oxen pulled log cars made with concave wheels on a pole road tramway. This bridge over School House Creek was reportedly constructed of living tree trunks whenever they grew in the right location. They were trimmed, topped, and left in place as part of the bridge supports.

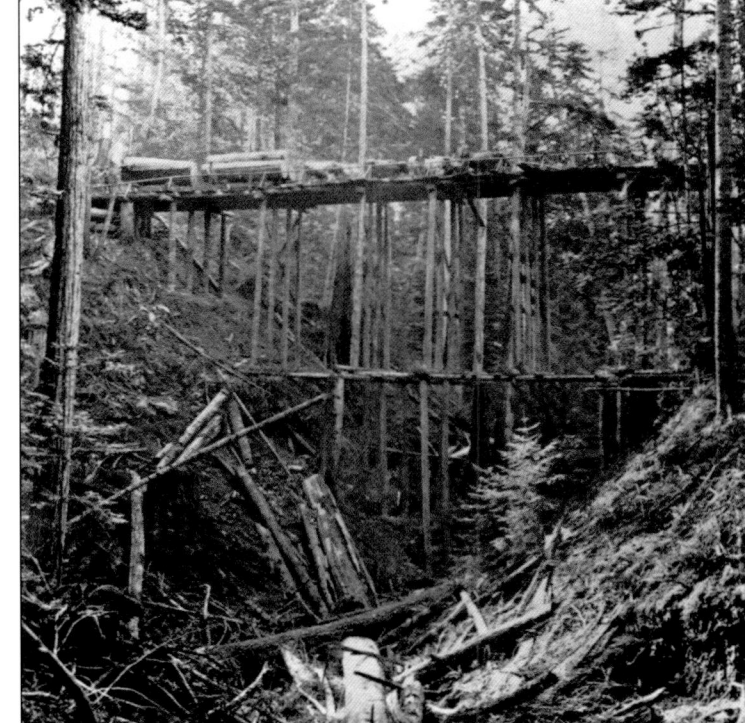

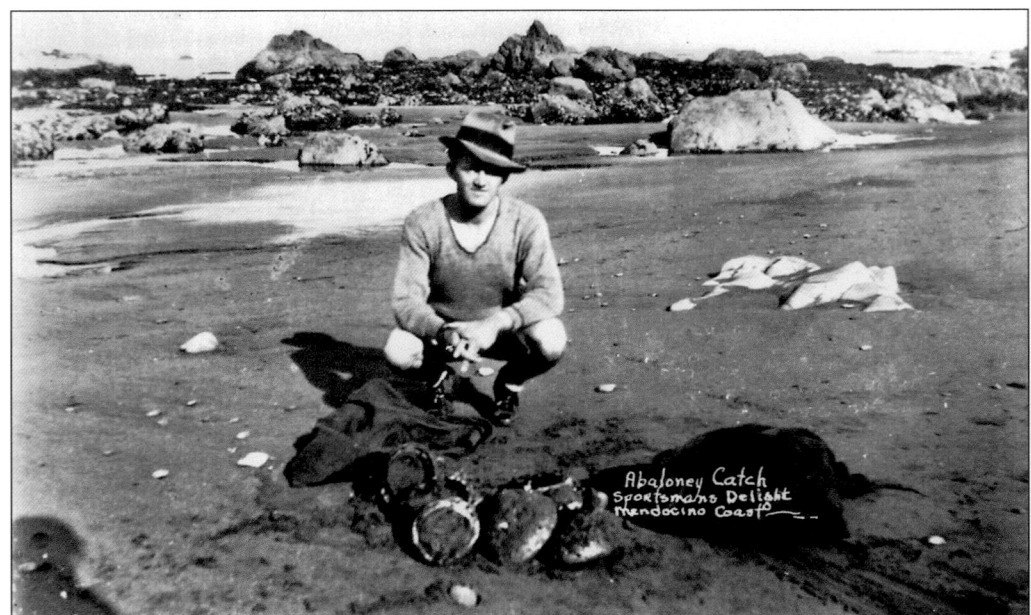

It has two eyes, one gill, and one big foot with tiny tentacles and has attracted sportsmen to the North Coast for decades: it is the yummy abalone. It is a sport fishing favorite, but is also illegally poached because it can be sold at a high price to restaurants. Abalone divers drown every year locally due to inattention to dangerous surf.

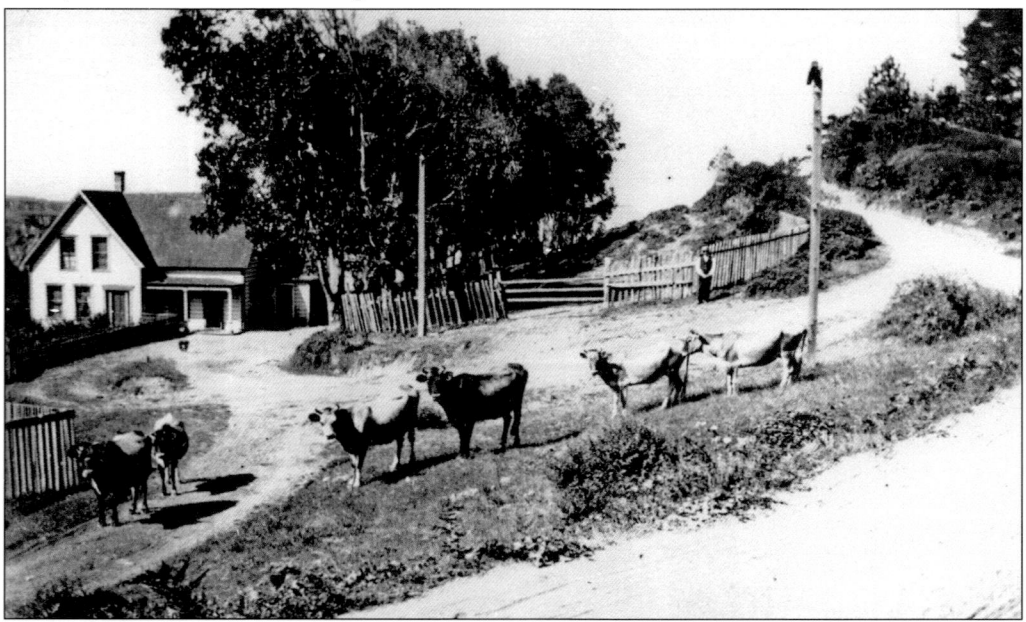

Today's lavish, forested Heritage House resort started as a farmhouse by the side of the road that would one day become the Shoreline Highway. Cattle in the road were a common problem for early coast motorists. Areas like this were popular locations for rumrunners to bring in booze during Prohibition. They off-loaded whiskey from ships and sneaked it into isolated coves by small boats to be collected and taken south.

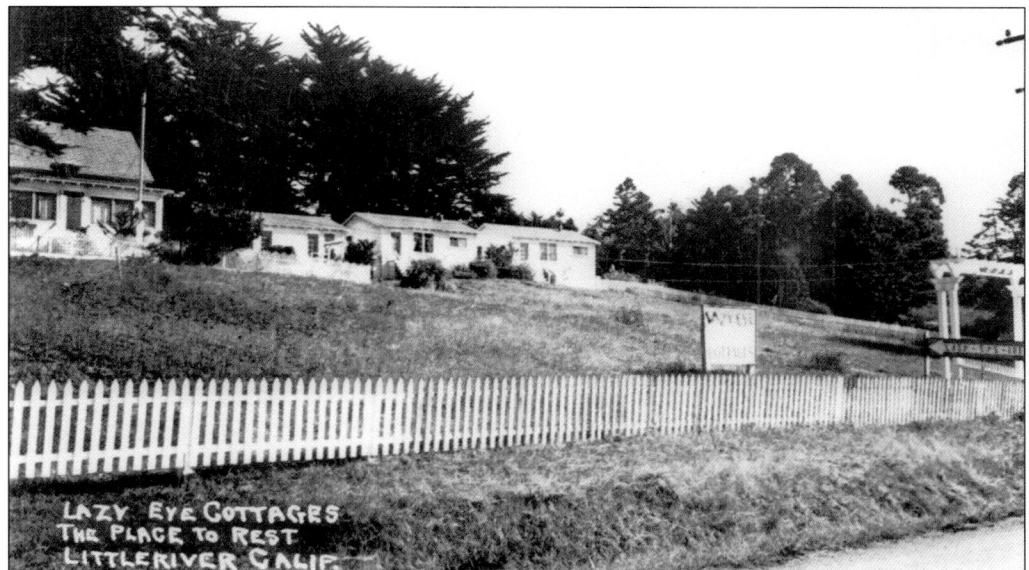

Cute names on roadside tourist cottages have been a tradition in Little River for more than 50 years. In this 1940s photograph, these lodgings offered relief to travel-weary motorists. Generations of families have come to the coast from the inland valleys to escape the summertime heat. This property is now the Inn at School House Creek.

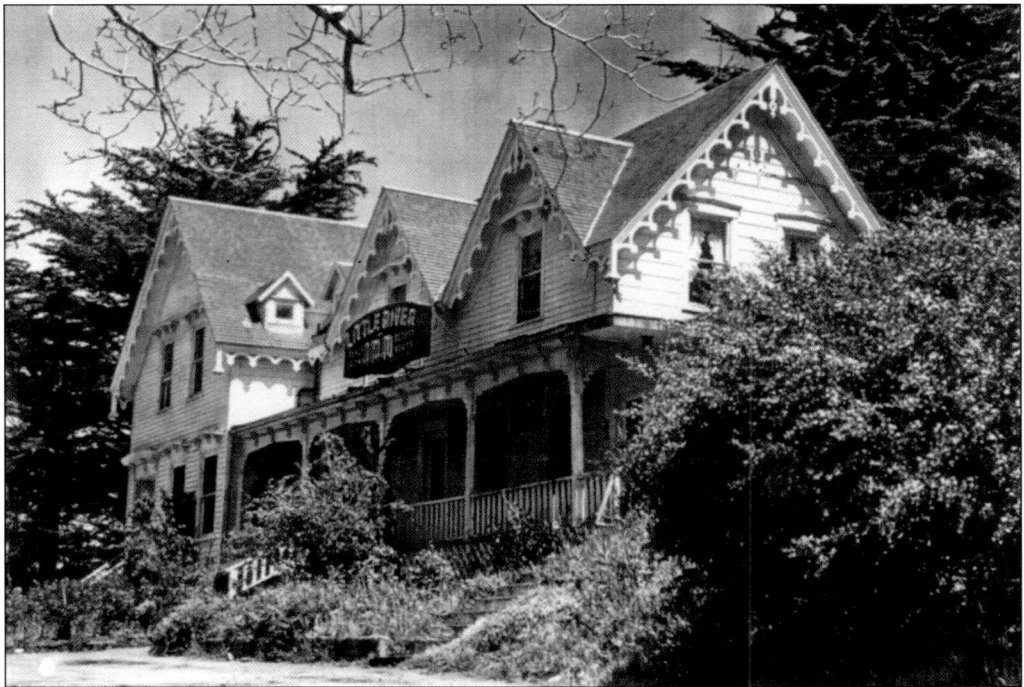

The Little River Inn was built in 1853 as early settler Silas Coomb's home but has functioned as a bar, restaurant, and lodging establishment since opening its doors to travelers in 1939. Many Hollywood celebrities have stayed here. Longtime owner Ole Hervilla was the local expert on abalone.

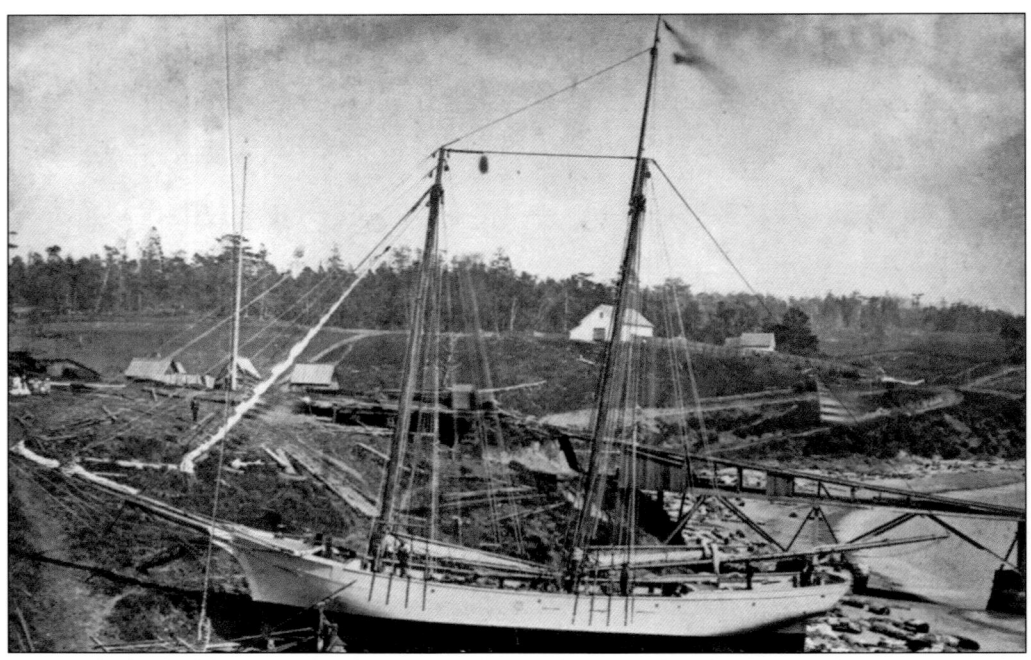

A Danish shipbuilder opened a shipyard on the north shore of Little River harbor in 1869. In the next 10 years, he built 14 schooners here. A wharf into the harbor survived until 1916. There was a wide turnout on the west side of the road winding up north from the river where travelers can pull over and look down into the shipbuilders' cove.

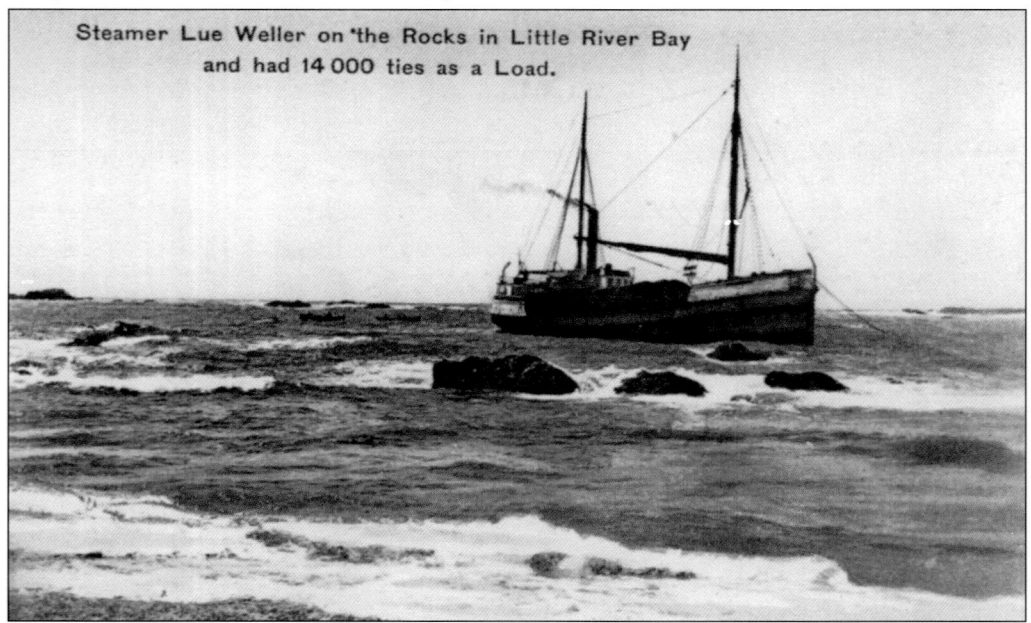

Literally hundreds of shipwrecks have littered the Mendocino Coast during the centuries. Some ships were total losses. Some ships could be refloated and towed to a local shipyard or to San Francisco for repairs. Other wrecks offered cargo that could be salvaged. Any cargo washing up on shore was immediately scavenged by local farmers and ranchers for useful items.

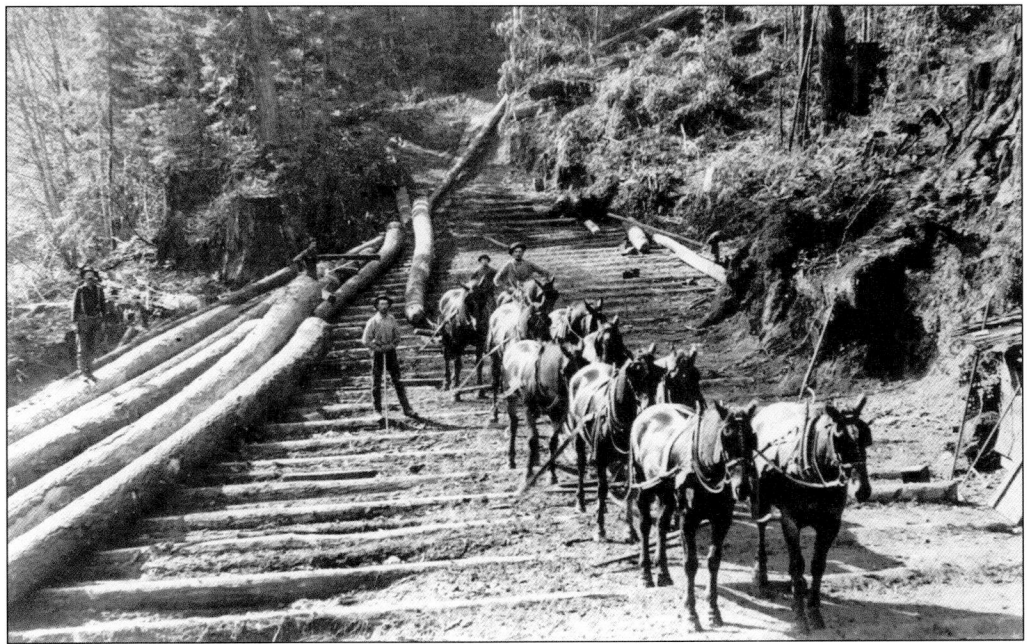

The logs on the left in this picture may have been destined to be ships spars and masts or pilings as they have not been bucked into shorter lengths. The tall, straight growth of these trees made them popular for maritime uses. On this corduroy skid road, horse teams were in use instead of oxen.

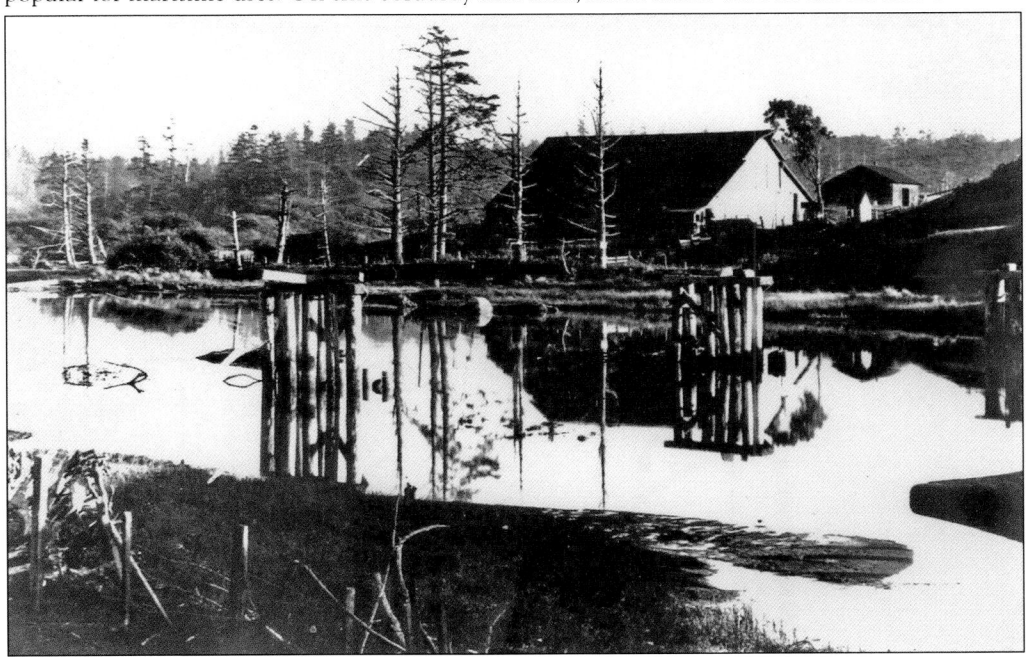

Capturing images in reflection was another skill early photographers liked to perfect. Here old pilings and a barn reflect in the still water of Little River or its millpond. The pilings could have supported a bridge or a framework to control logs floating downstream. There were sawmills here from 1864 to 1893.

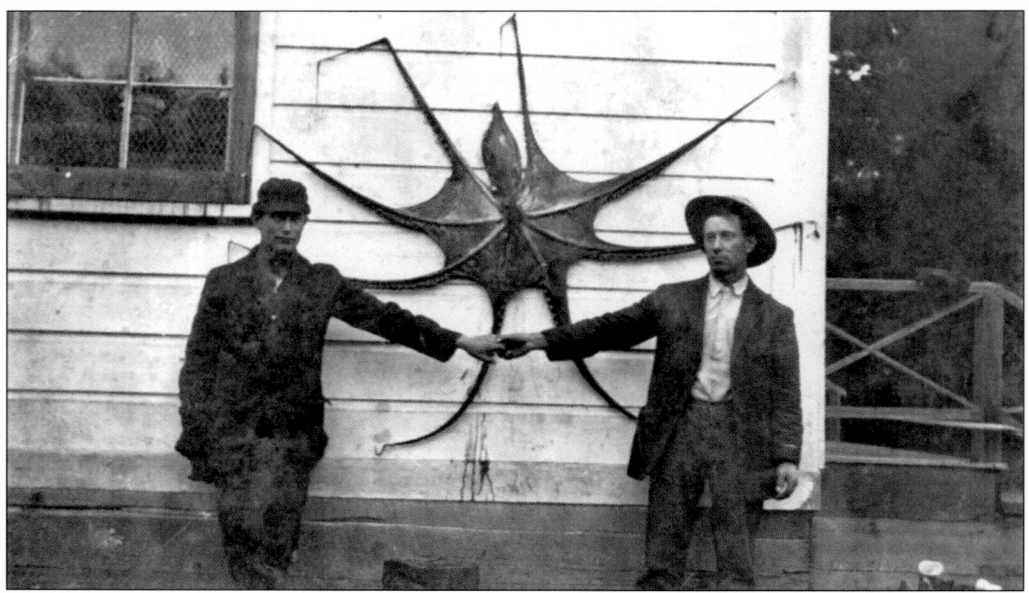

There must have been a story behind the large octopus nailed to the wall by the Albion harbor. The men held hands to show the size of the creature. Imagine the surprise of the fisherman who pulls in his net or reels in a line and finds a critter this long holding on to the bait.

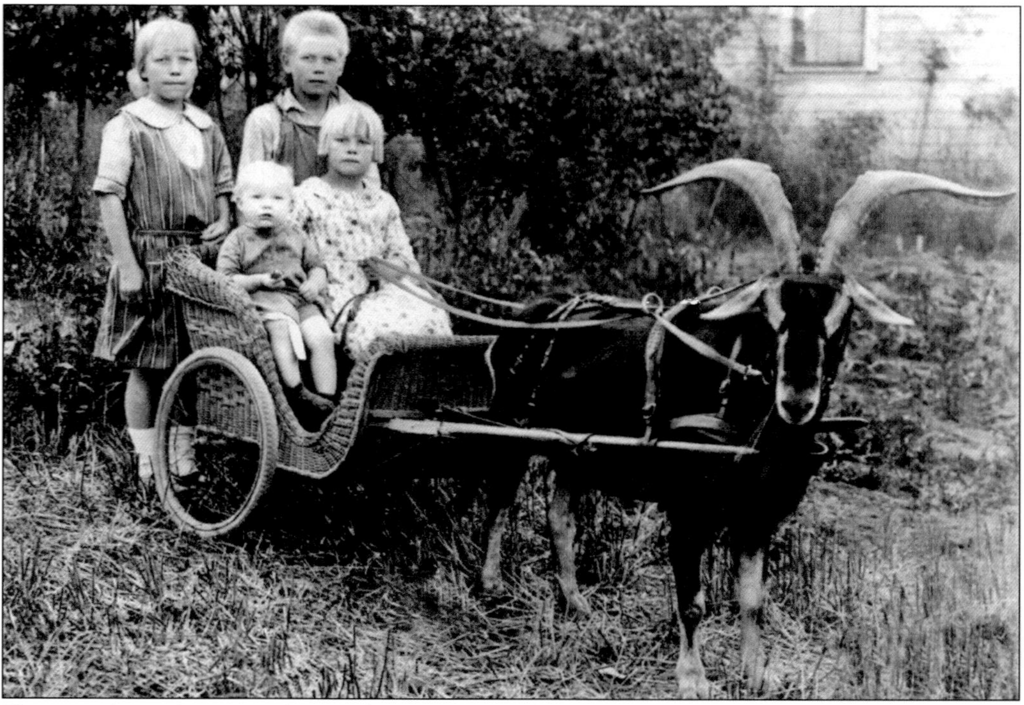

Photographers often went door-to-door in villages along the coast with this goat cart taking family group photographs. Many families on the Mendocino Coast more than 80 years have photographs of their elders as kids in this very same goat cart. This group of Finnish children includes the author's father-in-law, Andrew Tahja, the tall boy in back.

Three

Mendocino and Environs
10 Miles
Mendocino to Fort Bragg

The north bank of the Big River once held the reason for Mendocino's existence. For 80 years, sawmills operated here, drawing on timber resources upriver, and today all that remains are some pilings in the river. To the east now is more than 7,000 acres of the Big River unit of Mendocino Headlands State Park, established in 2002. It can be accessed by hiking, boating, or biking the old haul road, and Catch-A-Canoe and Bicycles Too on the south shore supply visitors with rentals. Wildlife, birds, and flowers are now the attraction where industrial logging once was.

Get oriented to Mendocino Village at the Ford House Visitor Center and the Kelley House Museum. Both are on Main Street and have knowledgeable docents. Gallery Bookshop at Main and Kasten Streets has every book ever written about the area.

Visitors find it is a great village for walking as everything is close. It is a historic preservation district, and locals work hard to maintain its appearance. Built by New Englanders, it was the set for years for the television series *Murder, She Wrote*.

Mendocino Headlands State Park surrounds the village with hiking trails. Farther north, the Russian Gulch State Park turnoff leads to Point Cabrillo Drive, the old highway for access to three state parks. Passing Caspar, the Shoreline Highway reaches Fort Bragg. Once dominated by the Union Lumber Company and sawmill on the headlands, the town is now focused on tourism.

The eventual use of the old mill site after environmental remediation is a subject of serious debate. A shoreline trail is hoped for, some park lands are promised, but what happens to hundreds of acres with stunning coastal access will require careful planning and community input.

Visitors should be sure to take in the Noyo Harbor area and watch the sea lions that like to haul out on the boat docks of the marina on the south shore to sun themselves. Tourists can also hike down to Glass Beach at the north end of town, stand atop the Pudding Creek Trestle, and then hike down the old haul road that offers miles of beach access for foot traffic.

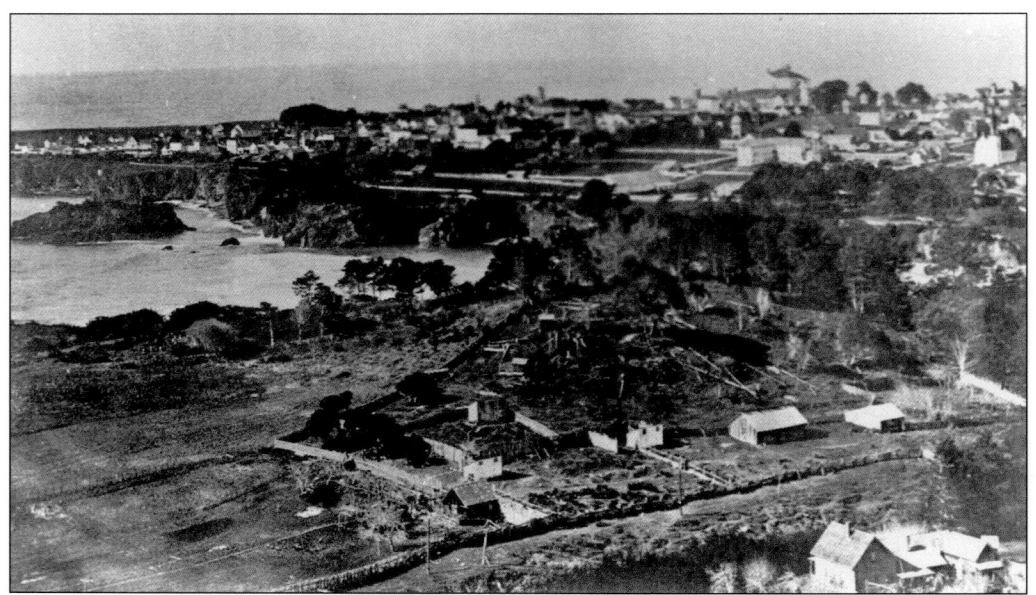

Before coastal travelers dropped down to cross Big River, they passed the Comptche Road turnoff (the stagecoach route to Ukiah) and came to China Gardens. Here the Asian population grew produce for restaurants and grocers in the village of Mendocino and for nearby sawmill and logging camp cookhouses. Today this area is the grounds of the Stanford Inn.

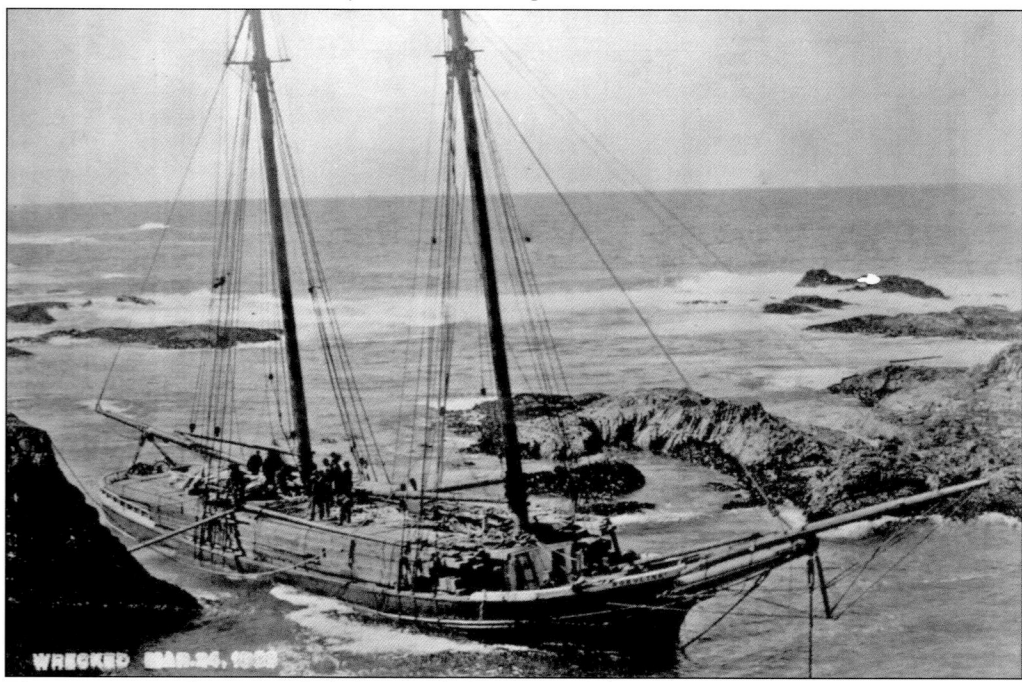

This two-mast schooner called the *Bobalink* finds itself where no ship wants to be: upon shore with a full load on deck. The crew has already put a plank over the side, and they can walk to shore. If the deck load is jettisoned, a high tide may lift it off the rocks, or that same tide could come in and smash it to splinters. In 1898, one life was lost in the wreck of the *Bobalink*.

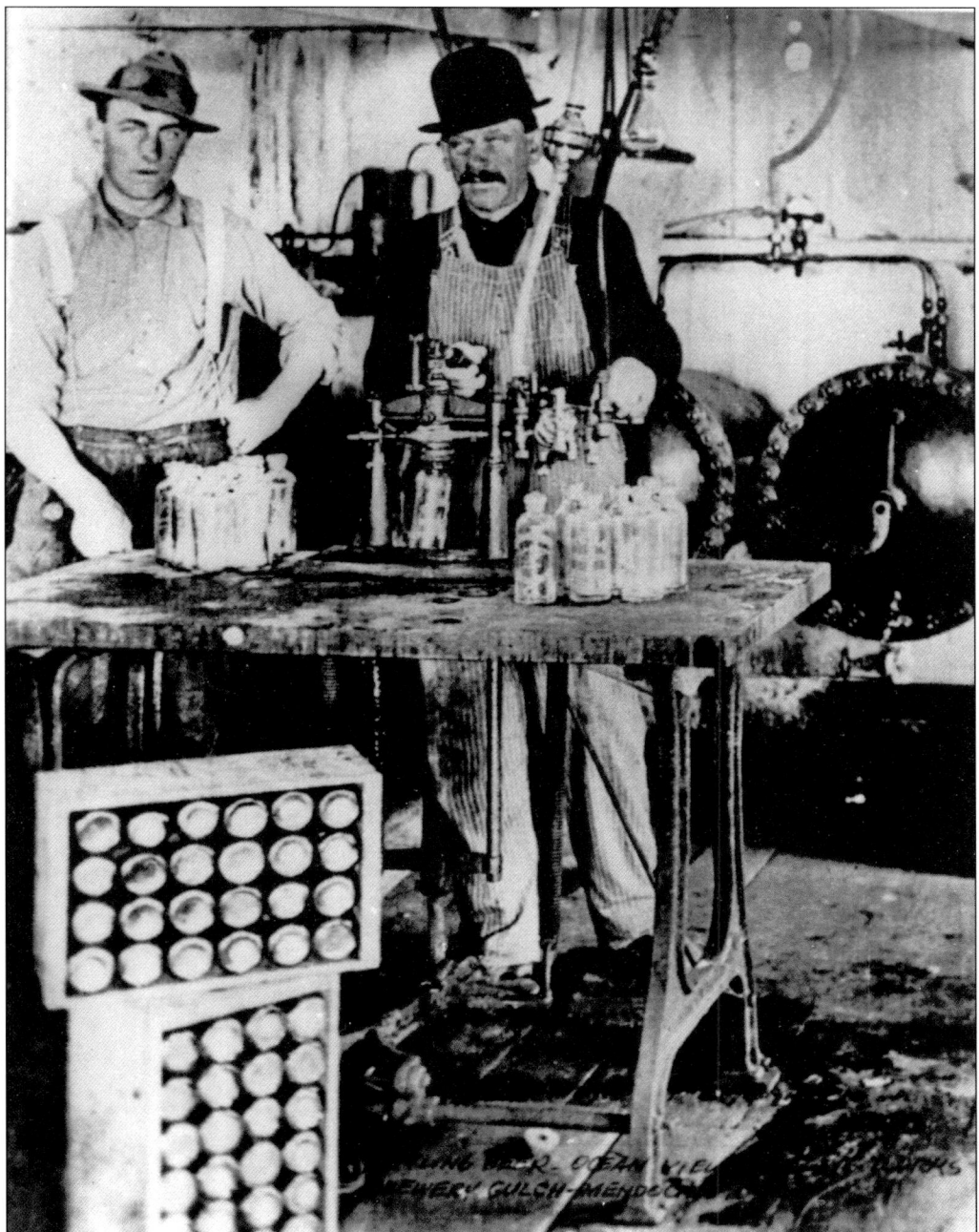

In the 1890s, the Ocean View Bottling Works in Brewery Gulch was one of several breweries south of Mendocino. Mendocino Village voted to go dry in 1909, ten years before the rest of the nation. The breweries tried to switch to bottling soda pop. At one point, Pine Grove Brewery north of Mendocino bottled 10,000 gallons yearly. Lumber mills allowed workers to take home scrap wood for heating and cooking fuel.

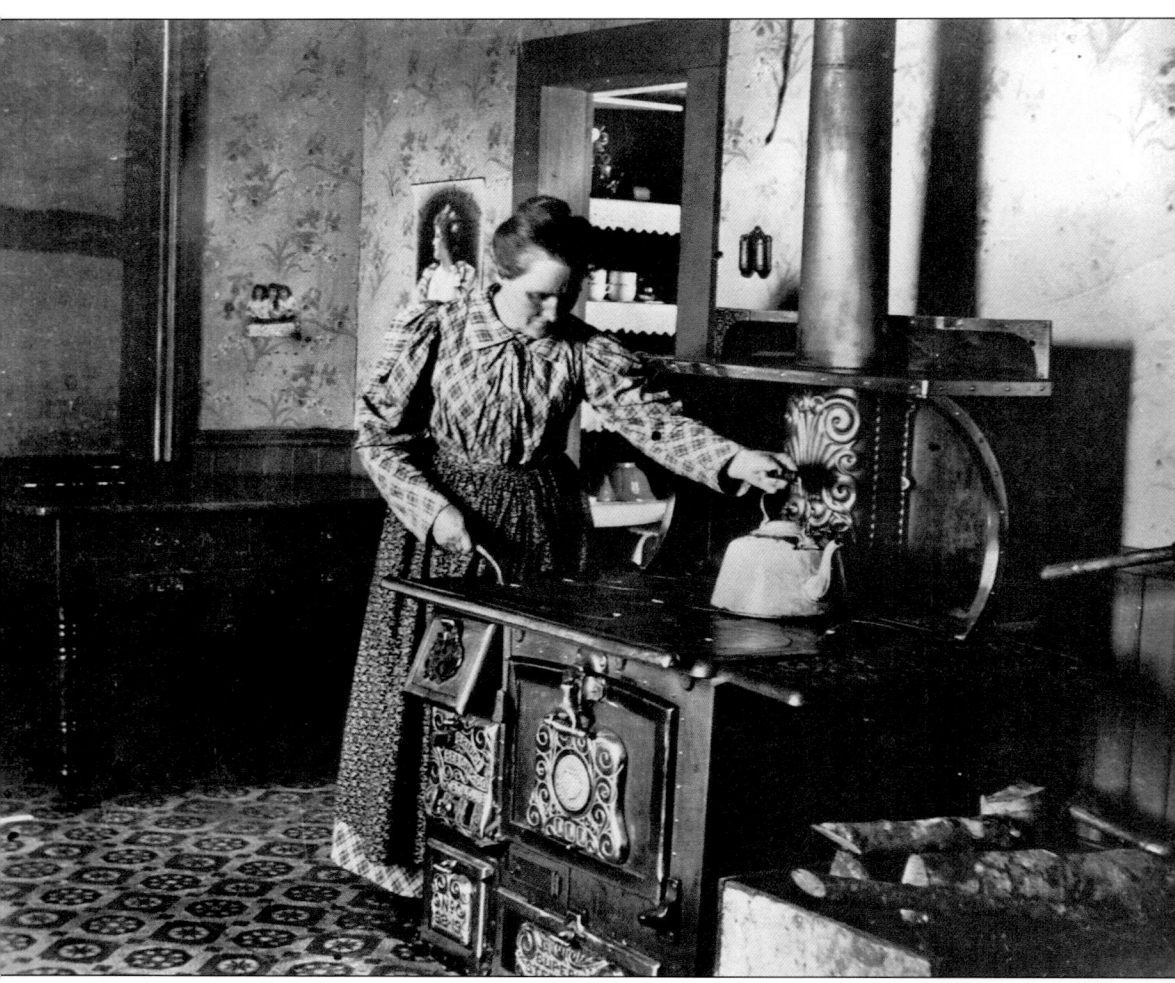

This housewife was probably proud of her wood range made by Bridge Beach and Company of St. Louis, Missouri. Her wood box is full, the kettle is heating, light shines in her pantry, and a calendar girl is over her shoulder. Wood ranges like these provided welcome warmth to a house in a climate that was often cool and damp.

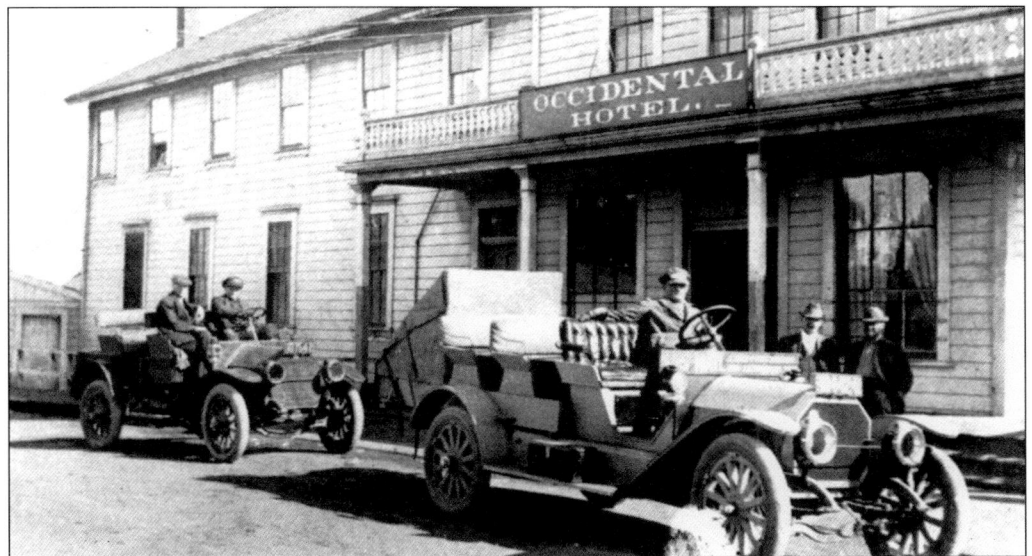

By 1914, horse-drawn stagecoaches had been replaced by auto stages. Outside the Occidental Hotel in Mendocino, passengers would load, and United States mailbags would be tucked in back. The Occidental Hotel hosted travelers from 1888 until it burned in 1941. Ed Stoddard owned this auto stage.

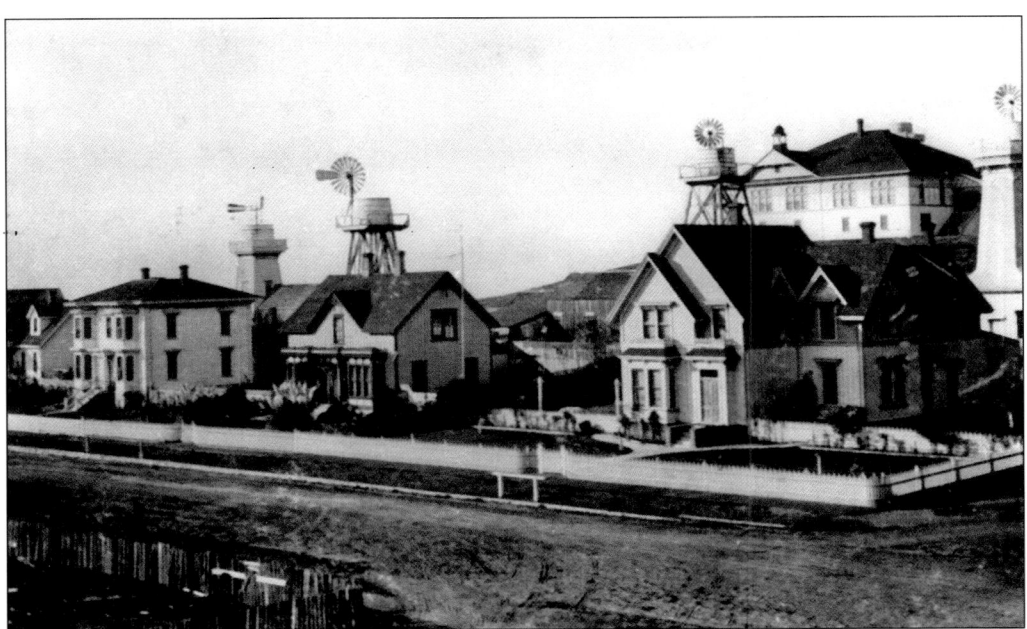

Pictured is Bankers Row in Mendocino with the high school on the hill behind the elegant mansions. From left to right are the Maxwell Jarvis House, built in 1878; the Brown House, built in 1880; and the Blair House, built in 1888. A trim fence line with gates, sidewalk, and hitching posts borders Little Lake Street.

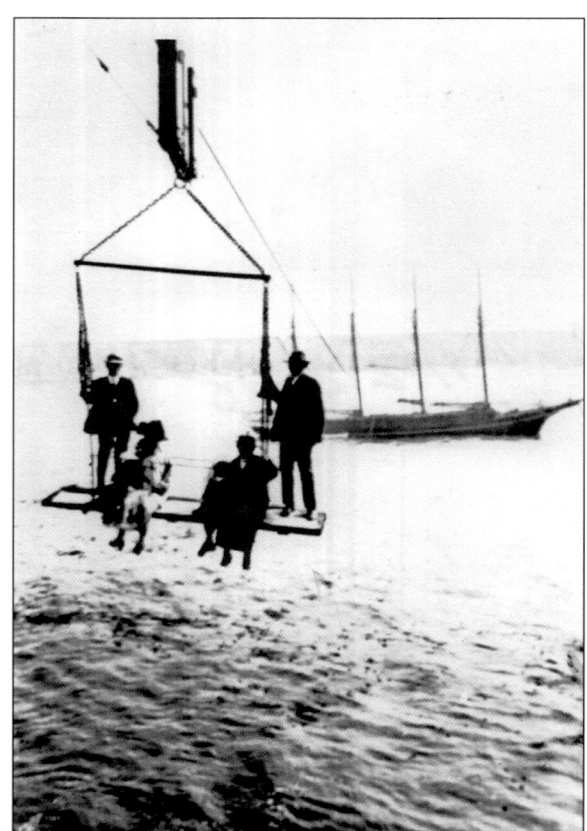

Women and children are seated, and men just hang on as a group slides down the cable to a ship probably bound for San Francisco. Having no wharves in Mendocino Bay meant bravery and a strong grip on the children to reach the ship's deck. Later improvements, seen in the photograph below, included a more secure box to sit in for the journey over the water.

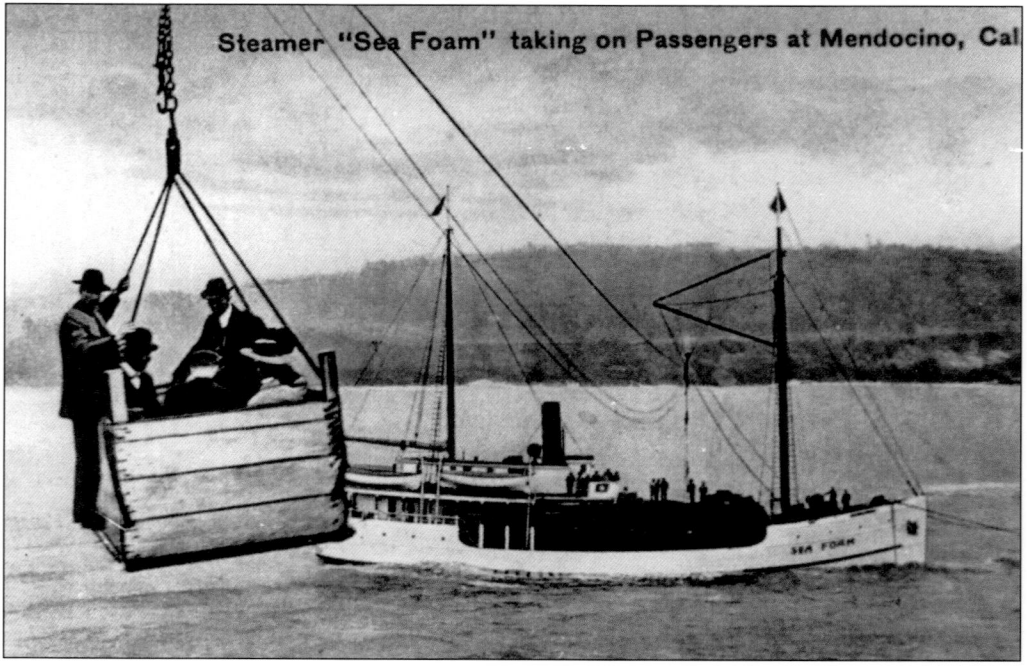

Steamer "Sea Foam" taking on Passengers at Mendocino, Cal

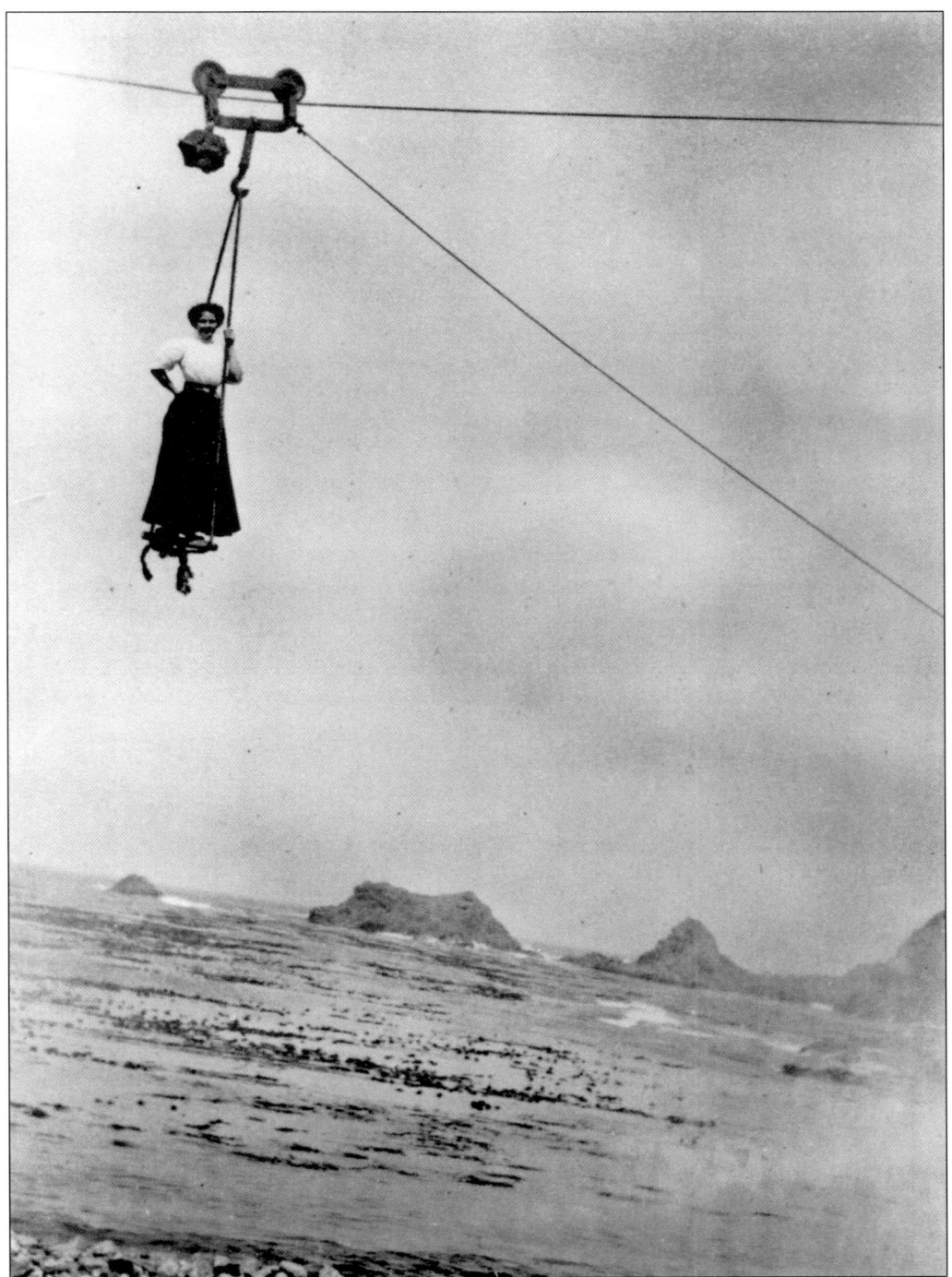

There's no doubt about it: this lady was showing off. Bundles of lumber slid down to ships on this "traveler," the mechanical unit on the cable, but so did this intrepid woman. Men saw nothing unusual in swinging down off the bluffs like this, but it was very unusual to see a woman do so.

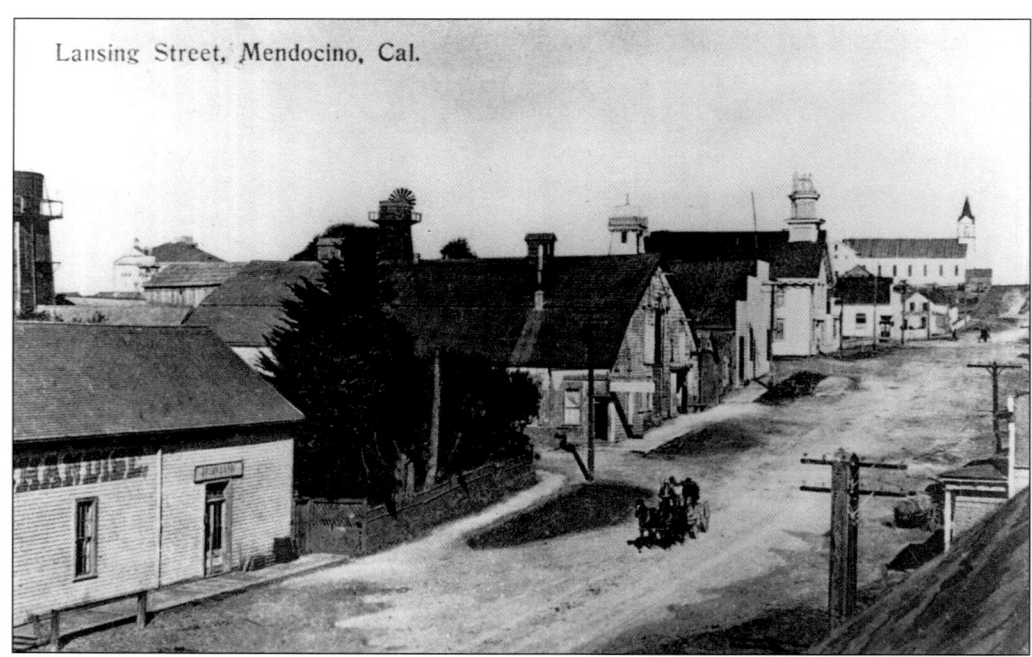

Cars may clog Lansing Street today, but things were slower at this time. Albion Street crosses behind the trees looking north. The Masonic temple is located just beyond the Ukiah Street intersection, and the Catholic church is visible on top of the hill. The merchandise store on the corner boasts a sidewalk. Water towers peek over rooftops.

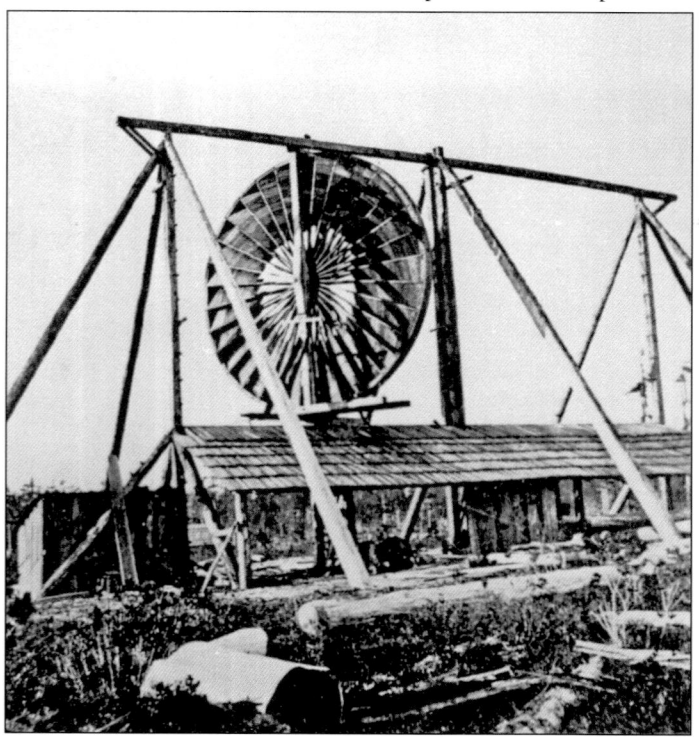

If windmills could provide power to pump water, why not try wind power at a sawmill? In 1890, the Heeser family tried it east of Mendocino. The angle of the curved metal blade wheel was fixed, and wind is fickle, so no one knew when, or for how long, power was available. It soon failed.

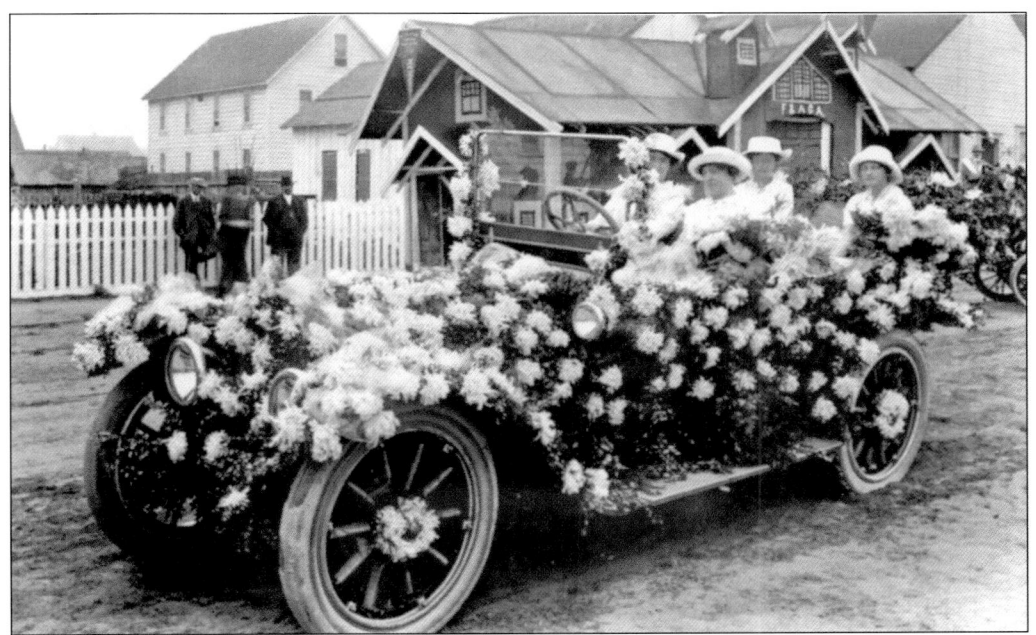

An entry in the 1913 Mendocino County Products Fair in Ft. Bragg is covered in flowers. Behind it is a replica of Mendocino's Apple Hall on a float. Below an automobile is done up in apples for the 1914 Mendocino Apple Fair. Parasols protect riders on a sunny day in an image from an old calendar page.

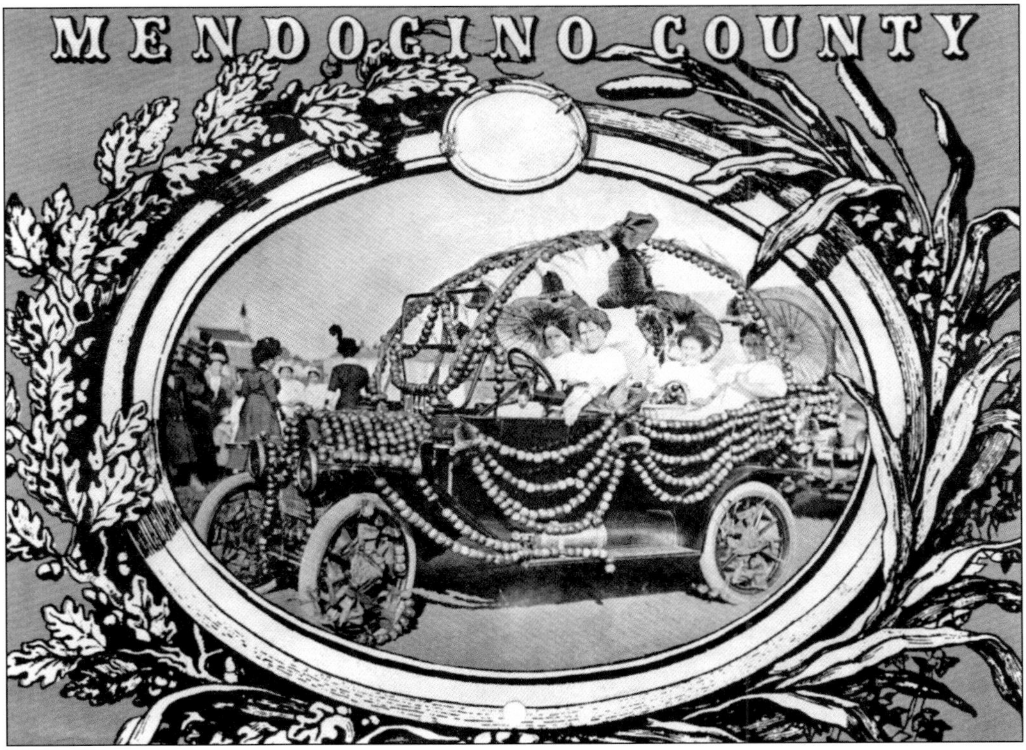

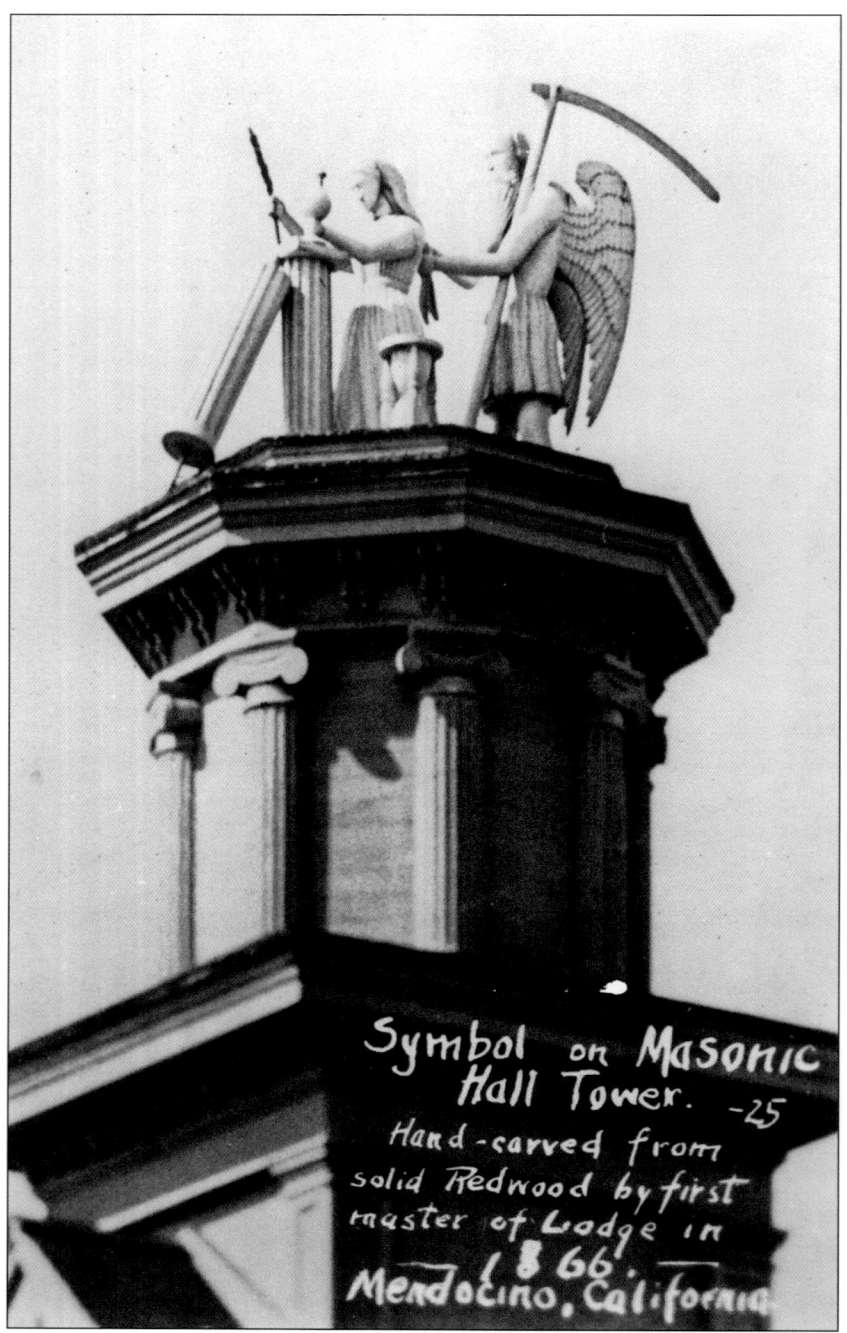

"Father Time and the Maiden" crown the top of the Masonic temple in Mendocino. In 1866, Erick Albertson was in charge of building the hall and carving the statue from a single block of wood. The female figure is standing at a broken column upon which an open book rests. She holds a tree branch, and there is an urn with an hourglass nearby. The bearded and winged male figure with a scythe braids her hair. All these elements are a part of the Masonic order's symbolism and ritual.

Visitors to Mendocino today don't understand why the Presbyterian church faces away from Main Street. One hundred years ago, there was a street in front of the church, but it is gone now. The church was built in 1868 at a cost of $7,000. The Masonic temple is visible to the left, but not much in the way of a town existed in between.

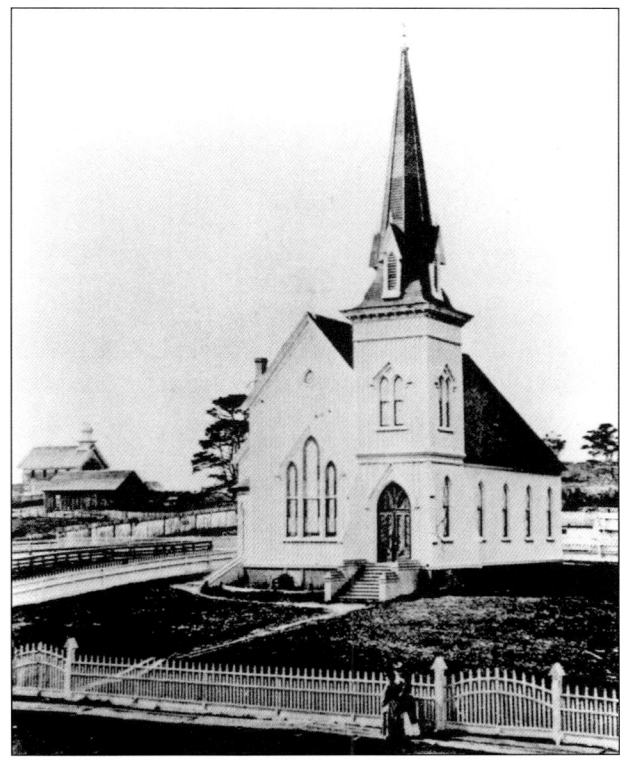

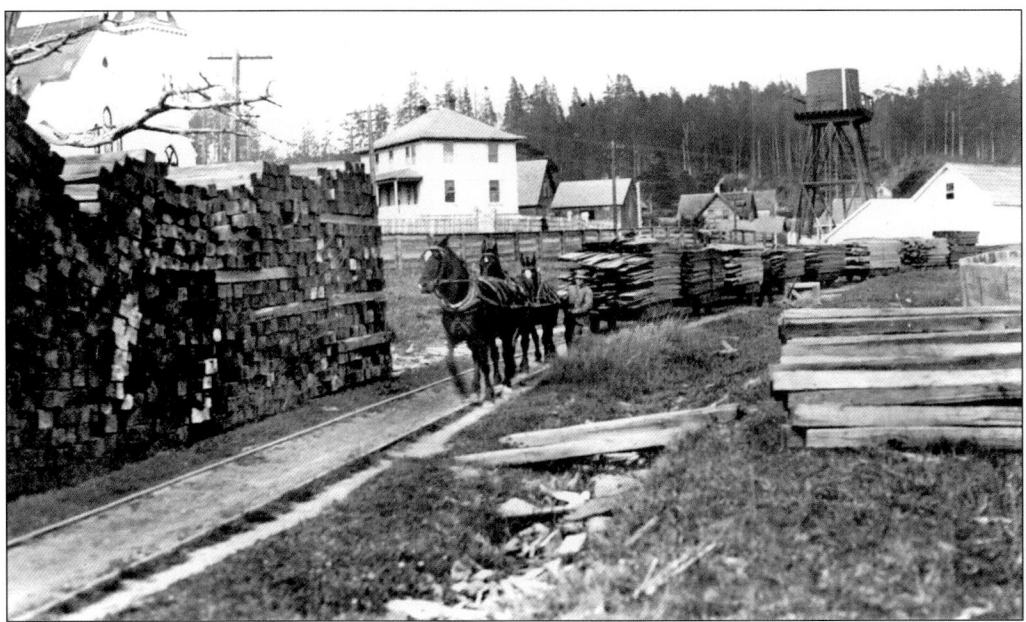

The church peeks out behind piled railroad ties as a horse team pulls lumber along the tramway to the shipping point around 1913. A steam engine pulled the lumber cars from the mill to the bluff top, and then horsepower took over. Stacks of drying lumber blocked all view of the ocean from the village.

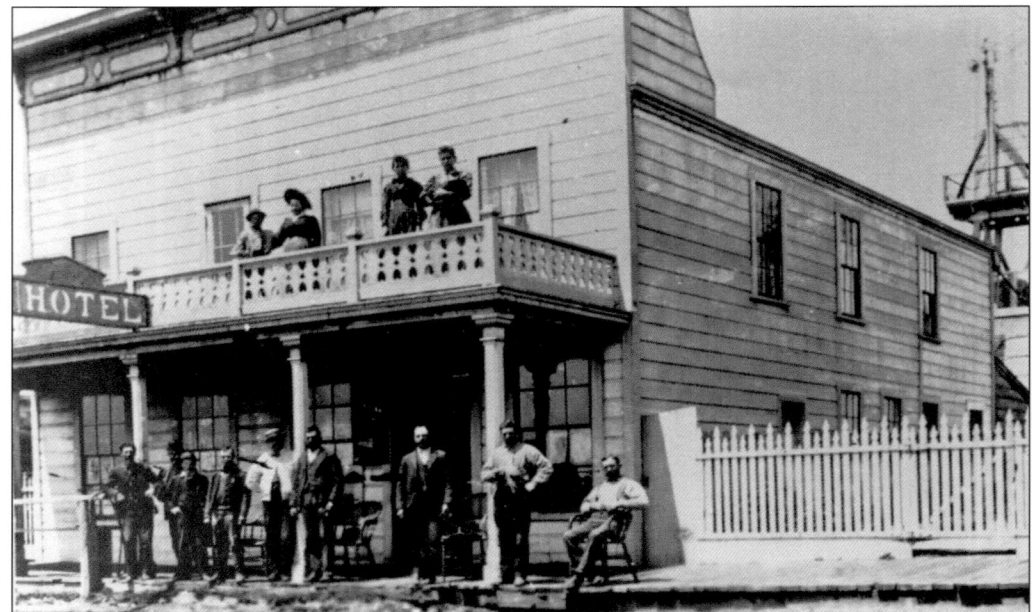

The Neto Hotel was on the west end of Main Street, near the intersection with Osborne Street. In the 1890s, guests and staff pause for the photographer. False fronts were a common feature in building design in Mendocino to make structures seem more impressive. There was a bar inside to generate additional income.

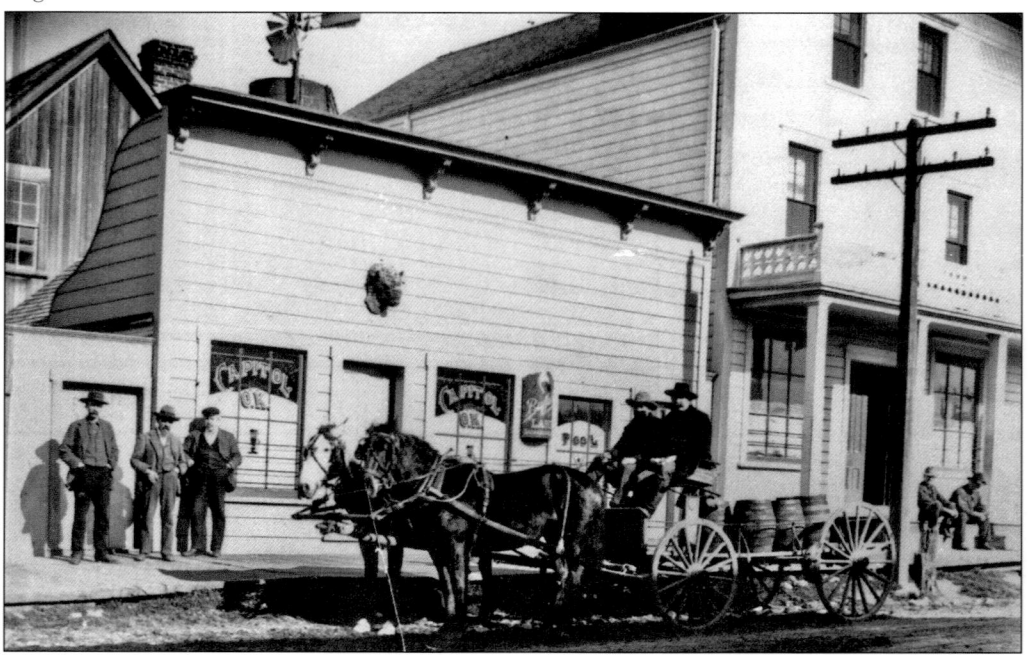

Opened in 1883, the Buffalo Saloon was another false-fronted establishment on Main Street. Barrels of beer are being delivered from the brewery north at Pine Grove owned by Martin Brinzing, who rides on the wagon. Note the stuffed buffalo head over the door. The windmill in the background filled a tank on a tower.

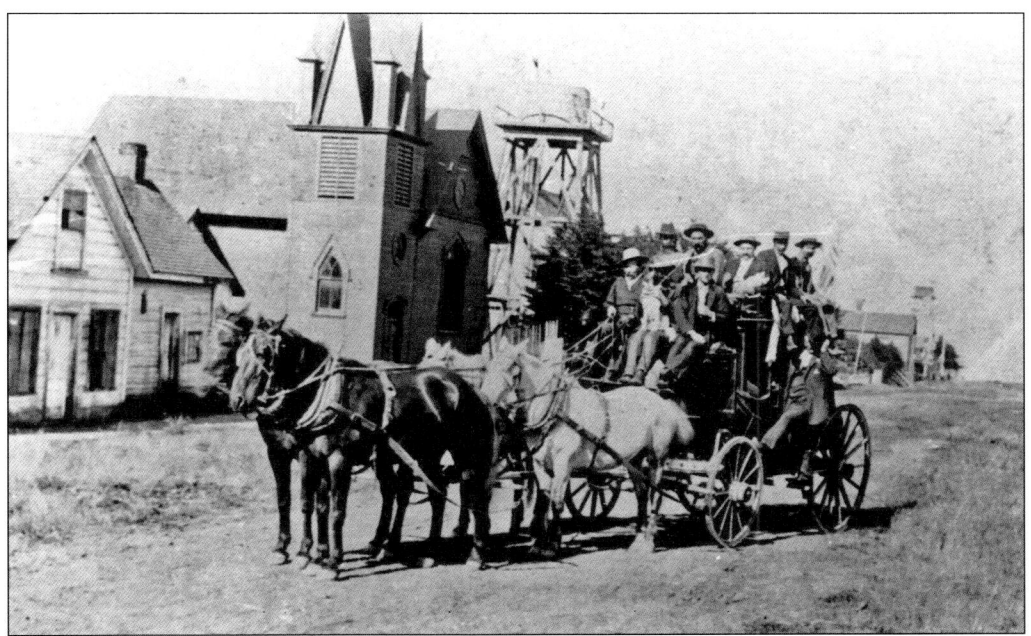

In the background of this image is the Baptist church, built in 1864. The stage prepares to leave town. Passengers could travel inside or on top, but cold weather was probably a deciding factor. Mendocino was what reference books call a "boss" hub town in 1886, with one stage line entering from the north, two from the south, and one from Ukiah.

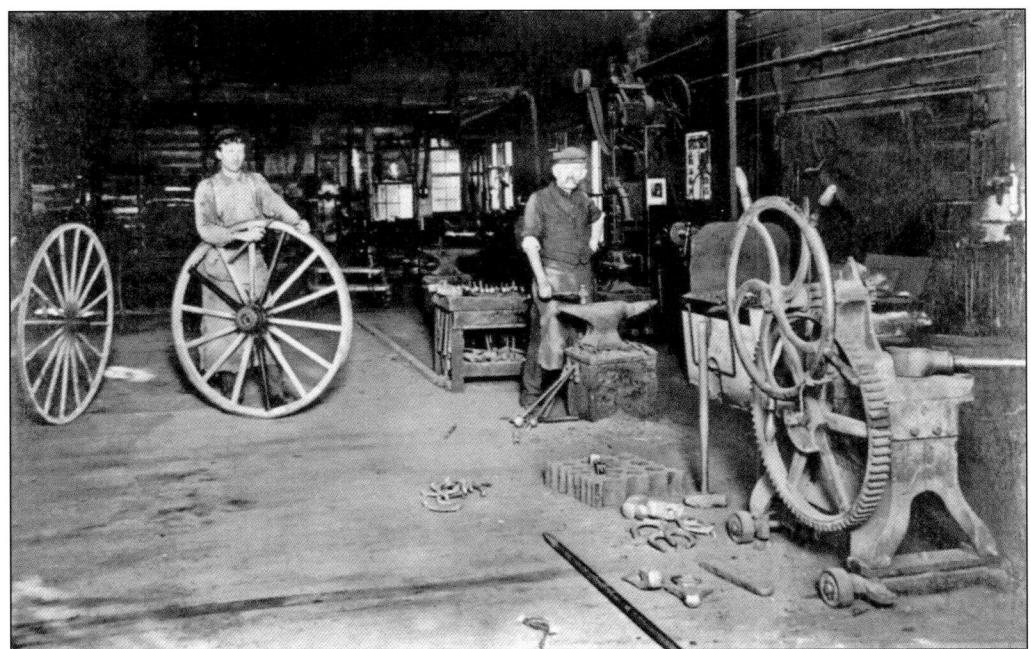

In 1912, Emil Seman and his son ran the town blacksmith shop. Wheel work and horseshoeing were practiced along with any other needed ironwork. Traveling blacksmiths shoed the oxen in the logging camps, and every sawmill also had a shop to take care of tool needs and repairs.

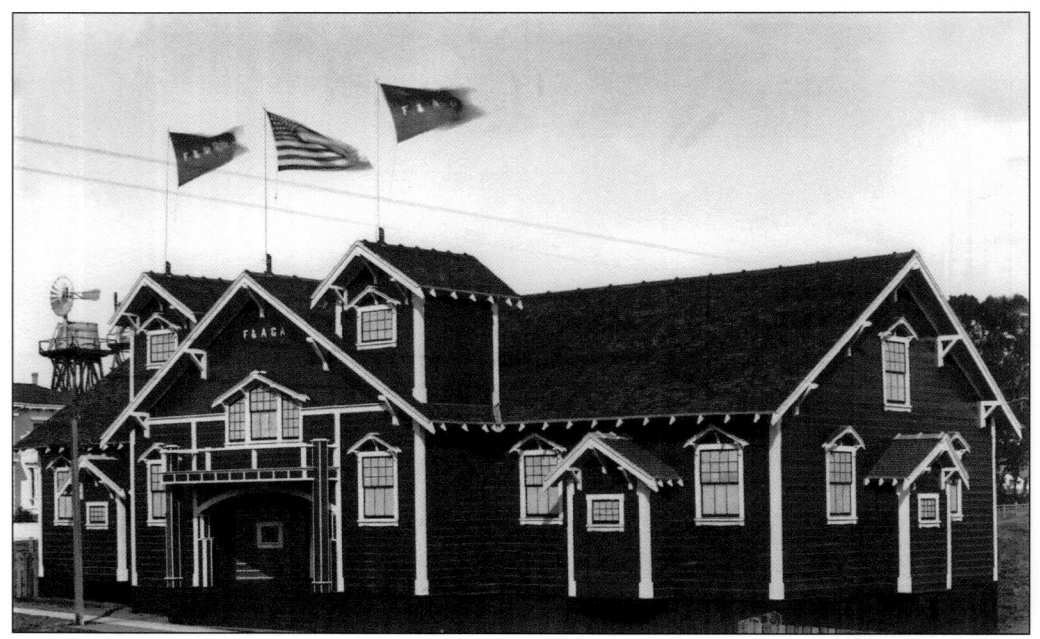

The first apple show in the Farmers and Apple Growers Association Hall was in 1912. Prize money was offered for the best fruit on the coast, and that money was often enough to pay property taxes for a year. Competition was tough. Today the site at Kasten and Little Lake is occupied by a Baptist church.

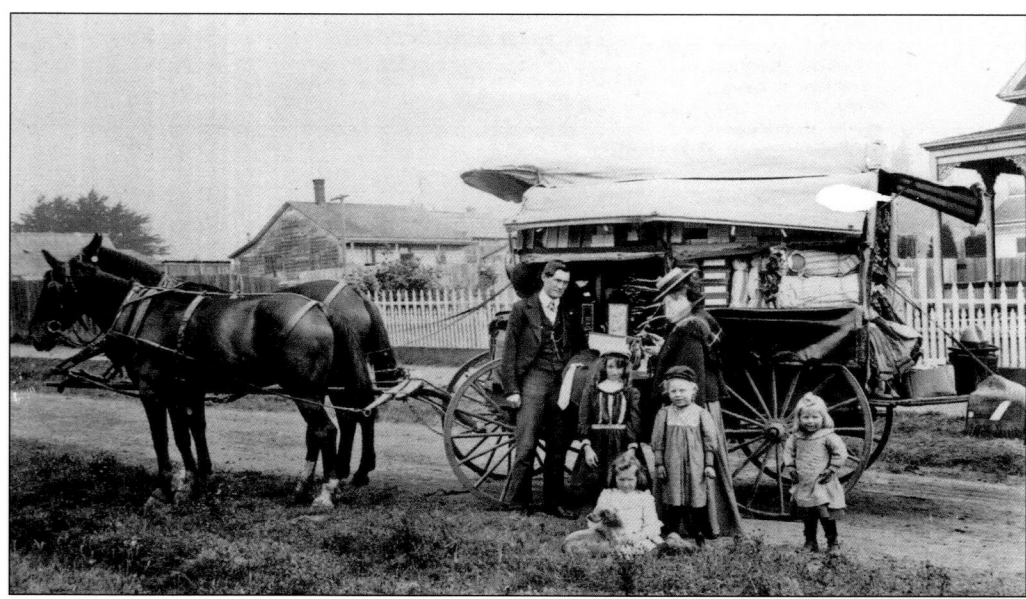

Mr. X. A. Phillips Traveling Emporium attracts the attention of a village resident and her children in 1908. Peddlers were welcomed outside of town by isolated rural women who found a treasure trove of needed articles delivered to their front gates. The picket-fence pattern in the background is still found in the village today.

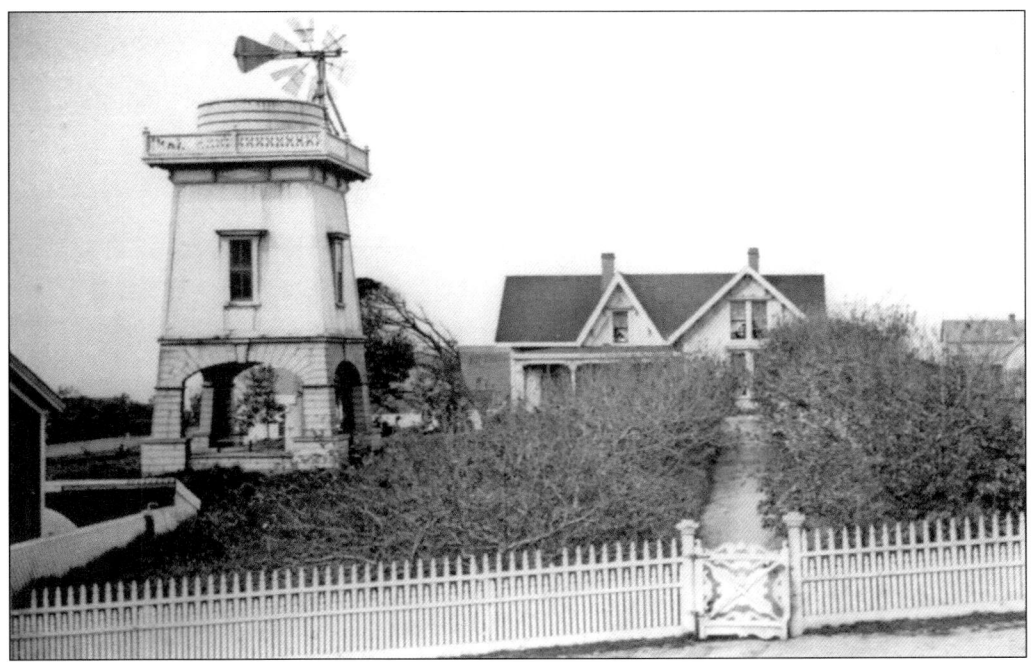

Eliza Kelley, wife of the richest merchant in town, didn't want a regular water tower for her home. She wanted something special and ornate—and she got it. Apple trees planted in the 1860s line the walkway around 1871. Today the home is the Kelley House Museum, and the photograph archives there provided many images for this book.

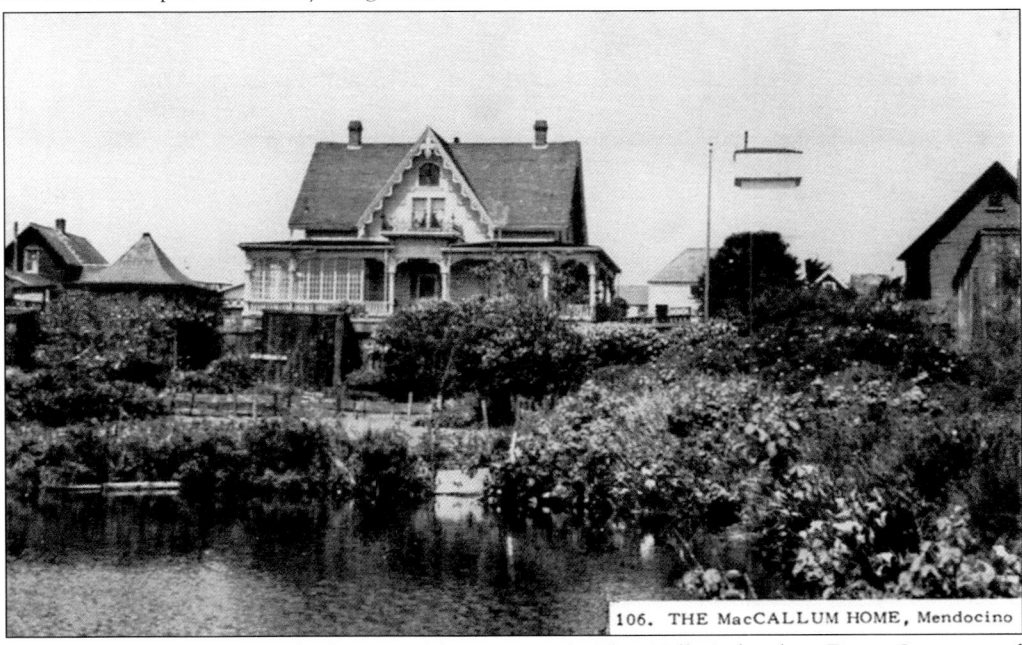

106. THE MacCALLUM HOME, Mendocino

The MacCallum House was built as a wedding present for Eliza Kelley's daughter Daisy. Constructed in pointed-cottage style in 1882, it originally had more architectural embellishment on it. Passed from family hands in 1974, it became a restaurant, bar, and later a bed-and-breakfast.

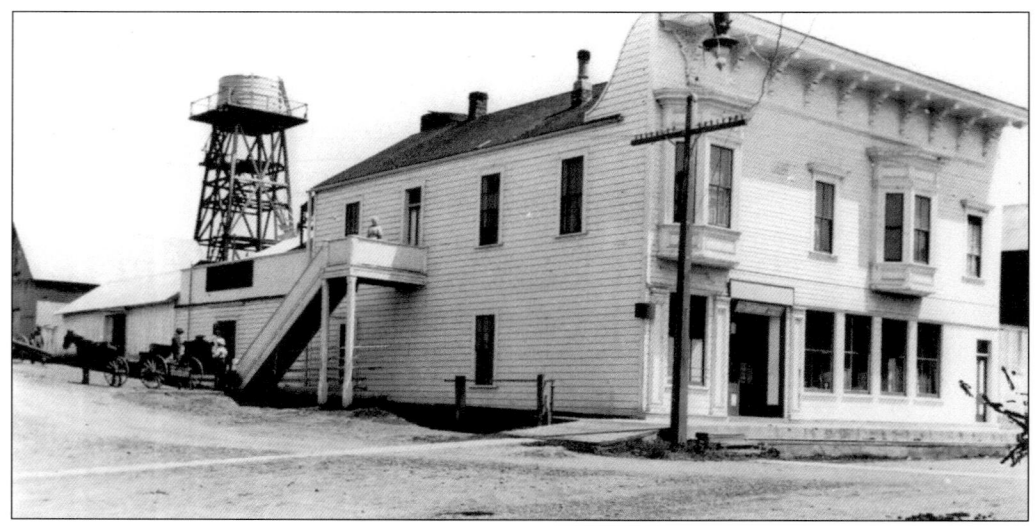

Even with its imposing size, the Jarvis Nichols Mercantile building on the corner of Main and Kasten Streets featured a false front too. An architectural element called a flying staircase gave access to living units upstairs. Built in 1871, the structure is home now to Gallery Bookshop, one of the best independent bookstores in Northern California (and the author's employer).

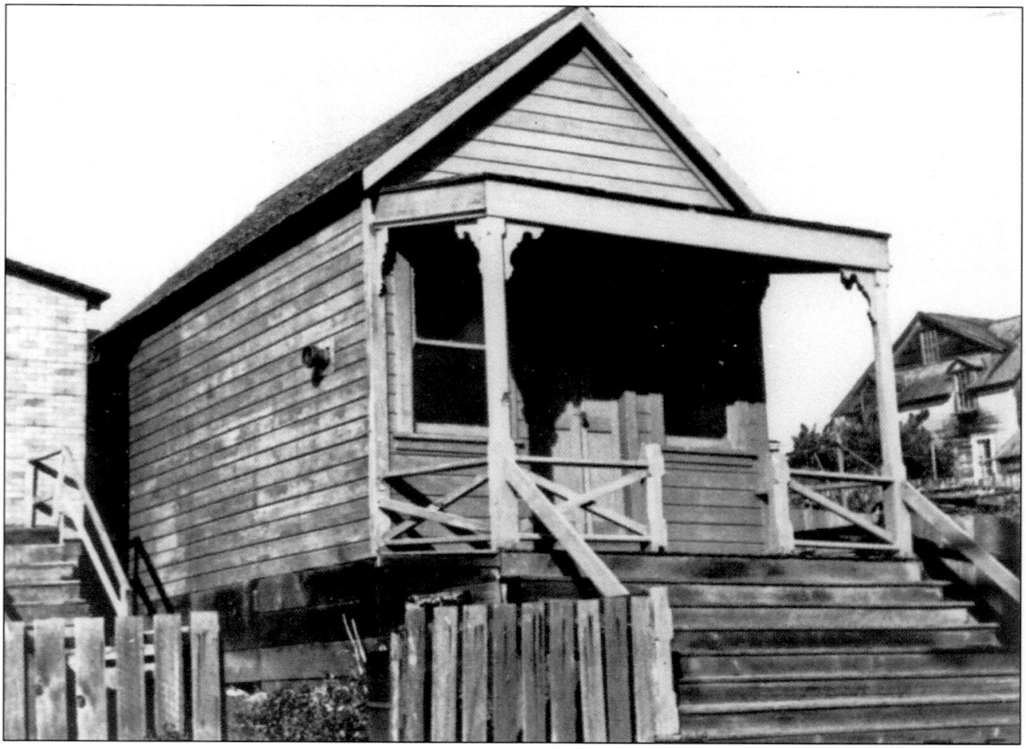

Mendocino in the past had a Chinese population numbering in the hundreds, and the Temple of Kwan Tai was their house of worship. Today restored and painted red and green, it is the brightest structure in the village. Dated from the 1850s by its construction, it is a California State Historical Landmark. Every February, the temple hosts a Chinese New Year parade.

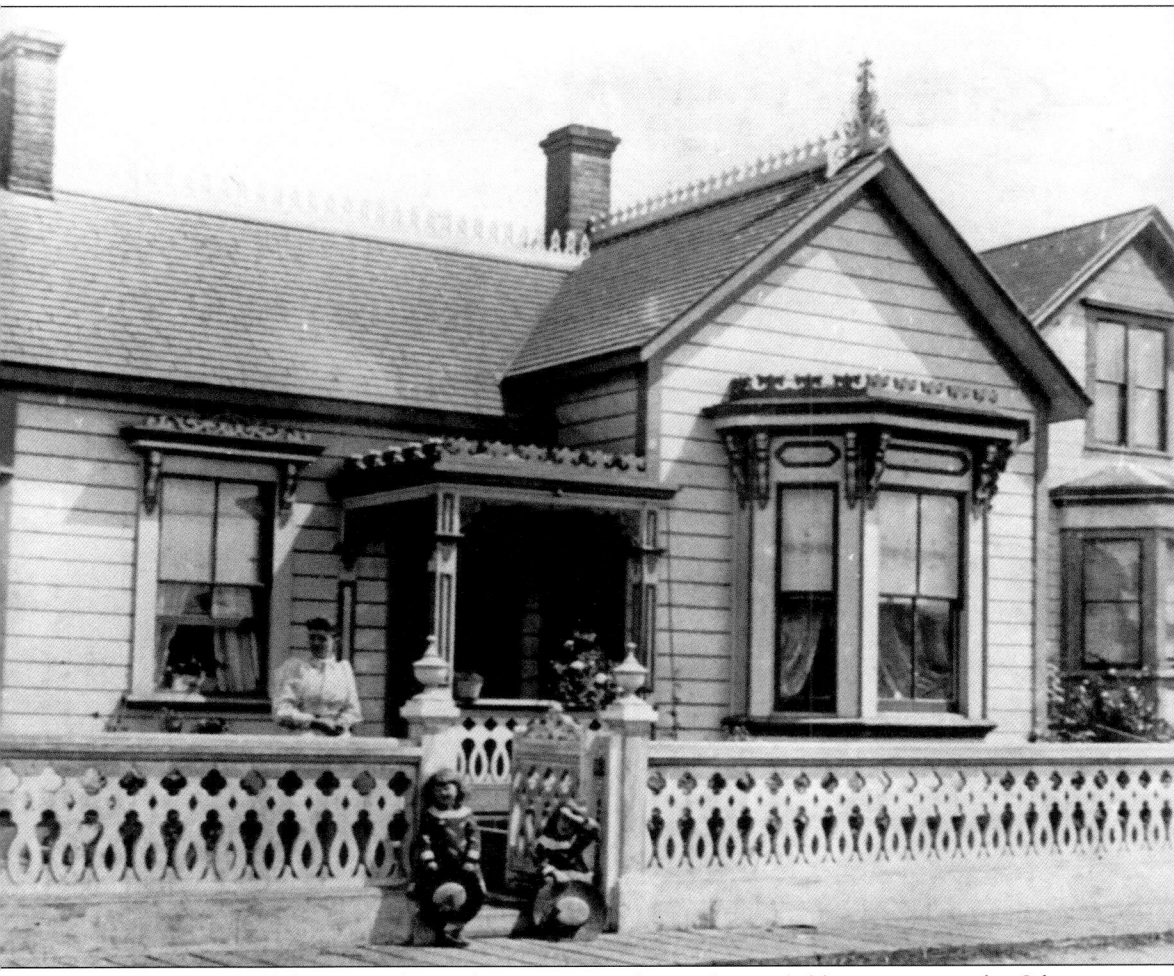

Gingerbread embellishments adorn a house as a mother and two children wait outside. Often ornate woodwork applied one generation would be stripped away the next as architectural fashions changed. Mendocino builder J. D. Johnson built more than 20 houses in the village, and many still stand today. He built many of the houses on Bankers Row on Little Lake Street, including the 1888 Blair House, which gained fame as Jessica Fletcher's house when the *Murder, She Wrote* television series was filmed there in the 1980s.

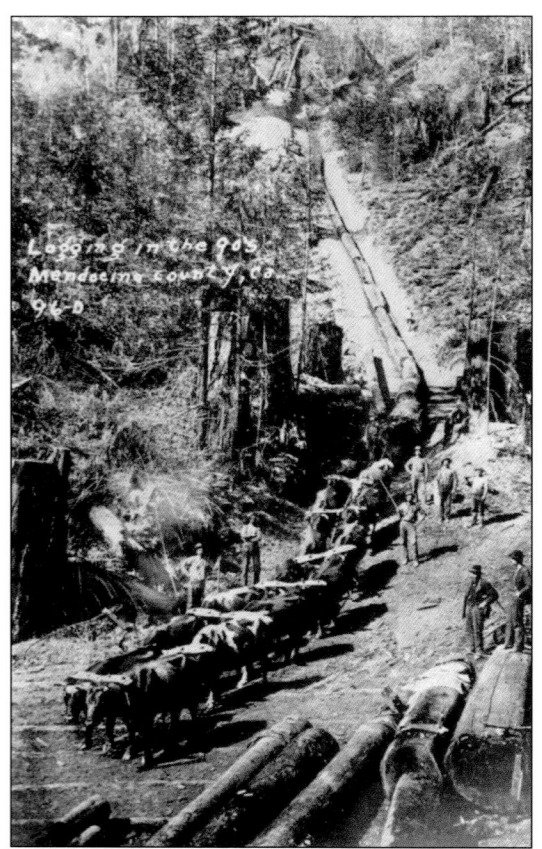

Loads behind bull teams were dependent on the size of the logs, the grade of the road, and the weather. The Durham breed of bulls were preferred at about 1,500 pounds each, and they plodded along at two miles an hour with a load in tow. The bull punchers who drove the teams were renowned for the colorful use of profanity to urge the bulls forward.

From 1855 to 1938, a sawmill existed down on the north bank of Big River. Logs were floated down river for miles to the tidal flats. For 80 years, every time this mill burned, it was rebuilt. This view is after the 1906 earthquake when the million-brick smokestack collapsed and was replaced by a metal one.

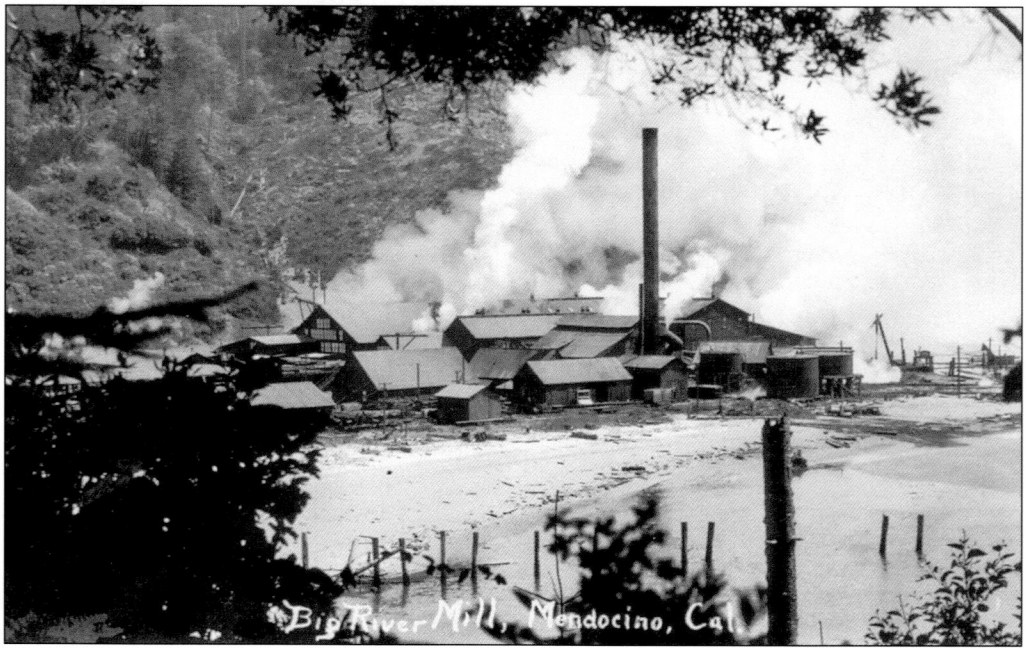

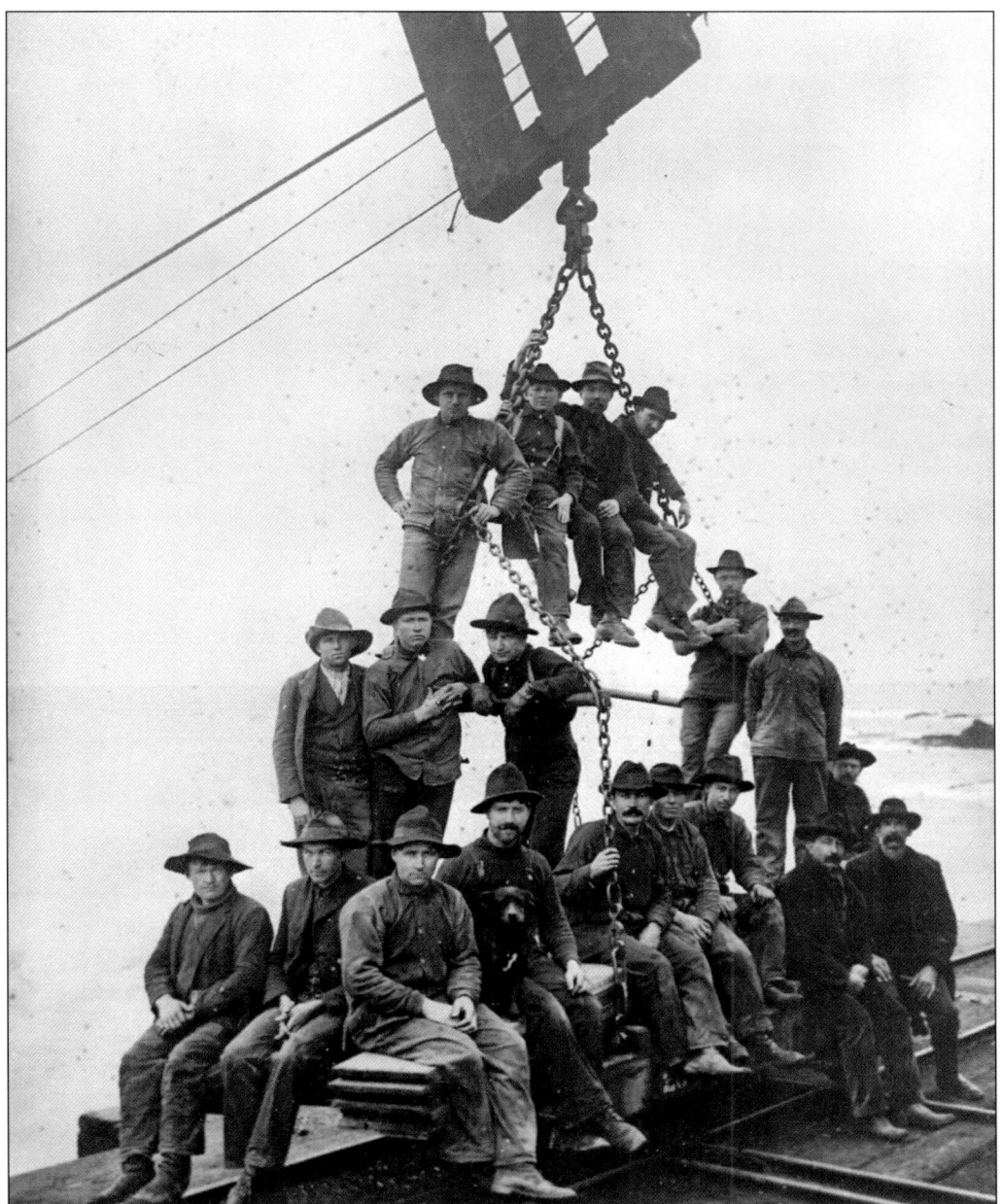

By 1902, a wire chute, or sling, had replaced the apron chute at the Mendocino Lumber Company's headland shipping point. Here some of the shipping crew and a dog sit on boards being bundled to ride the rigging down to the lumber schooners anchored in the bay. For fun, crew members had speed competitions loading vessels. Outgoing cargo included finished lumber, ties, tan oak bark, cordwood, posts, grape stakes, shingles, and farm produce. Coming up from San Francisco, the schooners brought stock for the mercantile establishments supported by woodsmen and their families.

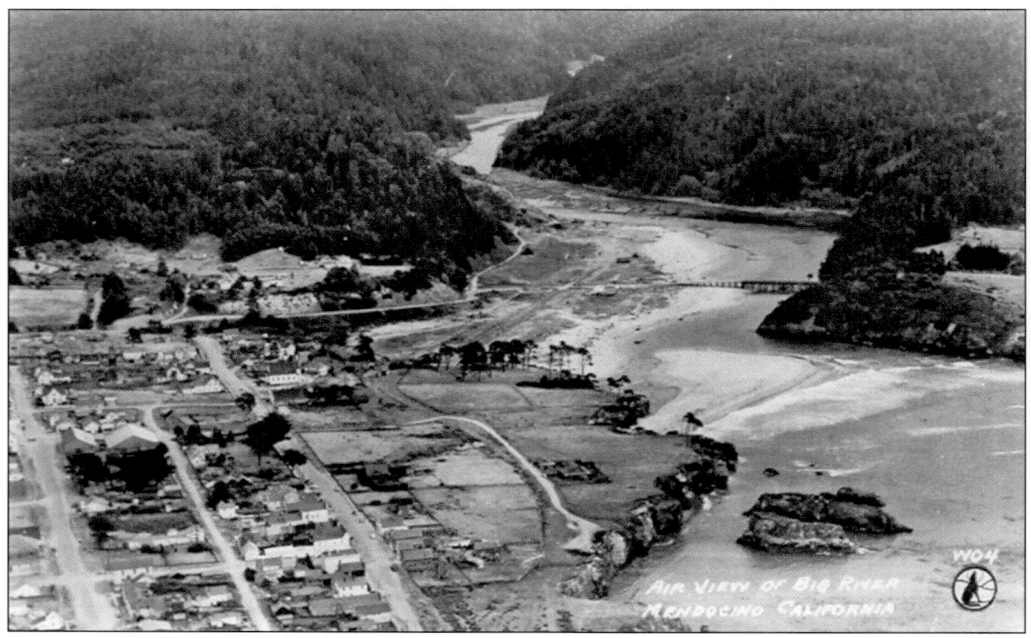

In the timber logging world, there are boom-and-bust cycles, and this was Mendocino in a bust time. Approximately 50 years ago, the sawmill down on Big River flat was long gone, as were the stacks of drying lumber on the headlands and the shipping point. The old low bridge over Big River was replaced with a high, modern structure in the 1960s.

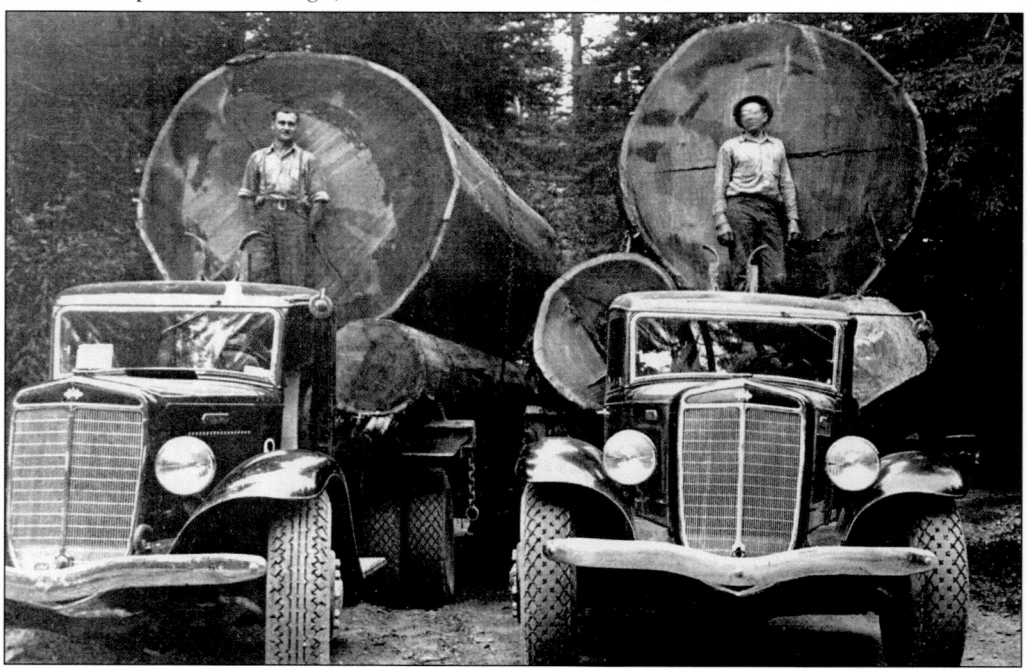

Just as the railroads replaced the oxen, log trucks replaced the trains. Mendocino Lumber Company's first log trucks along Big River appeared in 1935. Though the trucks had starters, the front bumper dips in the center for a hole for a hand crank—just in case.

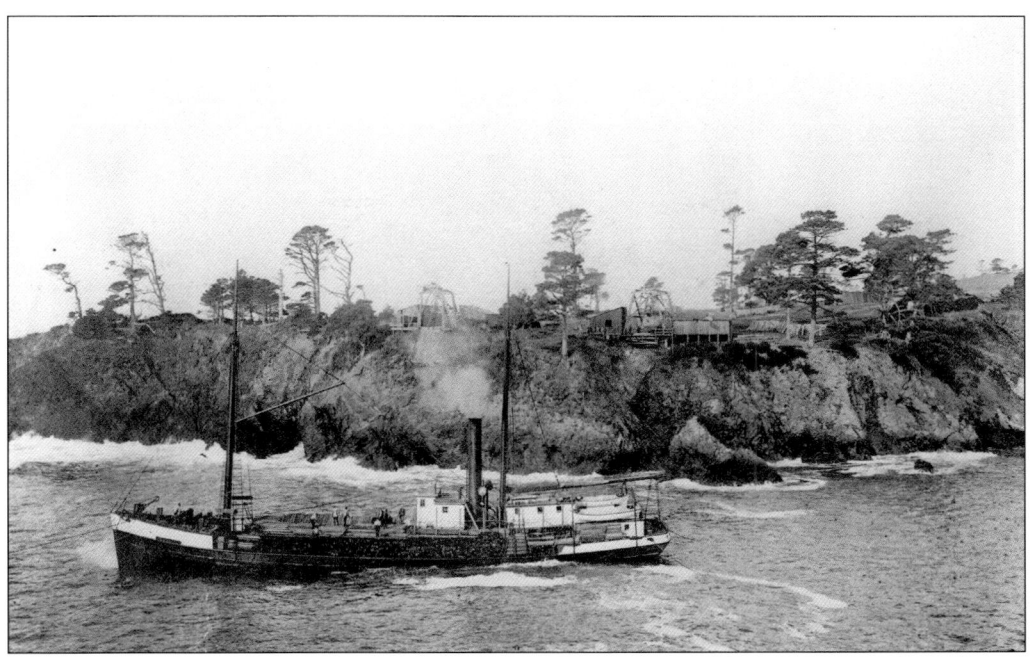

The coastal steamer *National City* takes on ties under the Russian Gulch chute, north of Mendocino, in the early 1900s. Boxed apples also shipped from here. This fast vessel was built in 1906 and later sold to Peruvian interests. Railroad ties from here are in the roadbed of many trains in Peru.

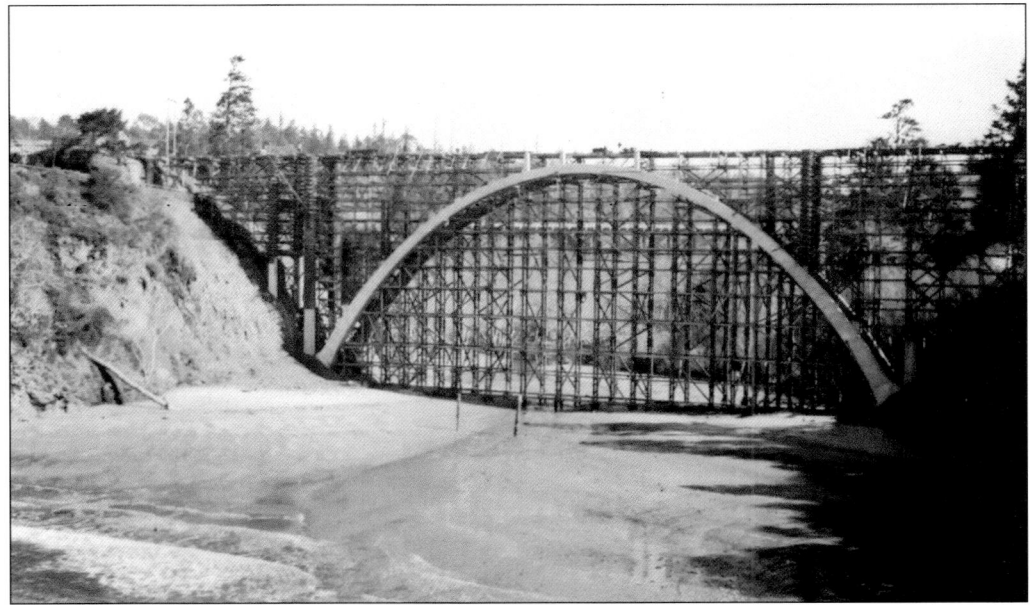

The bridge over Russian Gulch was a Depression-era WPA project finished in 1940. The smooth arch used lots of timber bracing during construction. Similar bridges were built in northern Mendocino County along Highway 101. On both sides of the Shoreline Highway is the 1,300-acre Russian Gulch State Park with a beautiful beach, campground, and waterfall.

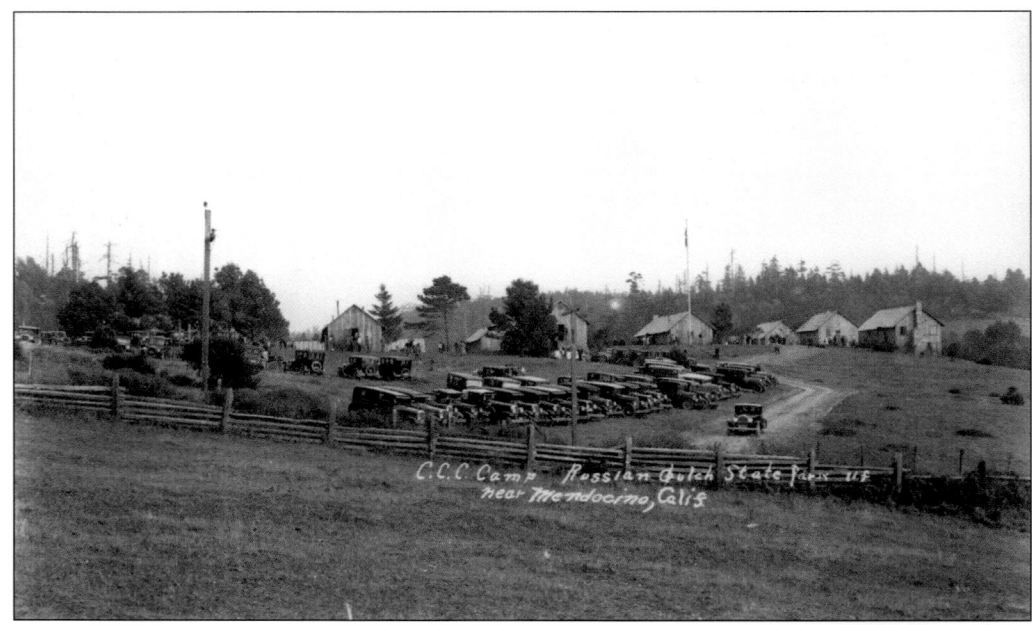

There was a Civilian Conservation Corp camp at Russian Gulch for 10 years during the Depression. These workers helped develop parklands and campgrounds along the coast. At the Mendocino Woodlands Camp on Big River, they built 200 buildings of wood and stone. This camp is now a historical landmark because its historical integrity has been maintained for 70 years.

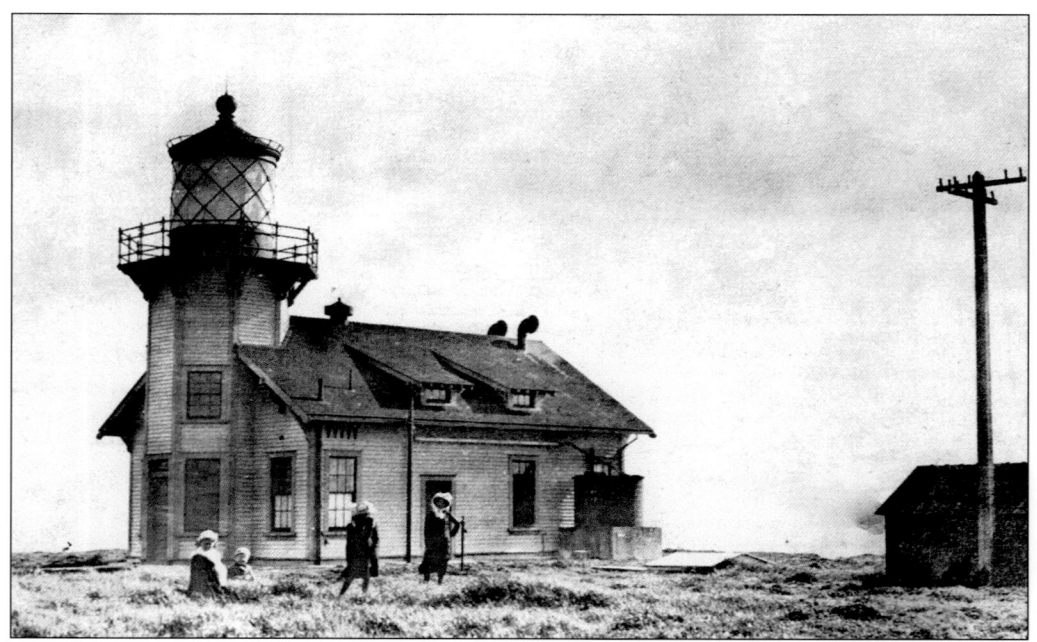

The 1909 Point Cabrillo Lighthouse on the loop of old highway west of today's Highway 1 between Russian Gulch State Park and Caspar has been lovingly restored with its original Fresnel lens in place. The 300-acre site has the former lighthouse keeper's house as a unique bed-and-breakfast location.

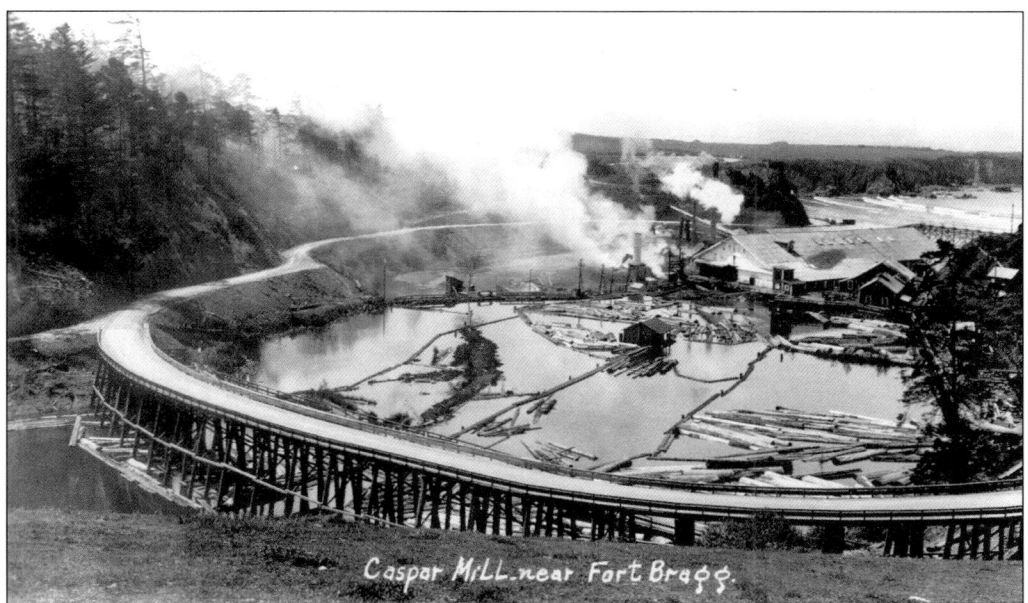

Caspar Creek was dammed to make a millpond, and the old state highway crossed over it. The grade on the south bank remains the same today, and back then, smoke filled the sky from the mill. When logs slid down into the pond from the north bank, cars on the bridge were splashed.

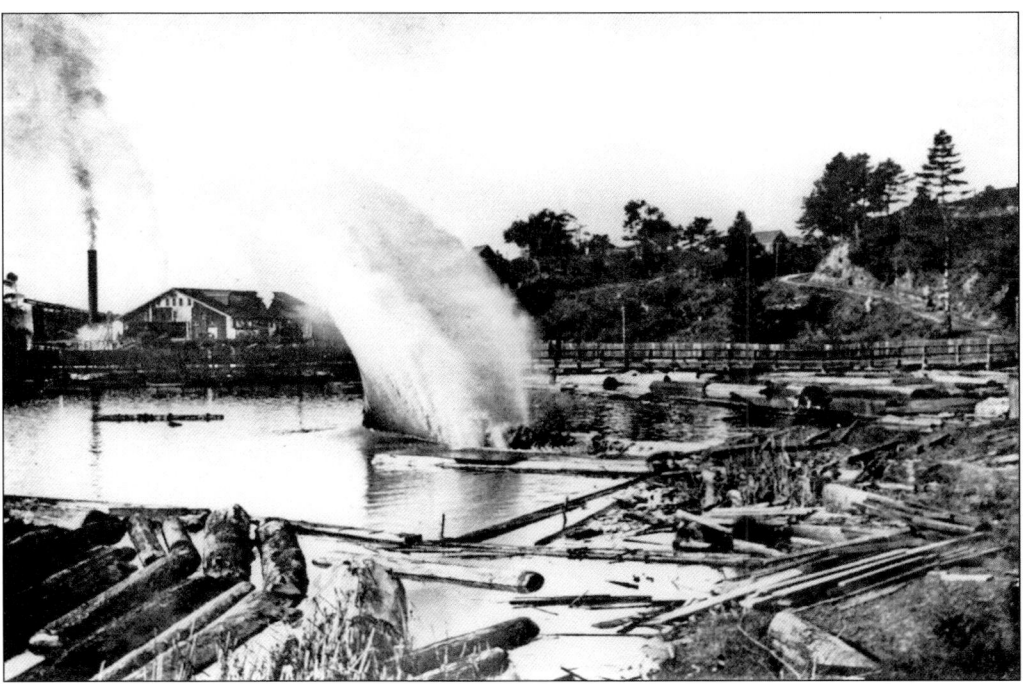

Photographers loved to try and catch on film the very moment a log weighing 20 or 30 tons slid 130 feet down the hill at 40 miles per hour and splashed into the millpond. Logs arrived at this millpond until 1944 from a railroad siding. In 1912, Caspar Lumber Company owned 80,000 acres of timberland.

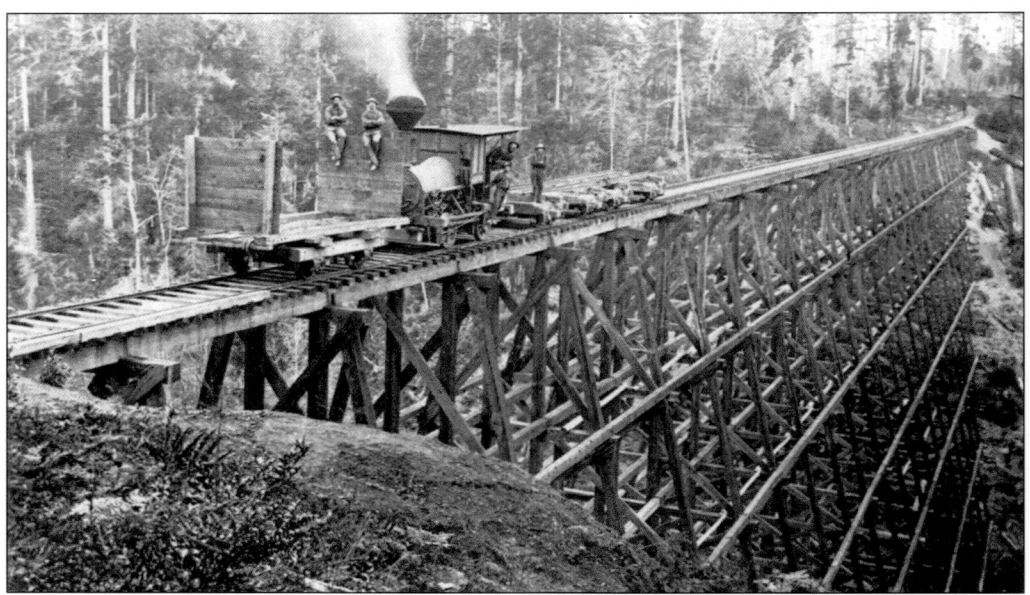

The Caspar Lumber Company built a 1,000-foot-long, 146-foot-high trestle over Jughandle Creek to access more timberland. An engine named *Jumbo* proceeds over this structure at 10 miles per hour. The trestle fell down in the 1906 earthquake and was promptly rebuilt. Today Jughandle Creek State Reserve has a coastal access point on the west side of the Shoreline Highway and a hiking trail up the canyon.

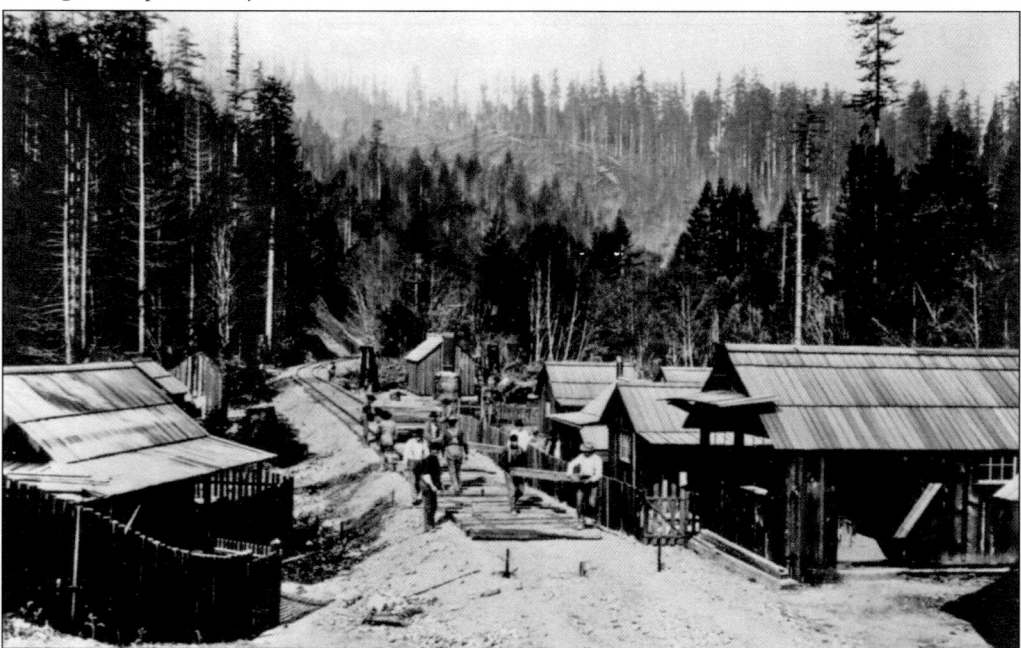

In 1914, the Caspar Lumber Company railroad was at the end of the line. A camp was in place with loggers' cabins, shops, a store, a cookhouse, and an icehouse. Trees awaited chopping, and work was ready to begin. When the area was logged out, the railroad tracks were built up further, and the whole pattern was repeated. In 1924, this company had 30 miles of track into the timberland.

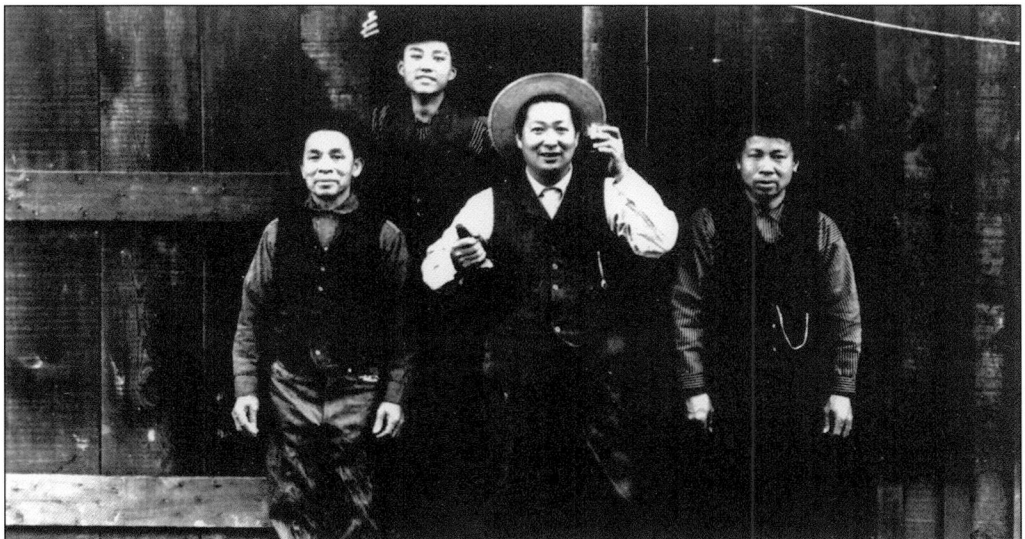

Hundreds of Chinese lived and worked along the Mendocino Coast. They performed menial jobs, worked as cooks and gardeners, and ran Chinese groceries and laundries. When they died, they wanted their bones sent back to China. Every big town locally had a Chinatown or China Gulch area. Here Wah Bow, Caspar Mill's head cook, and his kitchen helpers salute the photographer.

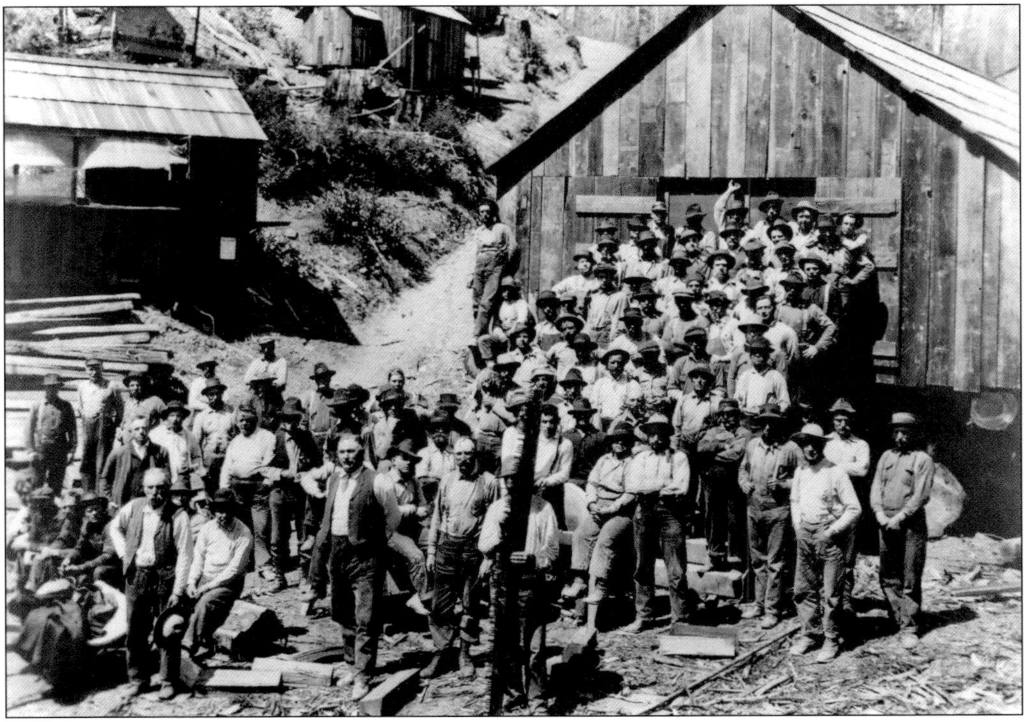

The crew of a Caspar Lumber Company logging camp lines up for a photograph with a tool of their trade: a crosscut saw. The lumber company owned 80,000 acres of forest lands and a railroad reaching 18 miles inland. This timber holding eventually became Jackson State Forest.

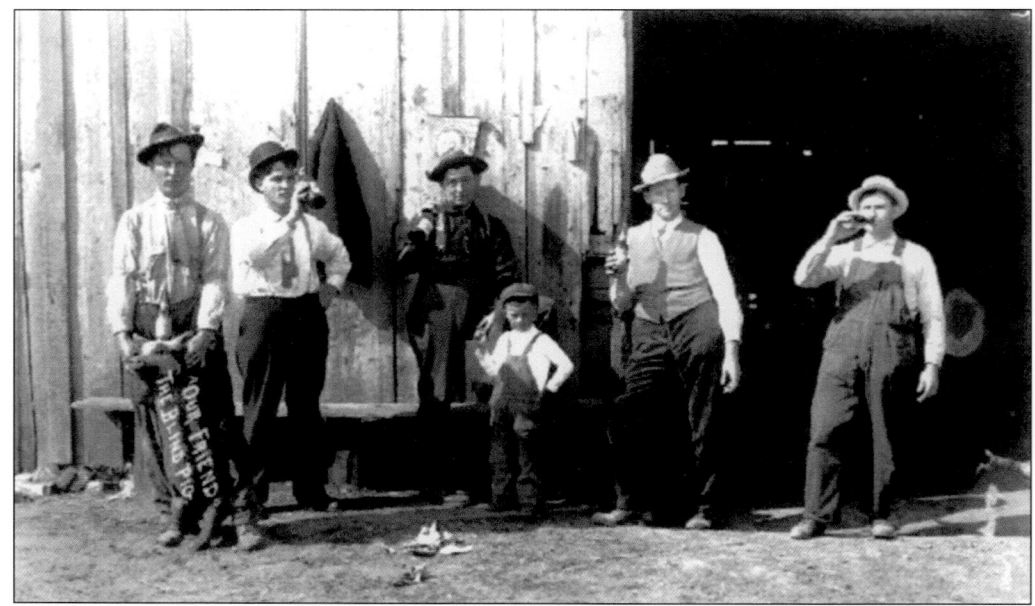

A colorful part of Mendocino Coast history was the effort to circumvent Prohibition laws in the early 20th century. A store owner would brag he had a blind pig trained to do amusing tricks. The merchant would charge admission to see the performing pig out back. Liquid refreshment was provided while the pig might, or might not, put on an act. The man on the left holds the critter with the words "Our friend, the Blind Pig" written on it.

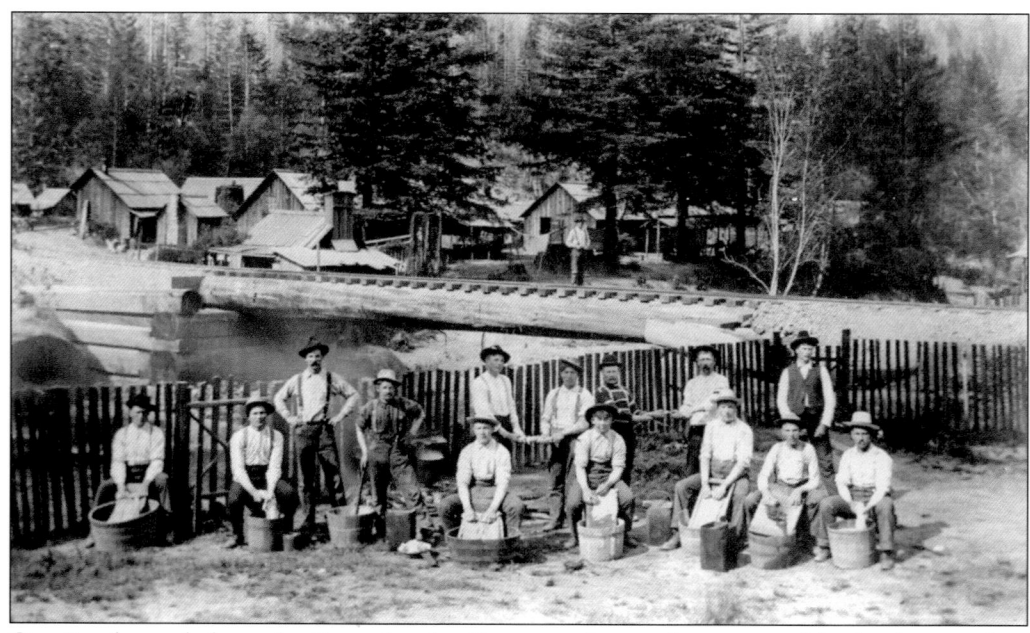

On a Sunday wash day at the Caspar Lumber Company, the woods camp posed for the photographer. An onlooker watches from the railroad bridge. For rare trips to town, where stores, saloons, and "women of negotiable virtue" awaited, loggers needed a clean set of clothes.

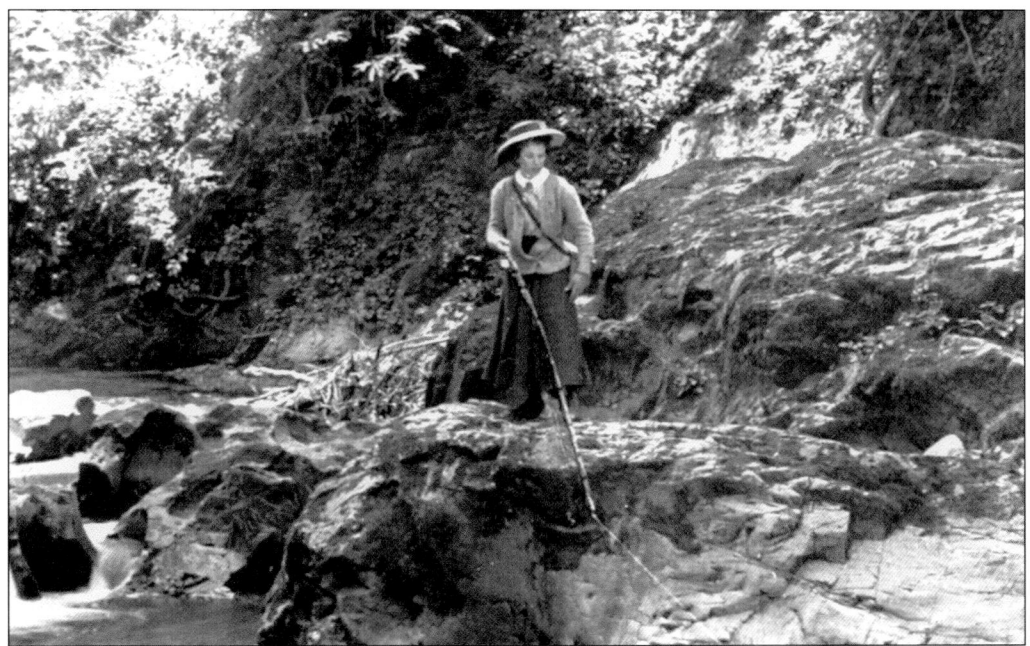

It was not just men who enjoyed the sport of fishing. Here a female angler watches her line along the Noyo River. When tourists began to arrive by rail and automobile, the Mendocino Coast promoted itself as a sportsman's paradise. The California Western Skunk Train would stop to drop fishermen off and pick them up on their return run later.

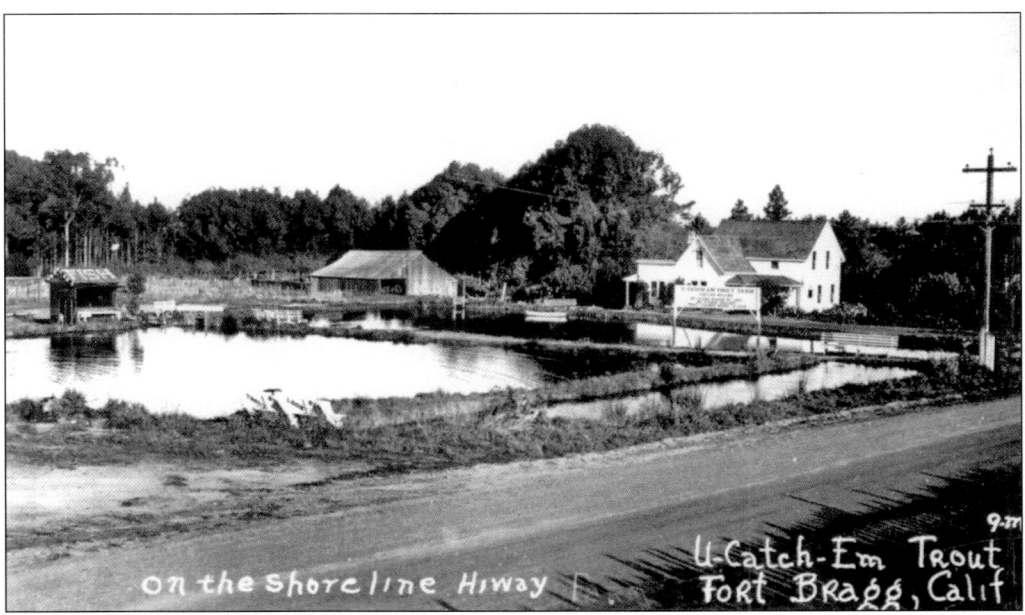

If a person could not make enough money to support a family as a photographer, it helped to have a sideline business to supplement income. H. H. Wornacott, photographer, and his wife, Mattie, ran the U-Catch-Em Trout Farm along the Shoreline Highway, south of Fort Bragg. Catching fish here was a lot easier than standing in a cold river all day.

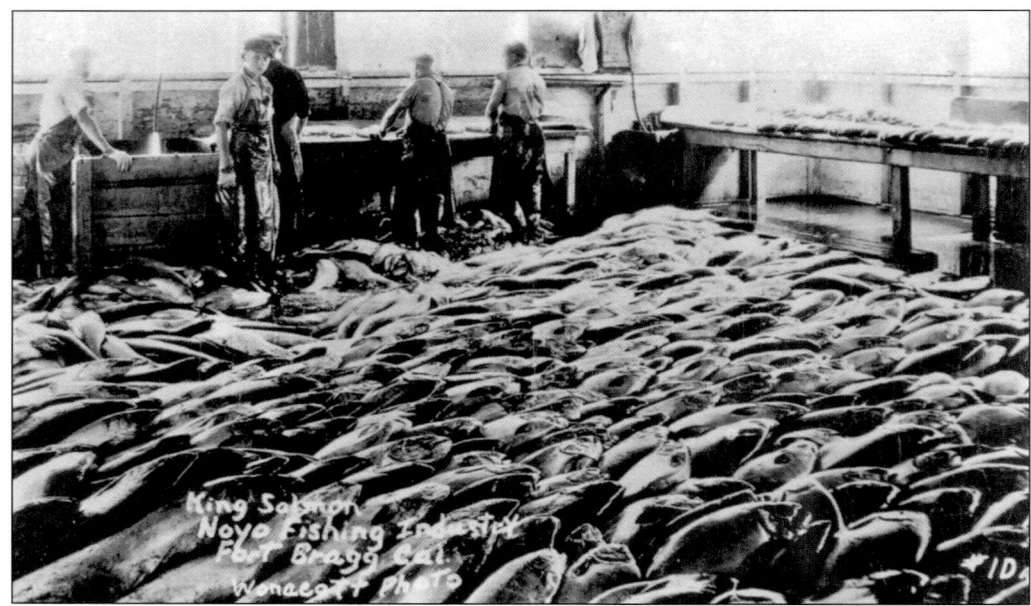

King salmon cover the floor of a fish-packing house down in Noyo Harbor in 1940. Salmon, crab, rockfish, and later sea urchin roe were packaged for sale down in the harbor. Today sport fishing boats take fishermen out into the Pacific to pull in, as every fishing-boat captain promises the passenger "that really BIG one" or to watch the whales go by during migration season.

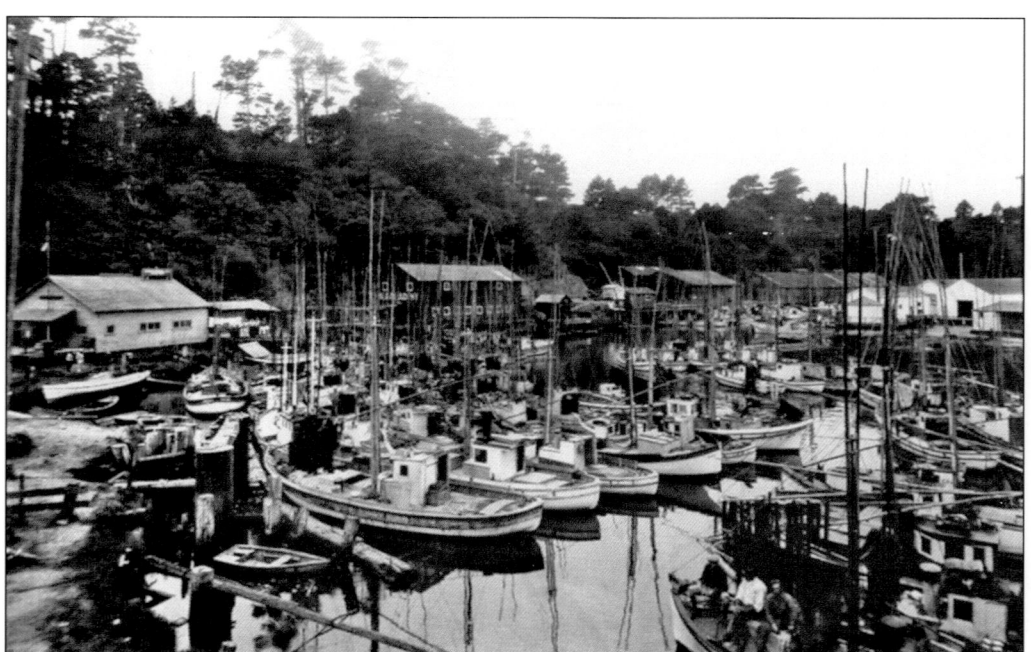

In the 1920s, a proper marina or small boat mooring area was decades in the future, so fishing crafts just tied up next to each other at whatever functioned as a wharf or deck. Today this area is covered with restaurants, but visitors can still watch fishing boats entering and exiting the harbor.

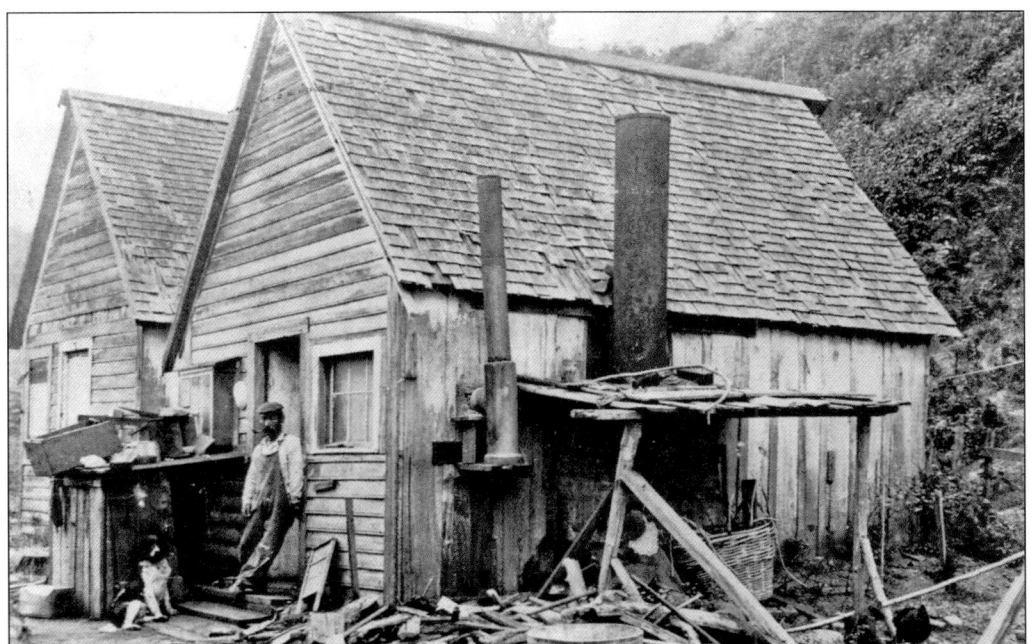

"Harry the Jap," who was reported to have been shipwrecked on the coast, settled on the Noyo Flat in the 1890s. He became a commercial fisherman and built a powered boat called the *Skipjack*. Names like "Harry the Jap," "Nigger Nat," or "Squaw Rock" were not considered prejudiced at the time. These words were just a part of the vocabulary of the era.

A lighter stacked with hay bales is tied upon the Noyo River. The old low bridge at water level is empty. The white barn in the background has pigeon roosts on the roof. The view is the south bank of the river in the 1800s. Today, taking North Harbor Drive, which takes off from the east just after the Noyo Bridge, brings visitors down to the harbor.

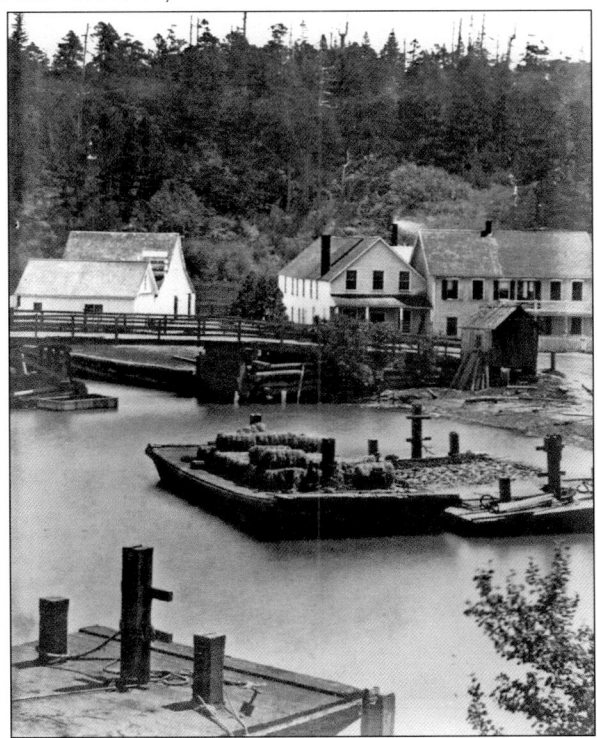

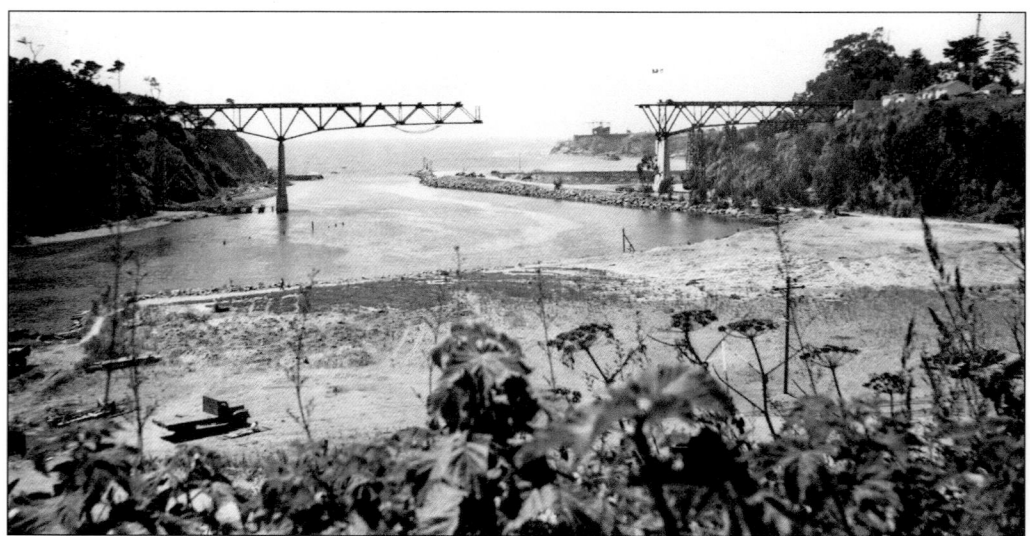

In 1949, a high line of wire cable (barely visible) is in place for moving materials for the Noyo Bridge, which was being built high above the harbor. The Noyo chute house at the shipping point can be seen on the headland. A jetty has been constructed to aid fishing boats entering the harbor. The flat land in the foreground is now covered in restaurants, and this bridge has been replaced.

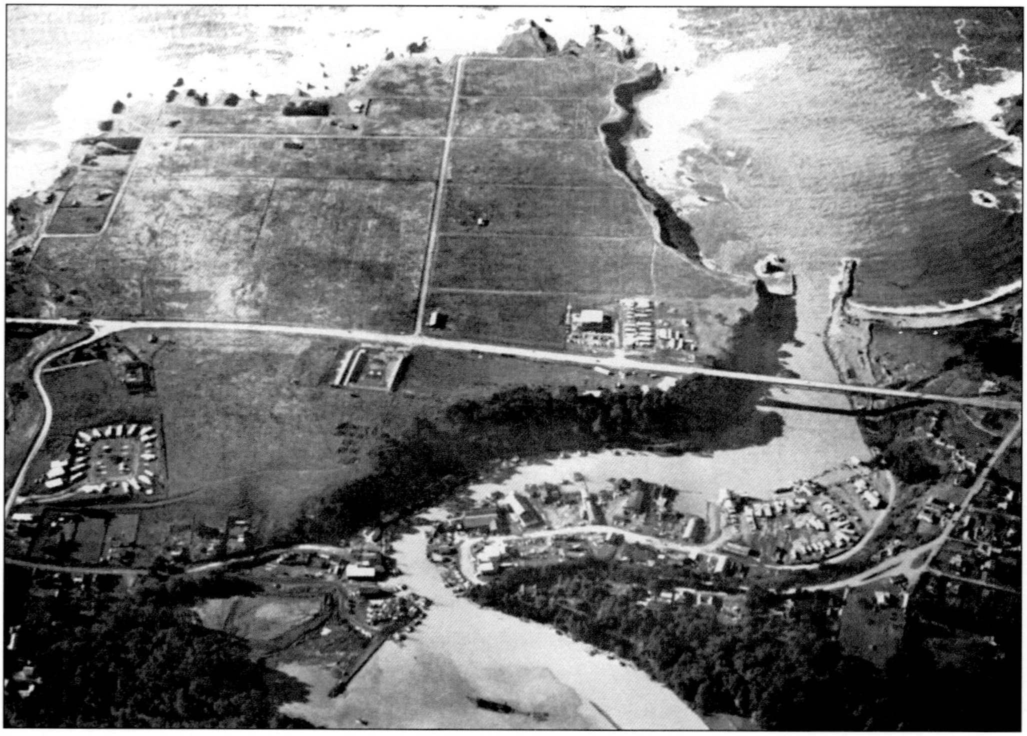

In the 1960s, the high bridge was completed over the Noyo River, but today's marina was still a mud flat on the south shore. The headland was called Todd's Point and had been a dairy farm, but a trailer park had appeared. Today the land is covered with a college campus, a subdivision of homes, Pomo Bluffs Park, and the intersection of Highways 1 and 20.

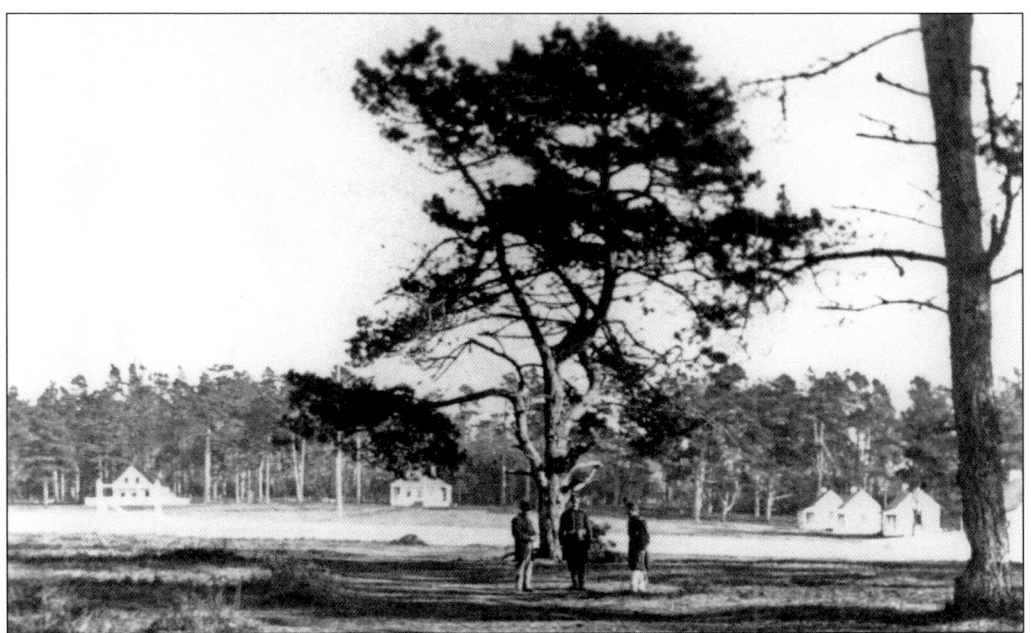

This was the fort that provided the name for the town of Fort Bragg. Established in 1857, it was the center of the Mendocino Indian Reservation. So who was "Bragg"? The post commander here named the fort for Braxton Bragg, a West Point classmate and friend. Though the fort closed in 1864, one of the buildings survives at 430 North Franklin Street.

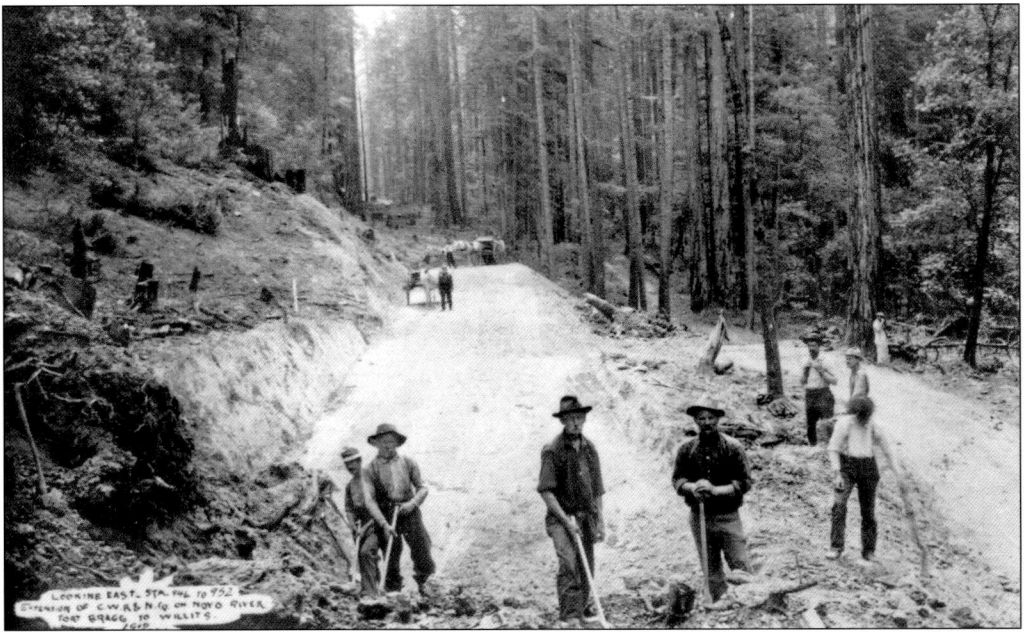

The Union Lumber Company had the biggest mill in Fort Bragg, and the owner wanted a rail connection east to the rest of the country. It took 25 years of construction as financing allowed, but by 1911, more than 40 miles of mountains had been crossed, and connections with Northwestern Pacific Railroad in Willits were completed.

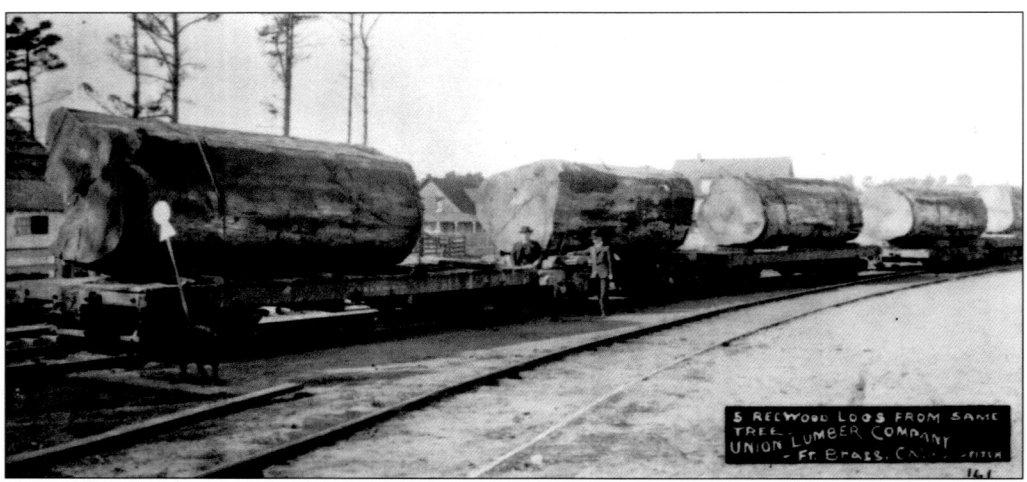

The logs that came into the Union Lumber Company sawmill were made into lumber and sold to provide income to construct railroad tracks a few more miles into uncut timber. In 1910, five logs from one tree arrived at the mill. This was the kind of photograph that company salesmen loved to show to prospective lumber buyers.

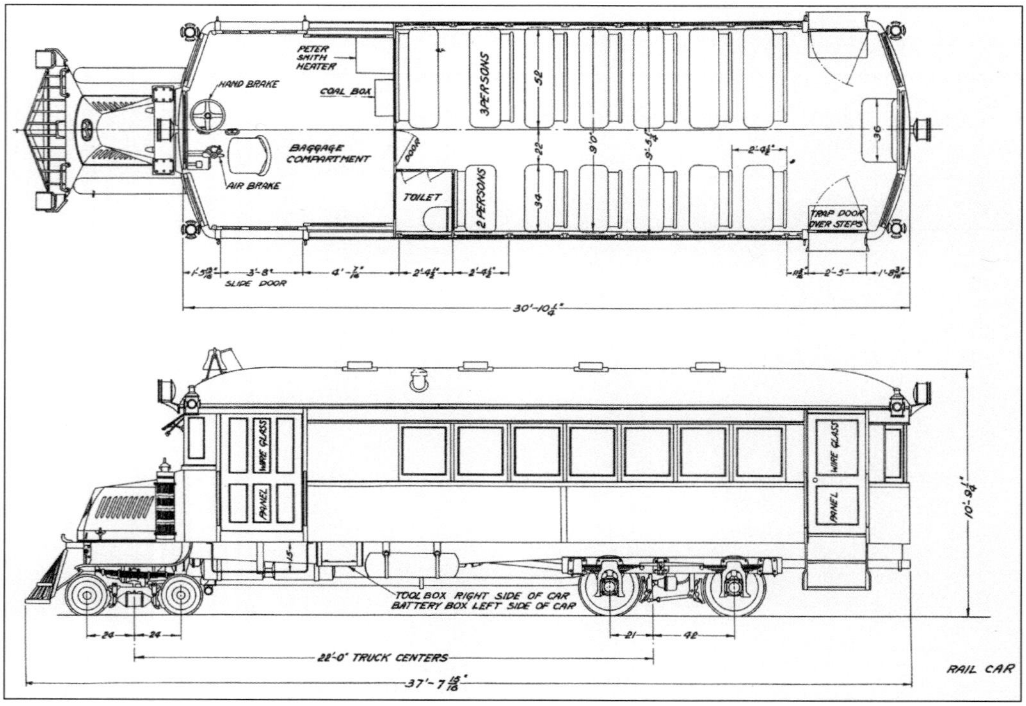

When highways improved, passenger train patronage decreased. The solution was a railroad track vehicle capable of carrying passengers cheaply. A Mack truck bus body, gas powered, on rail wheels was the solution. It cost $12,000 in 1925. But it didn't smell like a steam train—the gas exhaust stunk like a skunk. Today the excursion rail line is known as the Skunk Train.

Here, in the late 1920s, a young logger in Glen Blain, east of Fort Bragg, rides a track bike. Though this man was having fun here, the bikes were used for serious track inspection of rails, spikes, and bolts. The now-abandoned rail line went six miles into the Pudding Creek drainage.

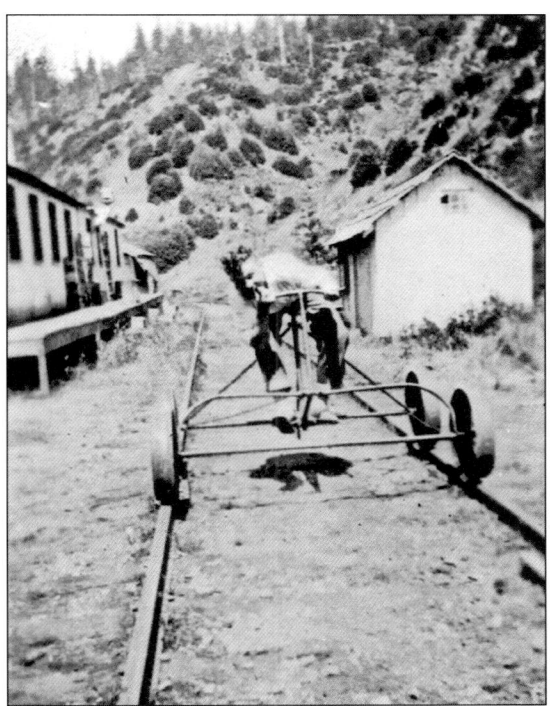

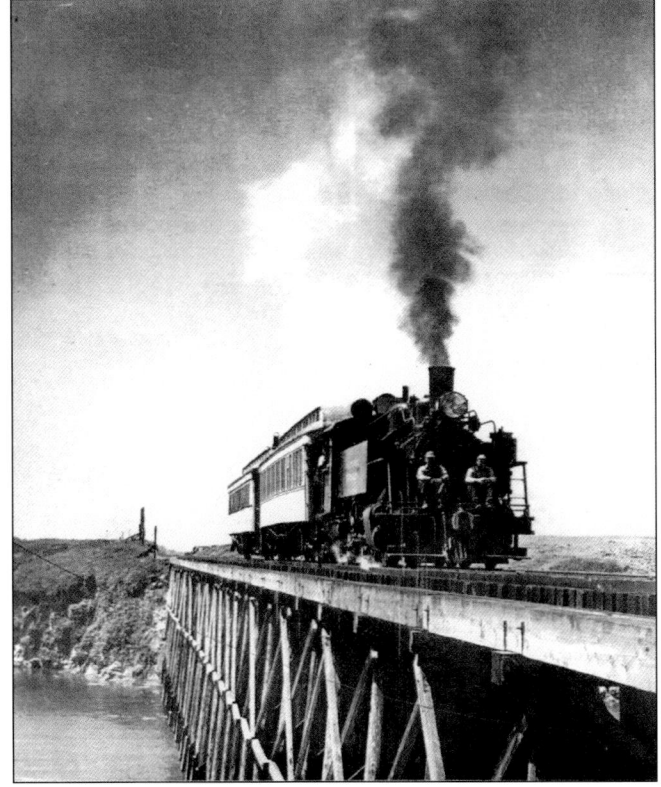

A 1949 excursion train heads out over the Pudding Creek trestle just north of Fort Bragg on the Ten Mile branch line. This trestle was 527 feet long and 48 feet high. Before it was abandoned, the 10-mile line extended 17 miles into the Union Lumber Company timber holdings. This trestle is now state park property. It has been rehabilitated and is accessible by foot.

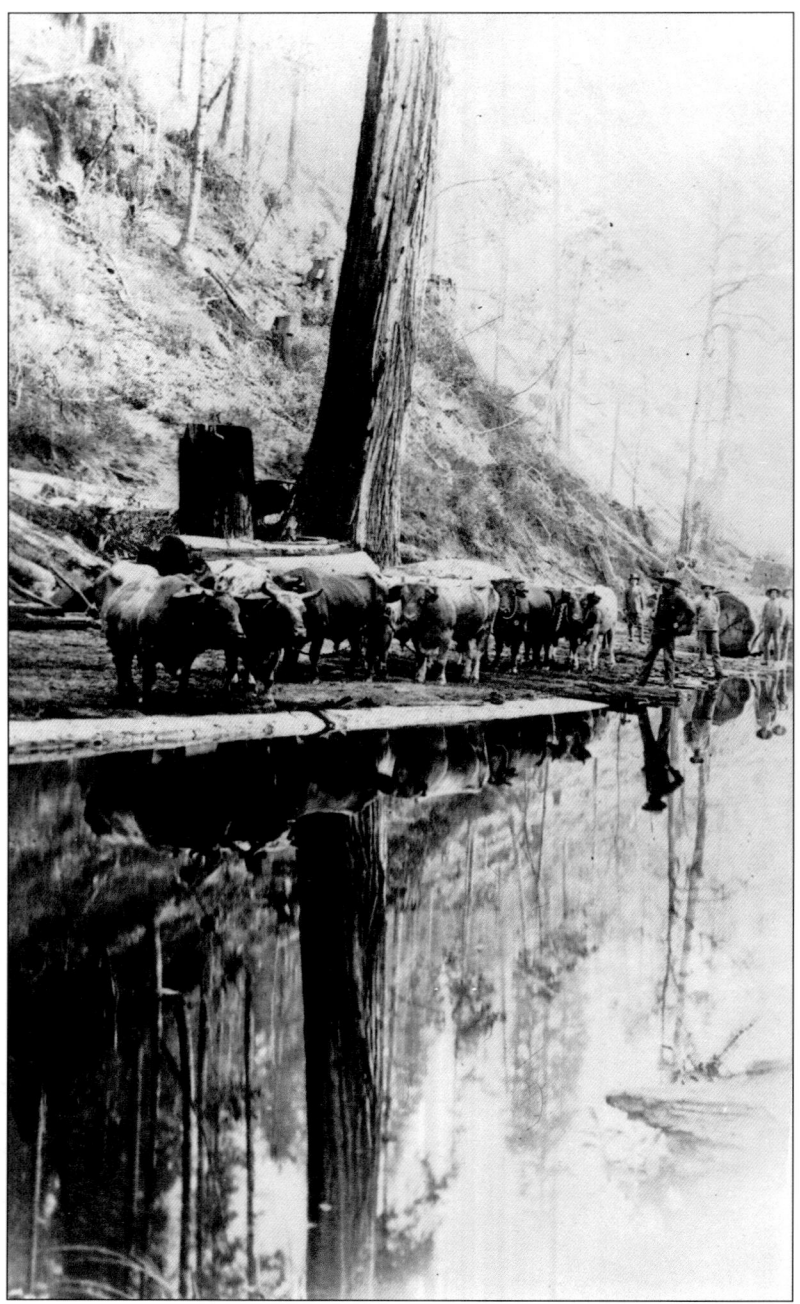

The Glen Blair area got its pretty name because the mill superintendent's wife thought Pudding Creek, or Duff River, referring to the muddy water color, was too mundane. Logging with oxen began in 1886, and they were used until the railroad arrived in 1907. There the photographer got another reflection view of oxen, trees, and loggers. That same mill superintendent's wife, Daisy MacCallum—later owner of the MacCallum House in Mendocino—surrounded her early home in Glen Blair with roses. One hundred years later, the mill and its buildings are long gone, but rose bushes grow wild in the area.

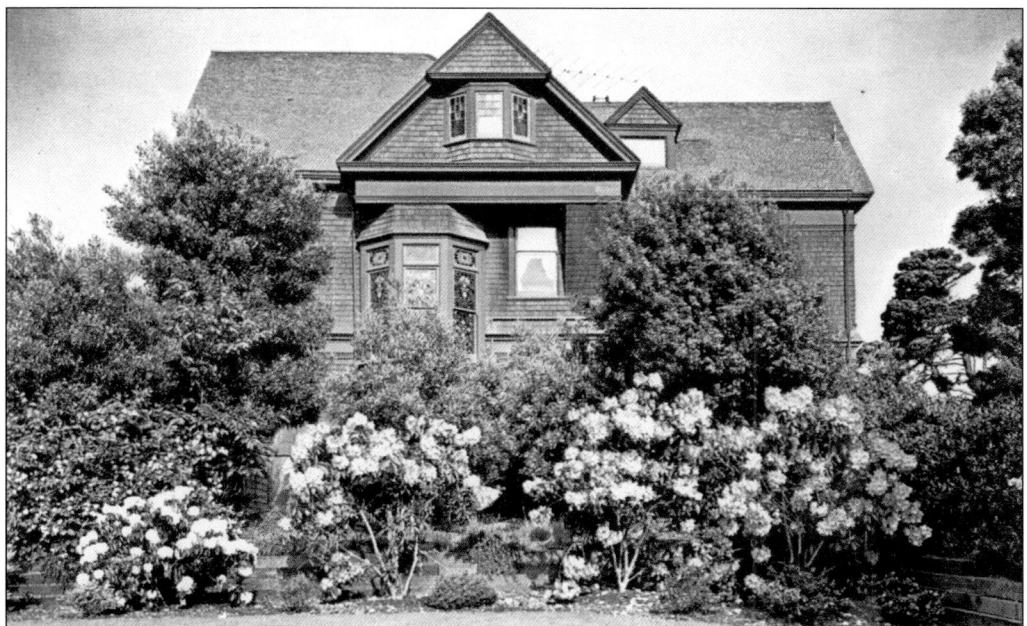

Built on the site of the military hospital for the original fort, the guest house was where the Union Lumber Company put up business visitors they wanted to impress. Built in 1892, it featured ornate woodwork inside and out and was constructed by local craftsmen of redwood milled next door. Today the building functions as a museum in Fort Bragg.

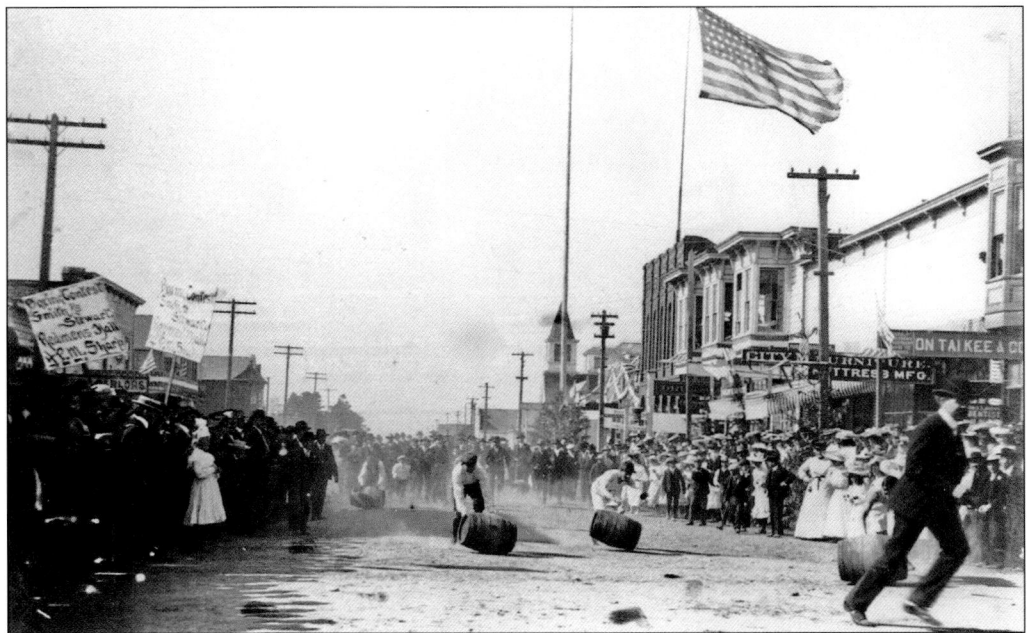

Around 1910, a pedestrian runs to get out of the way of a barrel-rolling race occurring as part of a Fort Bragg community celebration. By this time, Fort Bragg was the biggest city in Mendocino County, and it would remain so until Ukiah surpassed it in size after World War II. A Chinese merchant's store sign is seen on the right.

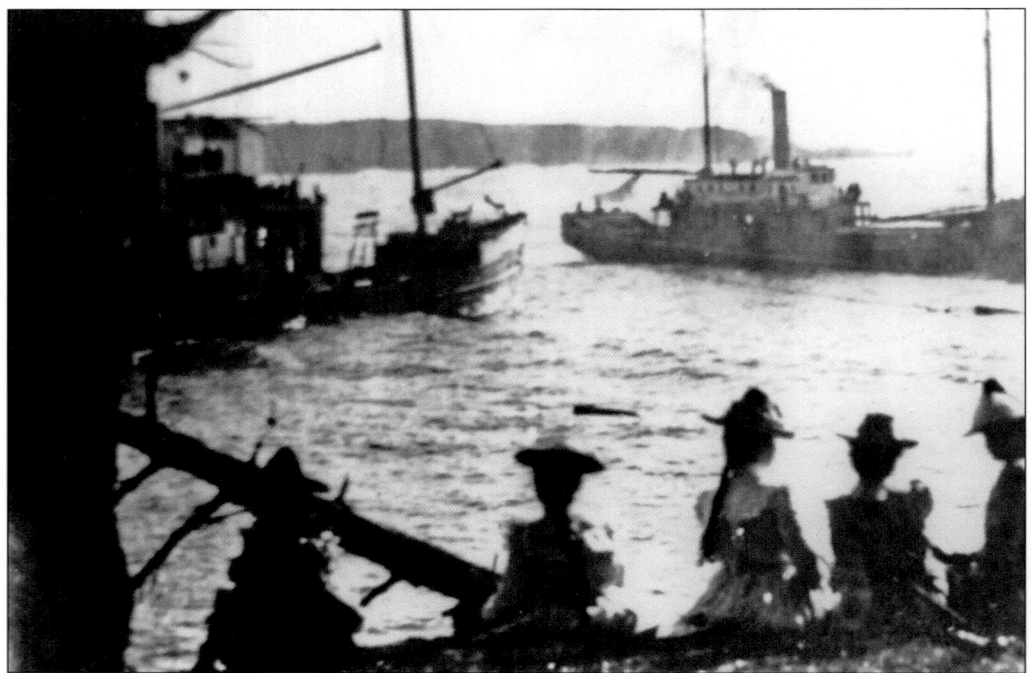

A picnic on the shore to watch the activity of the shipping point always provided diversions for the townsfolk. In 1911, they could have watched the largest ship ever to enter Noyo, the 420-foot steamer *Bjornson*, which arrived to take on one million board feet of redwood and tan oak bark bound for Australia.

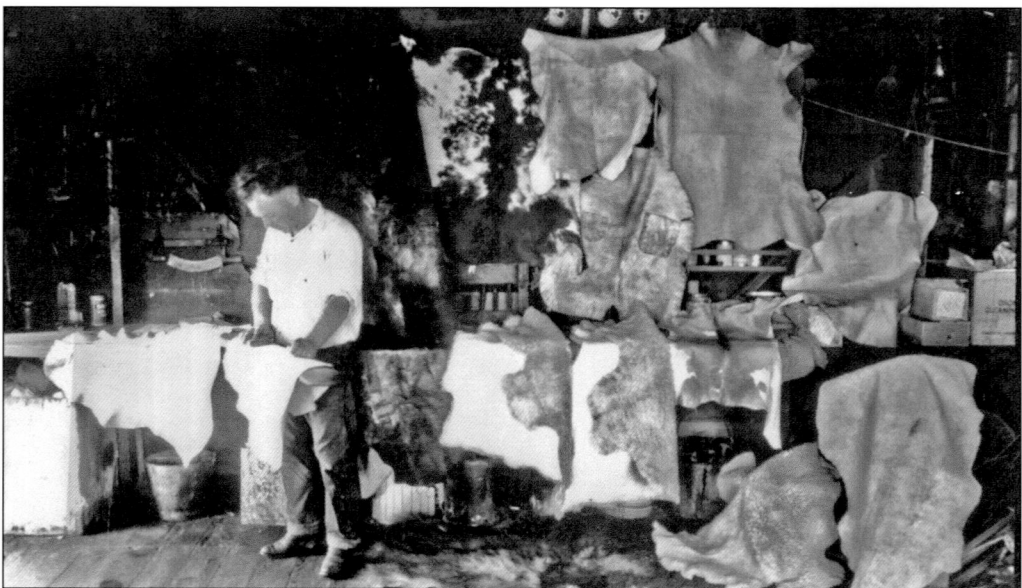

During the Depression, local folks turned to traditional crafts to supplement their incomes. Northwestern Fur Company was Larry Stone's enterprise in Fort Bragg. He tanned hides and fur animal pelts. Leather aprons were worn by mill workers and shipping-point crews for extra protection.

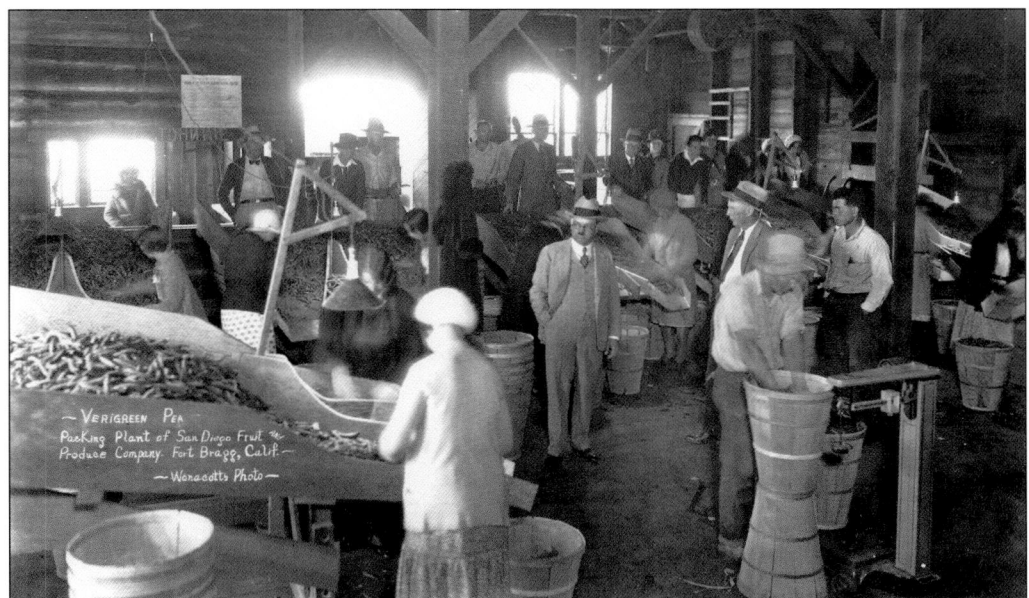

The Mendocino Coast has always been good for growing cool-weather crops. San Diego Fruit and Produce Company maintained the Verigreen Pea packing plant in 1932 in Fort Bragg. The wooden shipping barrels were probably locally produced too. The Depression hurt the local economy, and women began working outside the home.

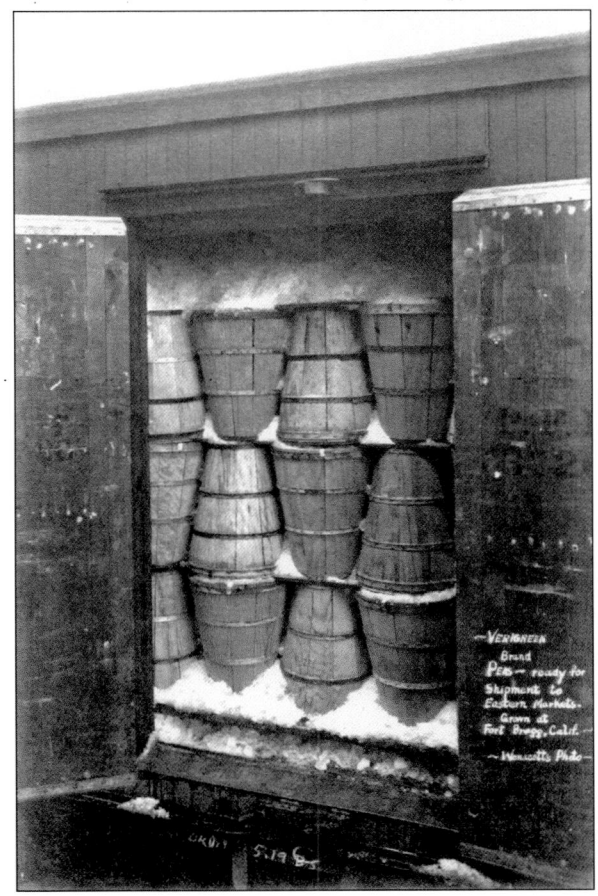

This is a view inside one of the cars of iced Verigreen peas ready to ship out to Eastern markets. From Willits, at the other end of Fort Bragg's train tracks, connections south in the Bay Area gave access to transcontinental rail lines. Huckleberries growing wild were another product collected and exported during the Depression.

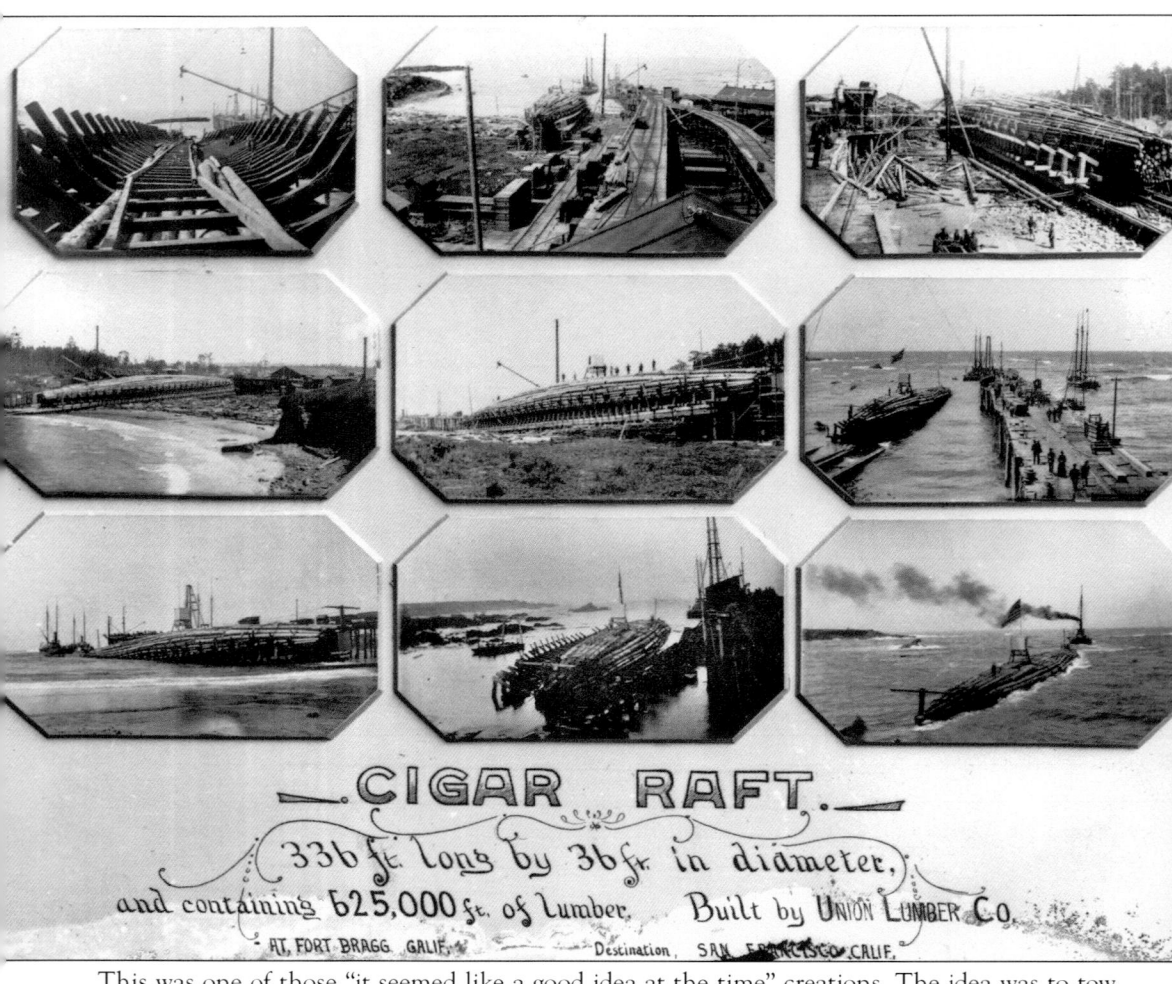

This was one of those "it seemed like a good idea at the time" creations. The idea was to tow whole logs to sawmills in San Francisco and San Diego and process them there. Rafts up to 1,000 feet long and held together with old anchor chain could be towed 60 miles in a 24-hour day, weather permitting. This cigar raft was hauling pilings. This modest 336-foot-long craft was assembled in the 1880s. Mills up and down the West Coast experimented with this transportation idea for 50 years.

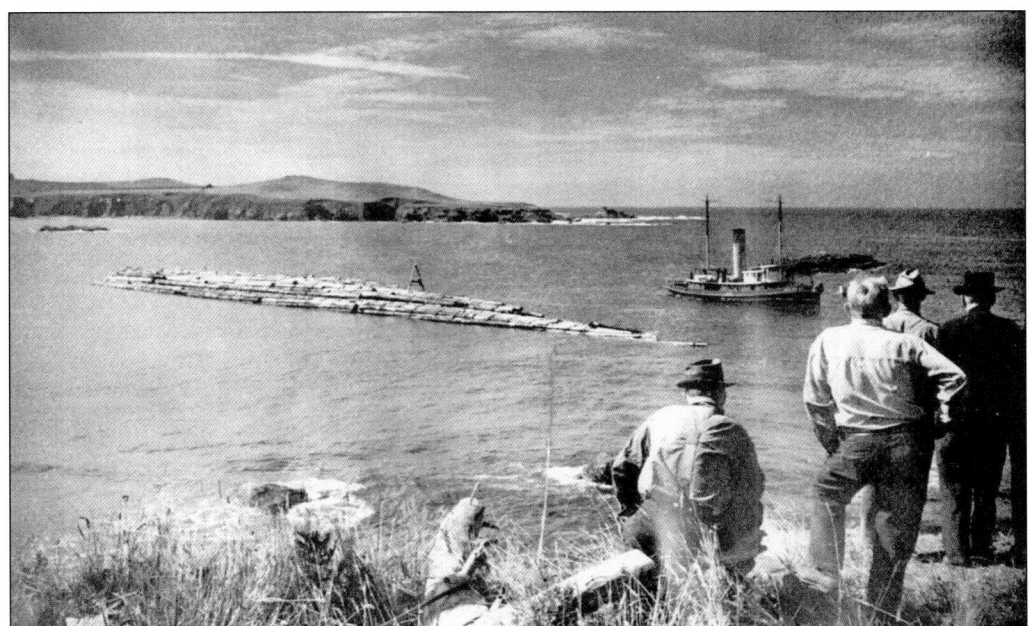

The problem with cigar rafts was that they often broke apart. The last time the sawmill in Mendocino ever operated was in 1938, when a raft came apart in Mendocino Bay. Logs were piled 10 feet high on the shore, and salvaged logs ran through the mill for four months. Part of the 35-foot-wide, 600-foot-long load was rewrapped at sea and towed south.

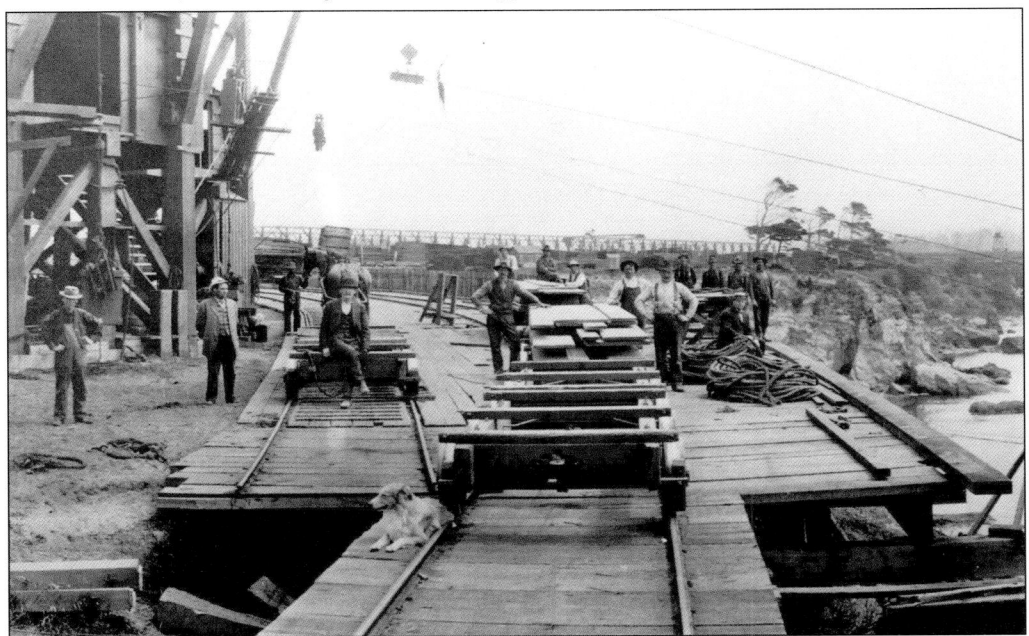

A shipping point crew and a dog stop for a moment at the Soldier Harbor shipping point at Fort Bragg. Cables overhead lowered lumber to ships. This area of coast has been off limits to visitors for decades due to mill operations. The mill closed in 1992, and a public coastal trail along the bluffs will be gained in the future.

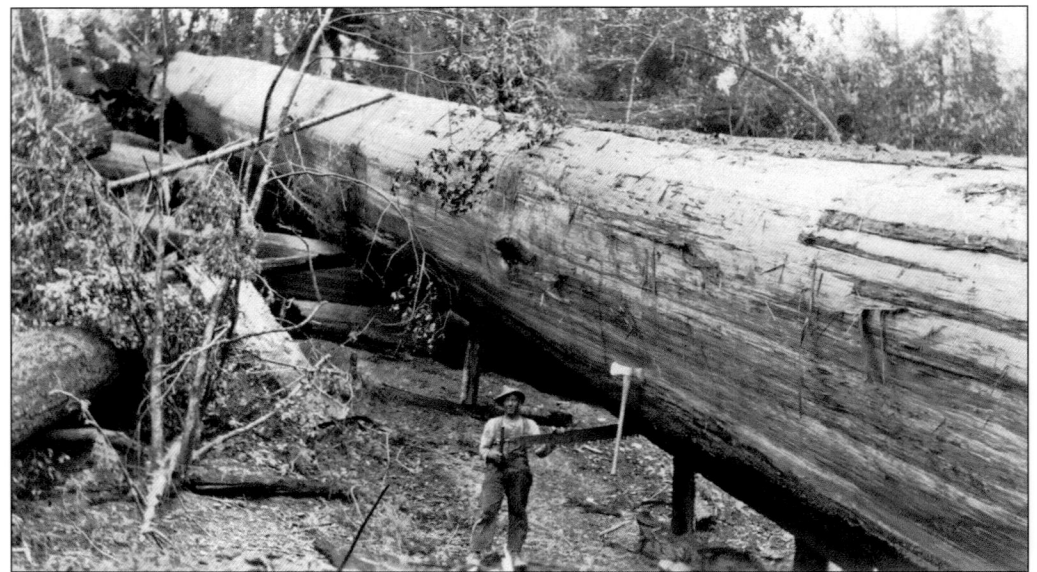

Big trees cut one year had bark and limbs cut off. The underbrush and waste would be burned off. The next year, a bucker would cut the logs into transportable size. This 14-foot-diameter tree was supported underneath to make the sawing easier.

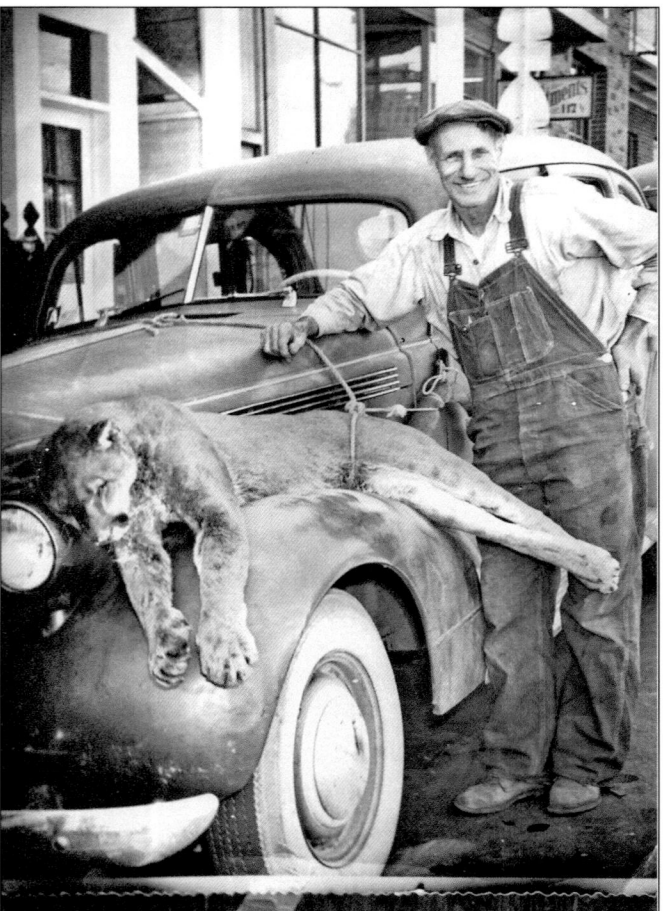

This guy looks happy that he has removed another varmint from the farmers' and ranchers' landscape; he brought the carcass into town 60 years ago to show it off. Mountain lions continue to be of concern on the Mendocino Coast, as they have been seen all the way to the ocean's edge in recent years, usually moving through parklands.

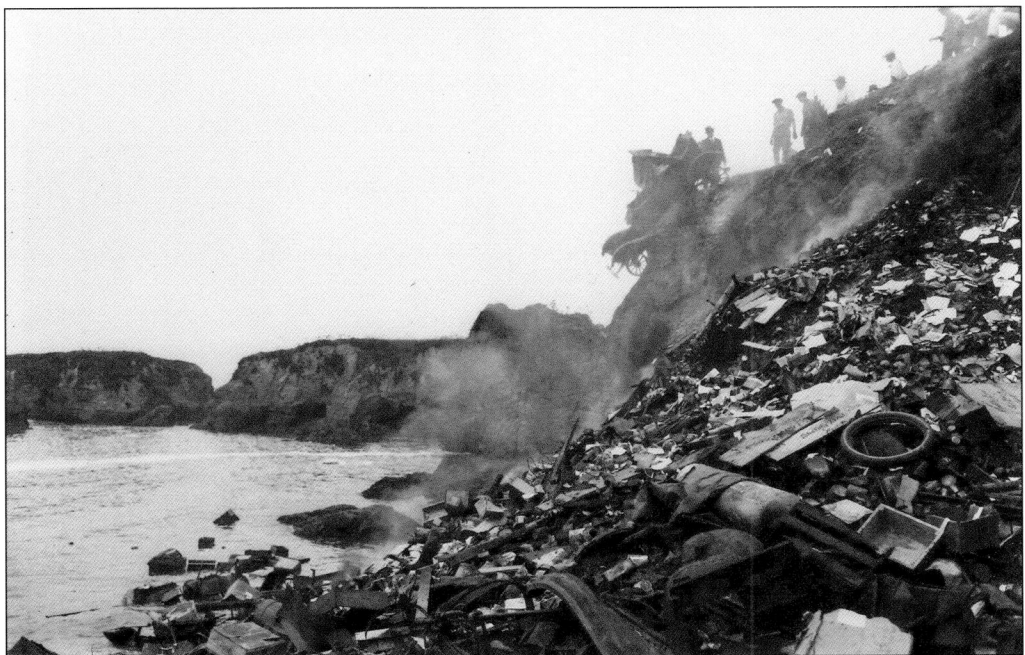

How did the Fort Bragg dump become a tourist attraction? The clunky metal objects were removed, and Mother Nature, in the form of the Pacific Ocean, took over. After 40 years of wave-grinding action, the glass becomes smooth, rounded pebbles. Glass Beach is a public park accessed from Elm Street off Main Street at the north end of town.

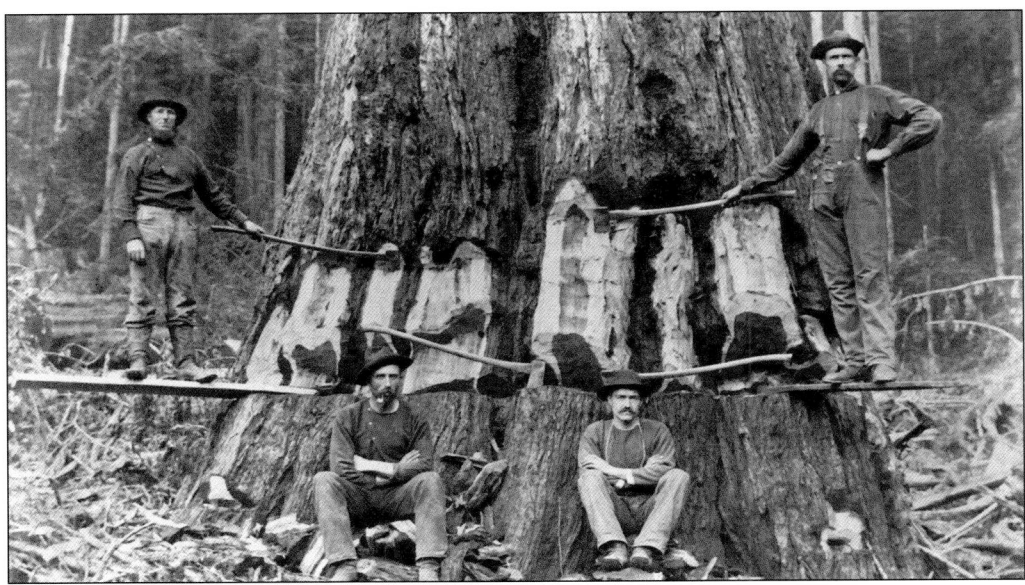

Around 1890, loggers stand on springboards inserted in the tree to begin chopping in the Cleone Woods, north of Fort Bragg. Flaring butts of logs were hard to move and sap-heavy and so were left behind. Today many moss-covered old stumps still standing have springboard slots in them.

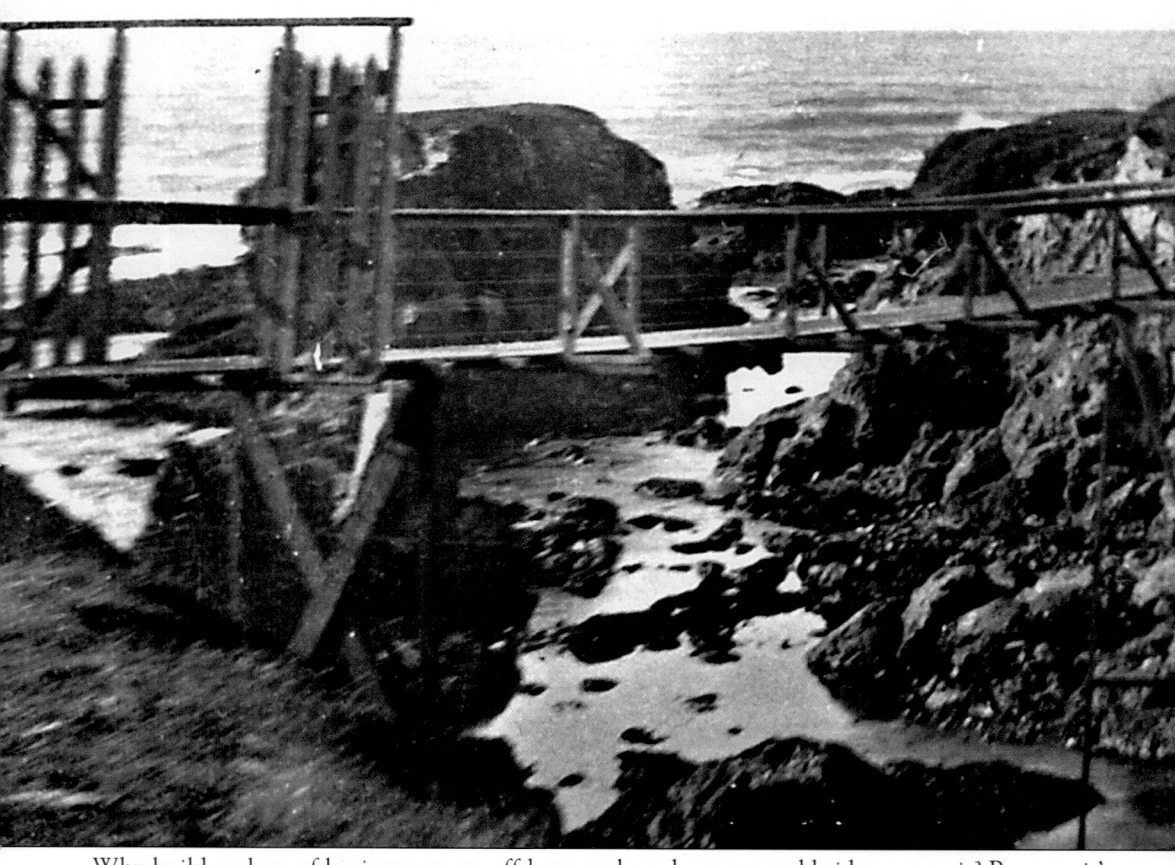

Why build a place of business on an offshore rock and put a gated bridge out to it? Because it's a whorehouse and illegal drinking establishment called the House of Joy. Old-timers remember many stories (unfortunately unprintable) about this place in Fort Bragg near the end of Fir Street. Inebriated men reportedly falling off the bridge to their deaths after too much partying led city fathers to tear down the house and the bridge. Prostitution was considered a necessary evil in mill

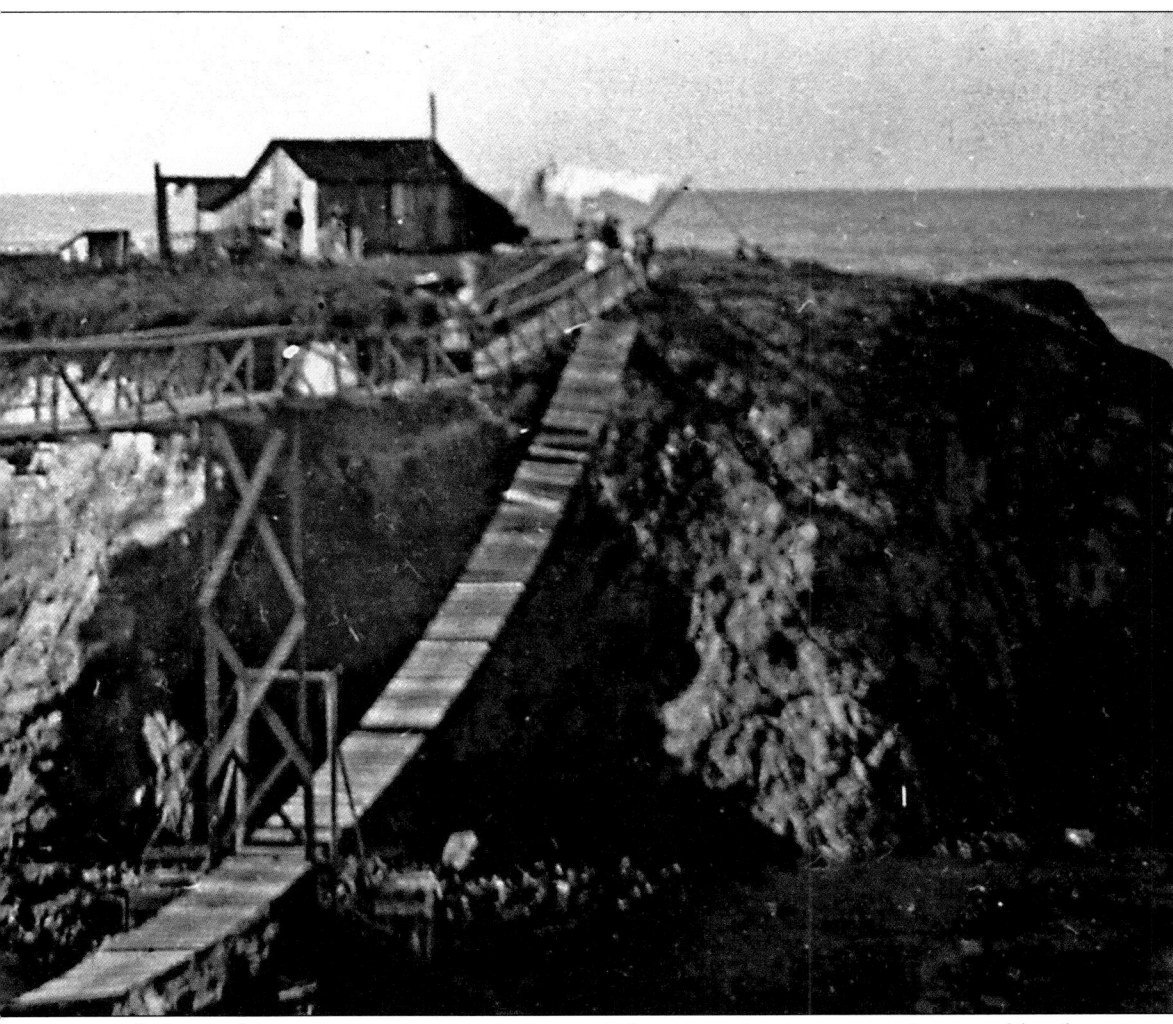

towns, because if there were no women to visit on infrequent trips to town, workers would pick up and move to a camp closer to towns with women of ill repute. An old logger in a 1975 oral history interview said: "Those girls, I always loved them. My old man would give me two bucks to go down to the whorehouse. I still had to work all summer to pay last winter's whorehouse bill."

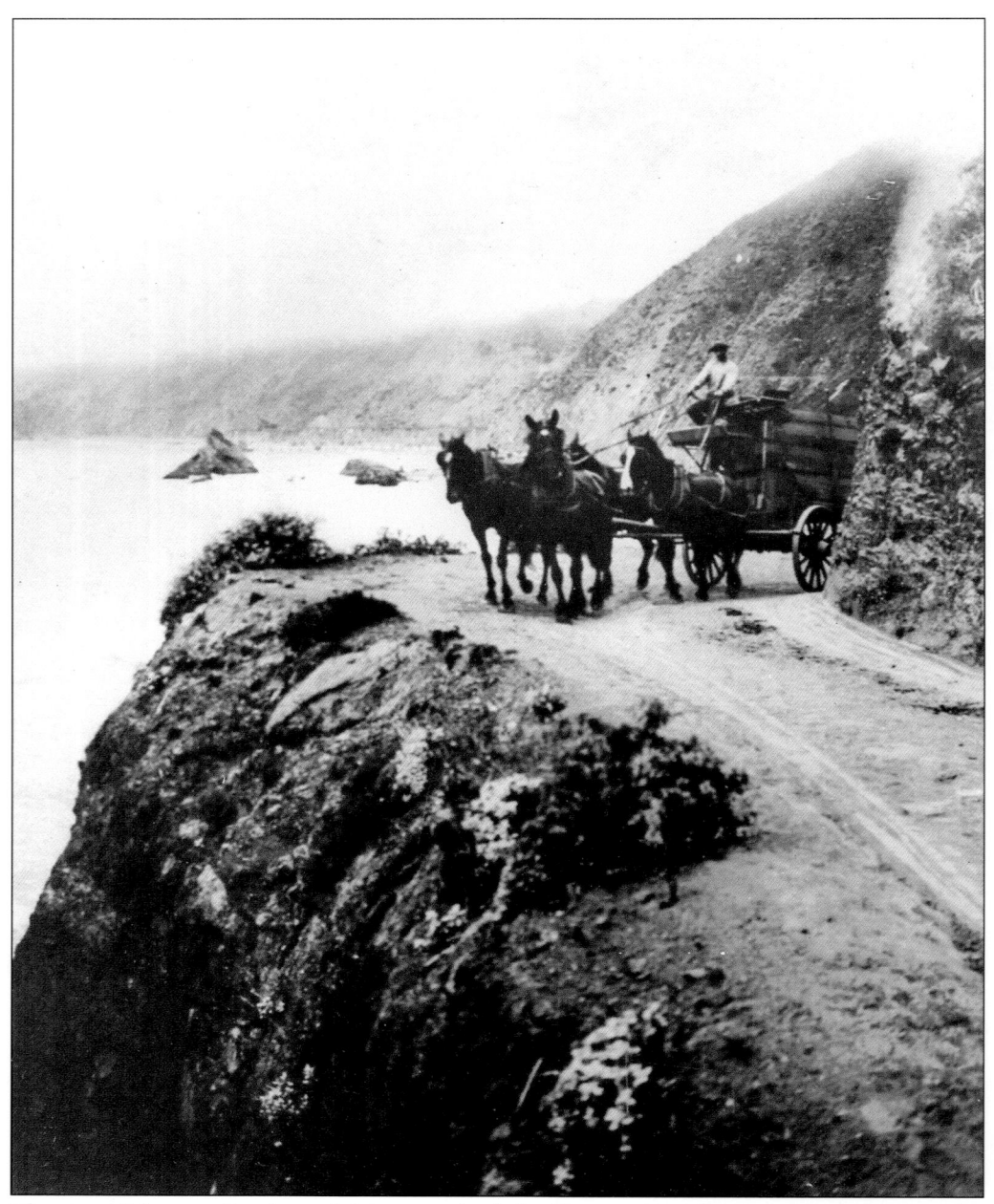

The view of the coastline beyond this wagon loaded with ties at Juan Creek can explain why today the area is called the Lost Coast. The road builders gave up on the idea of a shoreline highway when faced with Cape Vizcaino and other ridges abruptly rising from sea level to more than 1,000 feet in elevation. From here, the highway went inland along coast drainages to connect to Highway 101 at the Eel River. Today's intrepid motorists can turn north off Highway 1 at milepost 90.88, climb a gravel road, and drive north to reconnect with the Mendocino Coast at Needle Rock and Bear Harbor.

Four

NORTH COAST AND LOST COAST

50 MILES
CLEONE TO NEEDLE ROCK

The area north of Fort Bragg had fewer shipping points than the south coast but they were always busy. Again settlers came to exploit timber resources, and again the places they came to have since vanished. There was always the desire to have a good road connecting to Humboldt County, but it took until the 1930s to get it.

Many of the old ranches that supported small logging operations and shipping points like Howard Creek Ranch and DeHaven Valley Farm have now become bed-and-breakfast lodgings with owners who love to share local history.

The last 30 miles of the Shoreline Highway wind from Westport to Legget on Highway 101. These photographs, however, take travelers to the last little piece of far north Mendocino Coast called the Lost Coast.

Getting there is an adventure. Visitors should have a full tank of gas, food, water, and a spirit of adventure and all day to devote to the trip. This should only be attempted in summertime. Usal Road leaves the Shoreline Highway at milepost marker 90.88 for a bumpy but beautiful ride past long-ago vanished towns north to Needle Rock and Bear Harbor.

A visit to the area is entrancing if a person likes wide-open spaces and no people because that is the Lost Coast experience. Standing on a headland with miles of coast in view, the visitor might be the only human being around for miles.

Most visitors who use the Usal Road to access the Lost Coast take the quick road back to civilization. The Briceland Road runs back to Garberville and Highway 101. Go south to Legget and meet the Shoreline Highway again.

A great roadside attraction in Legget is the Drive-Thru Tree Park. There's nothing like a classic photograph of the tourist's car driving through a hole cut in a 350-foot-tall redwood tree to show the folks back home.

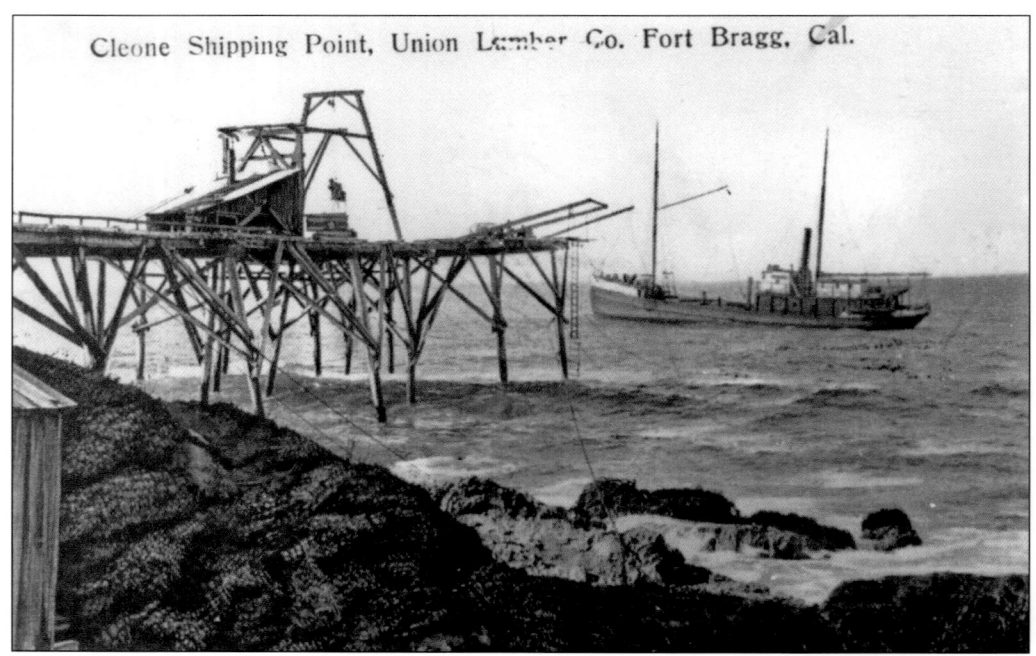

Timber products were shipped from Laguna Point until the 1930s, but today it features whale-, seal-, and bird-watching from a boardwalk accessible to the disabled. The MacKerricher family, which had purchased land along Laguna Creek for $1.25 an acre in 1868, deeded the land to the state in 1948, specifying that access to the park would be free.

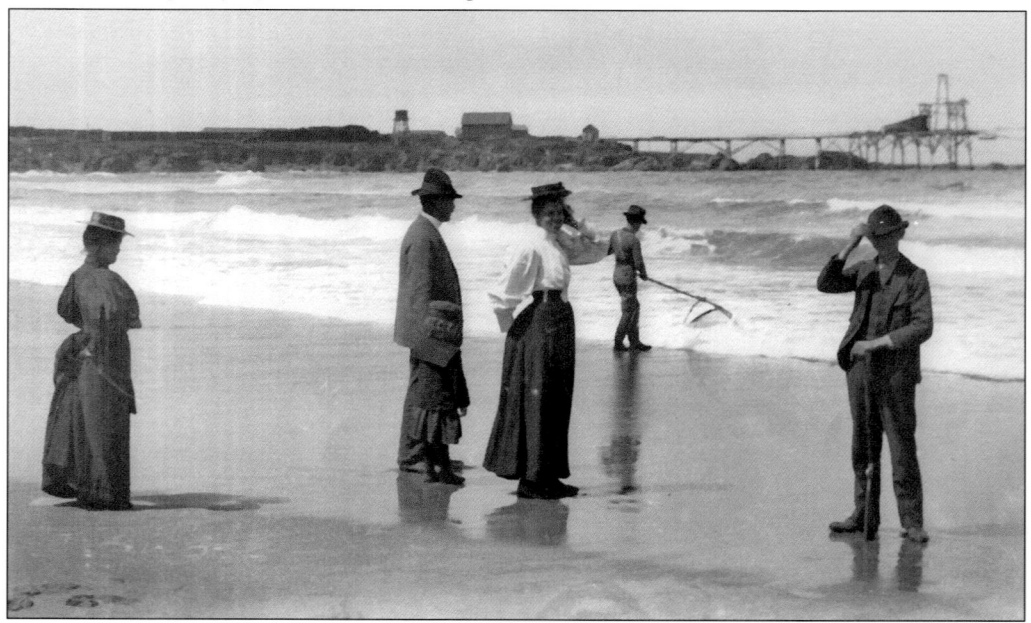

Spending a day at the beach has been popular for a century. These folks stand on what is now MacKerricher State Beach. Laguna Point, the shipping port for lumber coming out of the Little Valley and Cleone timberlands, is in the background. The man at the tide line is surf fishing with a triangular net on a pole.

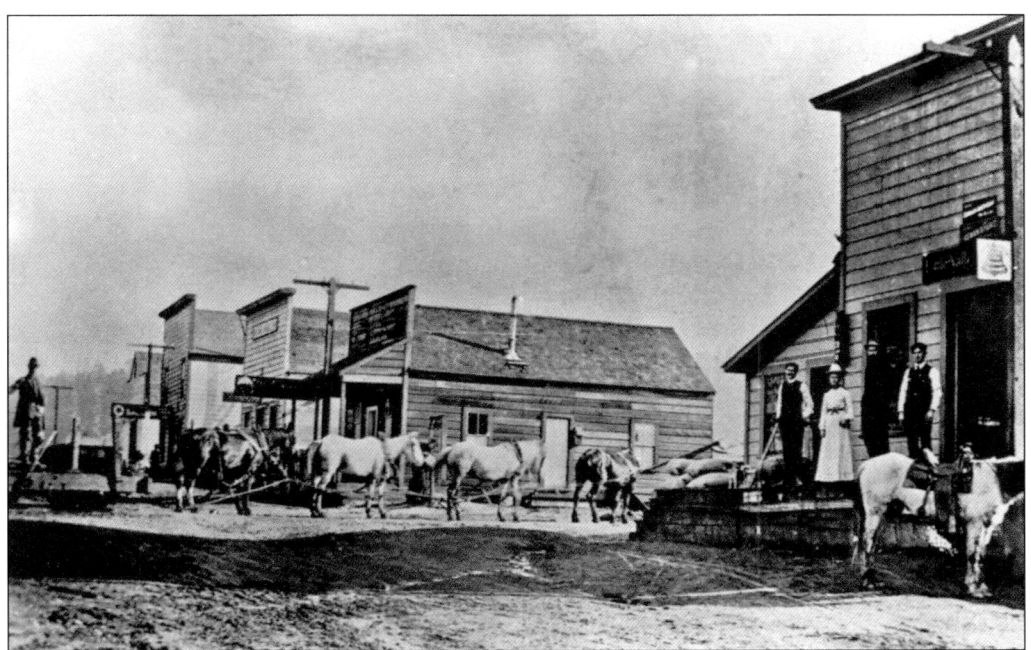

The Cleone Tramway was a railroad of iron strap rails, and horses and gravity provided power downhill. The mill was almost three miles from the shipping point. Ties, lumber, pilings, and tan oak bark ran downhill on small cars. Horses returned the cars uphill. Stronger rail was laid, but a locomotive was never added to the operation, which lasted 20 years.

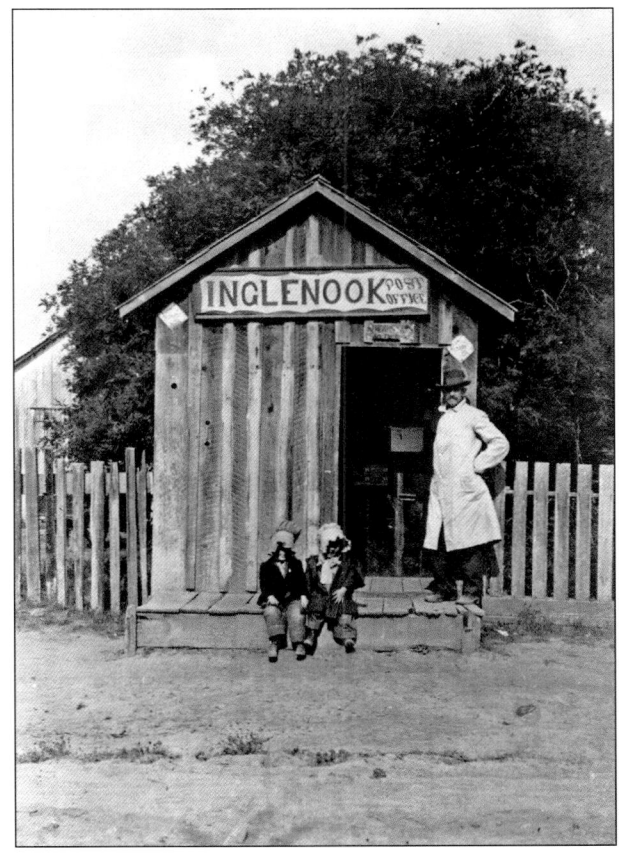

If a town keeps moving its center of population, how about a post office so small it could be picked up and moved to wherever the people are? That's what Inglenook did. Today one of the largest sand dune complexes in California borders the road to the west and continues for four miles north to the mouth of the Ten Mile River.

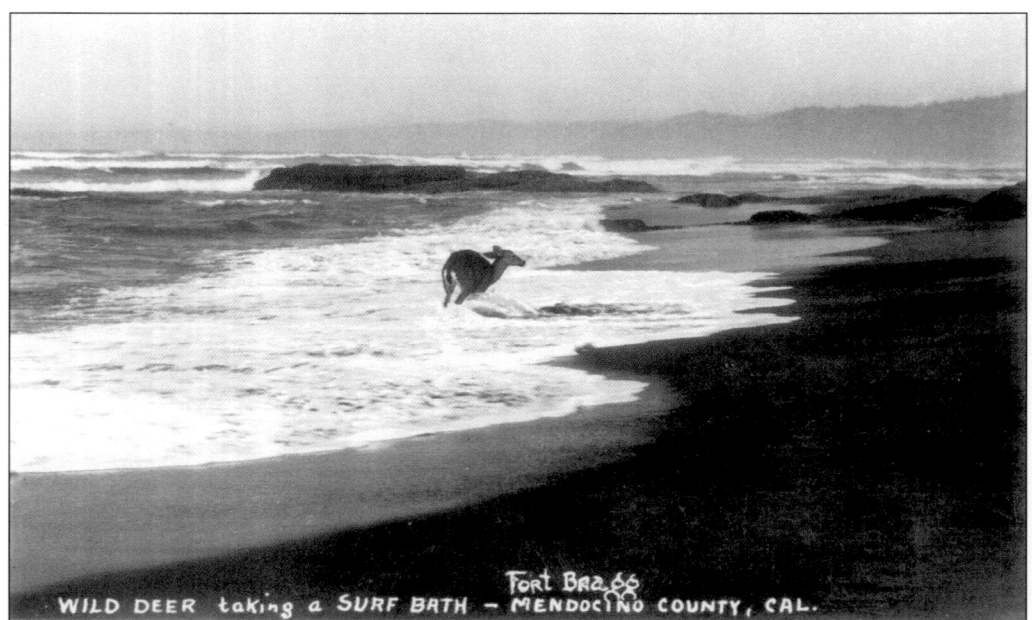

Shown here is an unusual photograph of a deer splashing in the surf. Deer and elk enter the ocean in hopes of getting ticks and fleas to fall off. Horses enter the surf for the same reason. Deer are common along the coast, and elk were reintroduced from Humboldt County in the 1970s and populate the Lost Coast to the north.

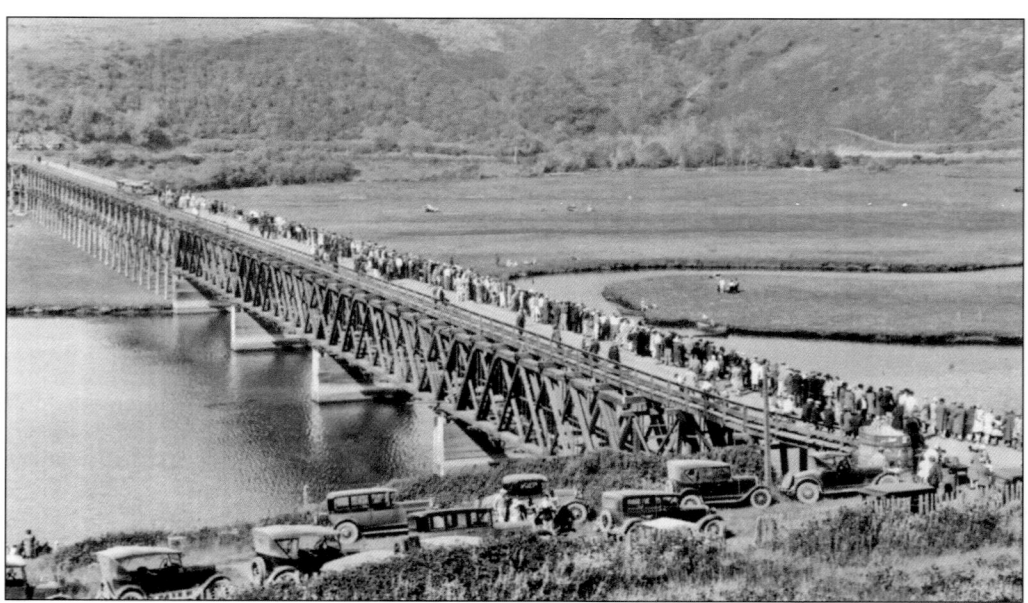

Why would so many people line up on the side of a bridge and peer over the side? In the 1930s, two local Finn swimmers, Sylvia Ruuska and her brother, were participating in a swim marathon in the Ten Mile River in preparation for an Olympic team tryout. They used the flat waters of the river for a demonstration, and fans lined the bridge to cheer them on.

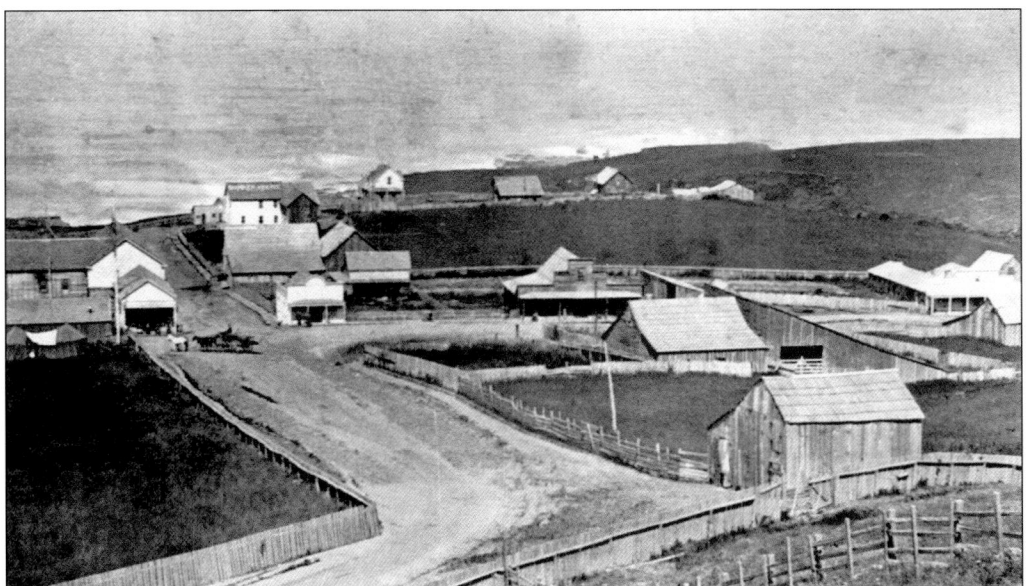

Four miles north of Ten Mile and a mile beyond the old shipping point of Newport was Kibesillah, which means Head of the Valley in native Yuki tribal speech. More than 20 buildings, including a newspaper and telegraph office, existed in 1870. When local sawmill machinery moved to Fort Bragg in the 1880s, the town vanished.

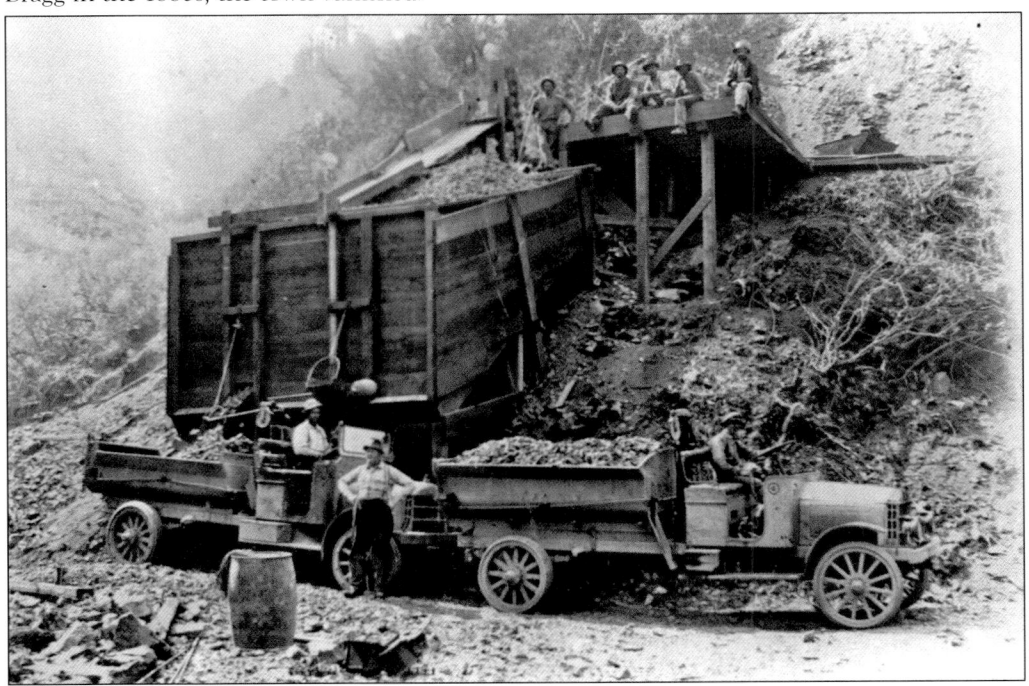

Twisting down the Shoreline Highway grade to Chadburne Gulch and climbing back up out of it makes drivers appreciate the concept of high-level bridge crossings. Access to the ocean is down a dirt road on the north bank. During the highway's construction, a rock quarry up this canyon provided roadbed foundation materials.

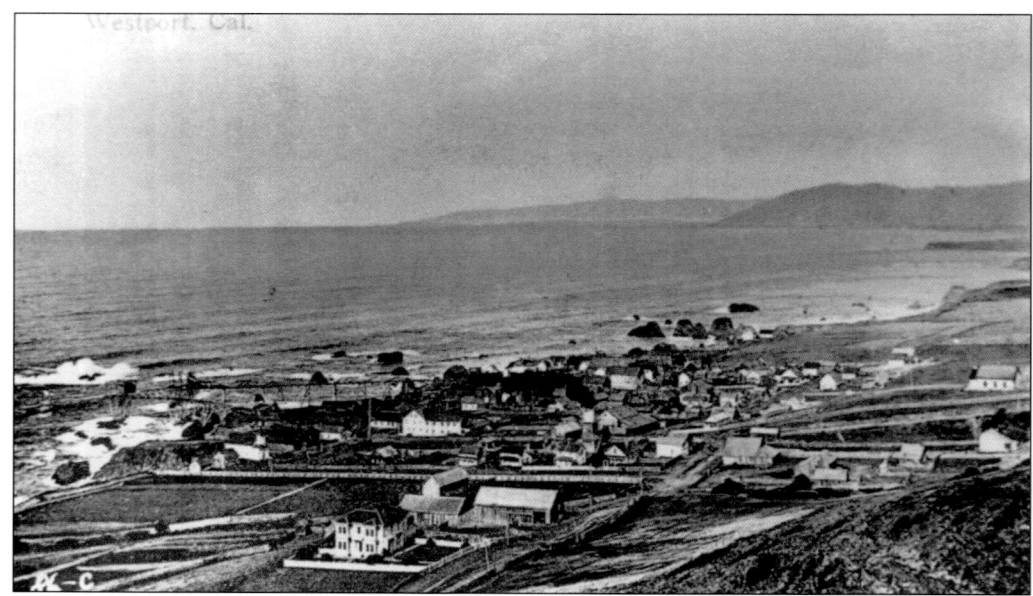

At its peak, Westport had 400 residents. A steam schooner is loading at the north chute around 1900. Big structures were probably hotels with the Switzer/Fee mansion in the foreground. Westport shipped tons of potatoes, oats, hides, and wool, along with wood products.

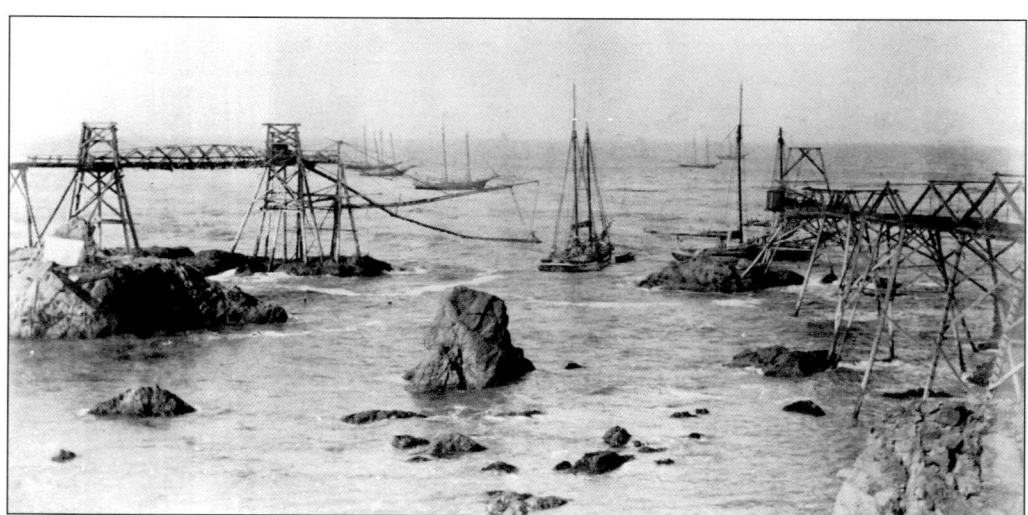

This Westport shipping point around 1896 shows two ships loading and five more vessels waiting to come in and take on lumber of tan oak bark. Notice the clapperman on the end of the chute on the left controlling the rate of speed in which boards approached the deck of the ship in the center of the photograph.

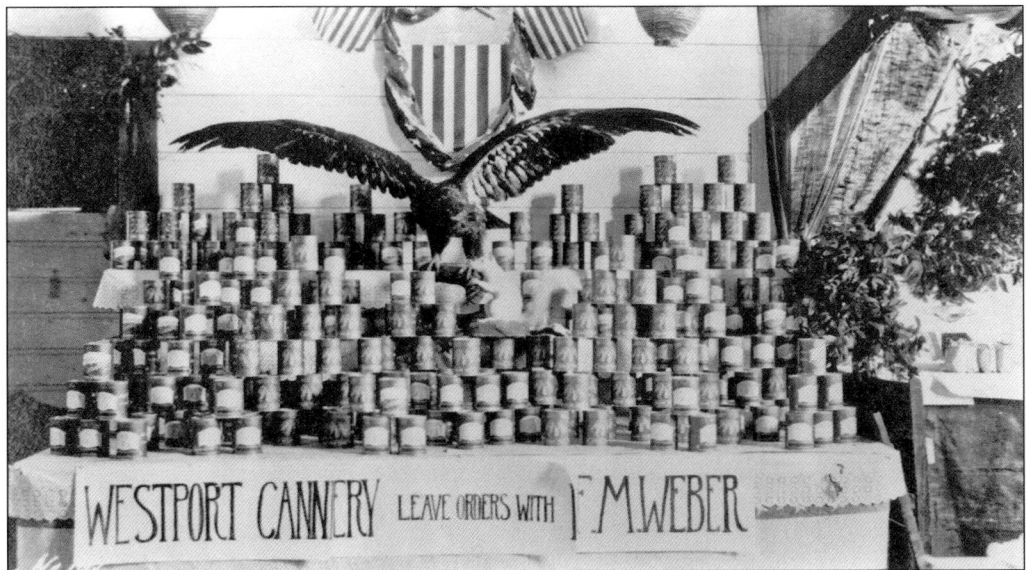

A mercantile store display from the Lewis Canning Company of Westport shows the brand names Westport, DeHaven, and Mendocino Coast for sugar peas and green beans grown locally. Many products like this went straight into lumber camp and sawmill cookhouses. Eagles were pests that got shot when killing lambs. This one was preserved and stuffed to add interest to the display.

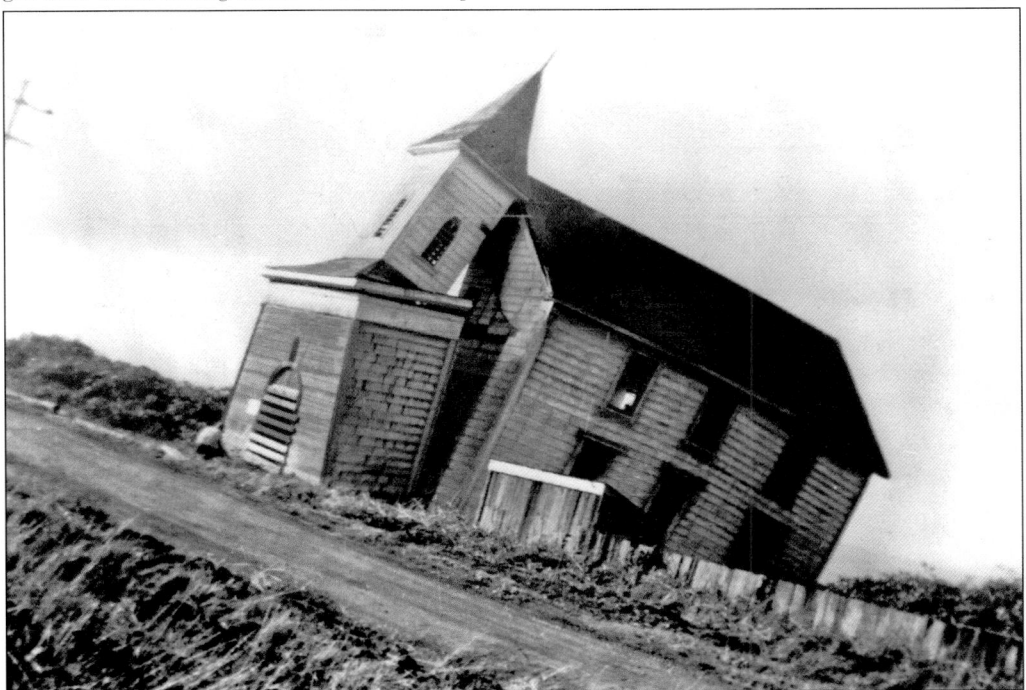

Westport residents claim this church would never have been lost off the bluff in 1952 if the highway department had not changed the road water drainage patterns, which inadvertently undermined the structure's foundation. The church and community center was more than 50 years old at the time of its plunge into the Pacific.

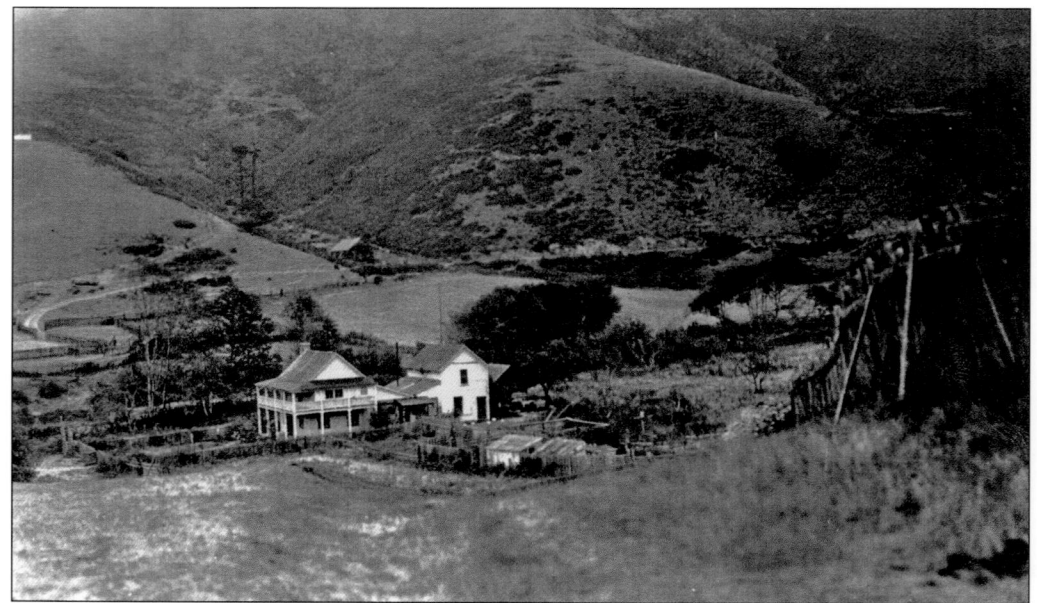

Howard Creek Ranch in 1871 had two houses built back-to-back, mimicking building styles seen in Maine. A later resident from Missouri added porches and verandas. Sheep were kept unfenced in areas with very short grass. Today, as an excellent bed-and-breakfast, the houses are filled with antiques, and there is a swinging bridge over the creek.

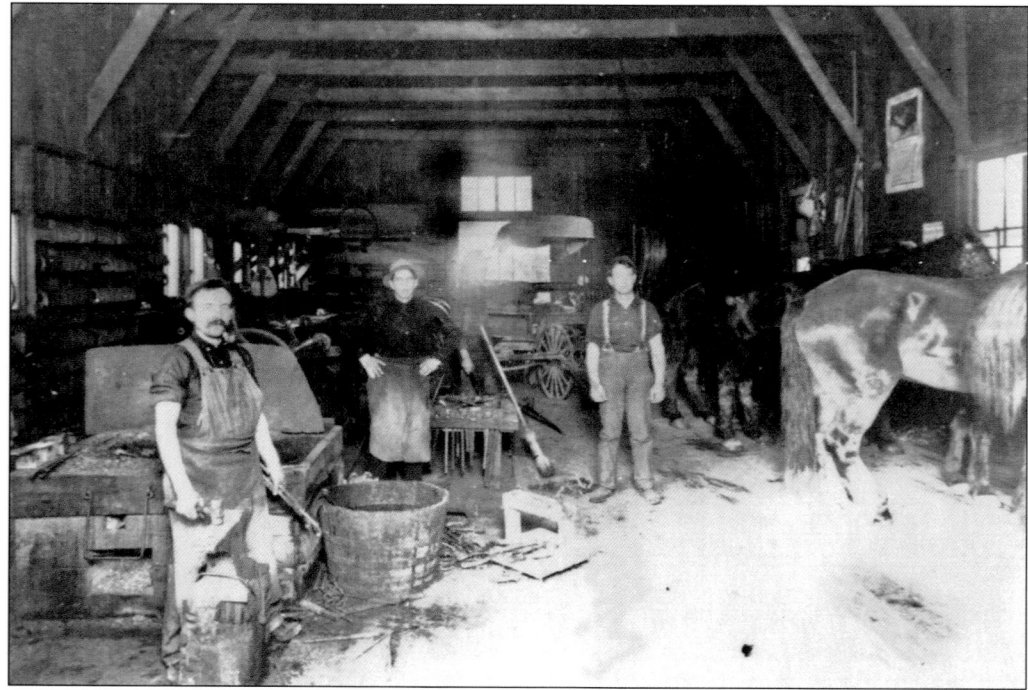

In 1910, Howard Creek Ranch had a blacksmith shop that took care of travelers' needs and probably did ironwork for small sawmills in the area. The drive-through bay of the big barn here sheltered the Hardy Creek railroad's little locomotive during the winter season.

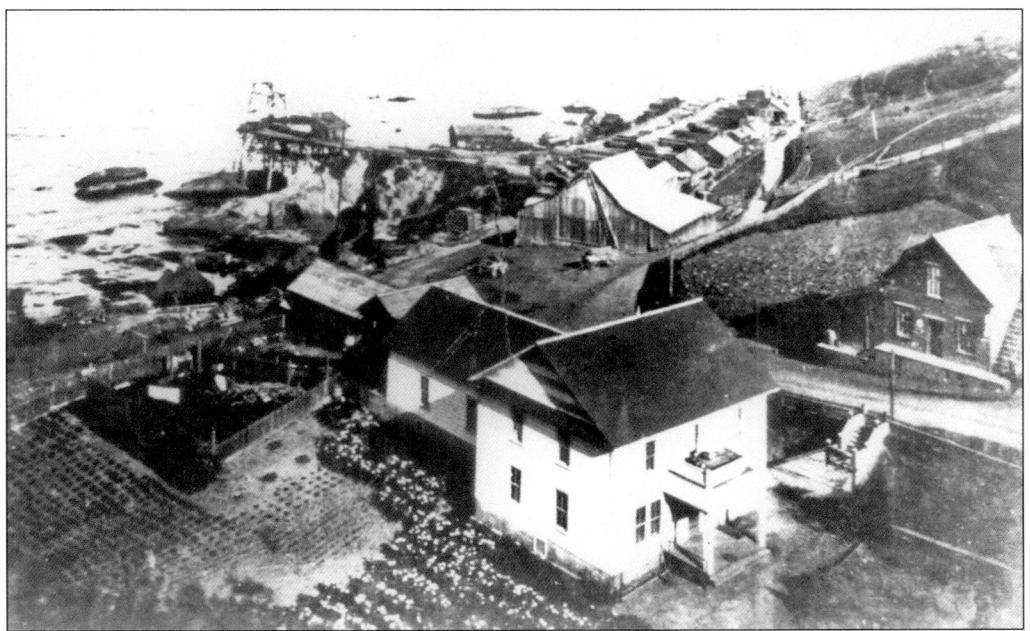

In 1912, Union Landing was the shipping point for timber cut north of Westport, operating from 1899 until the sawmill up Howard Creek burned in 1924. The landing has vanished as much of the flat bluff here has eroded into the sea. The headlands west of the Shoreline Highway here are now all part of the Westport-Union Landing State Beach.

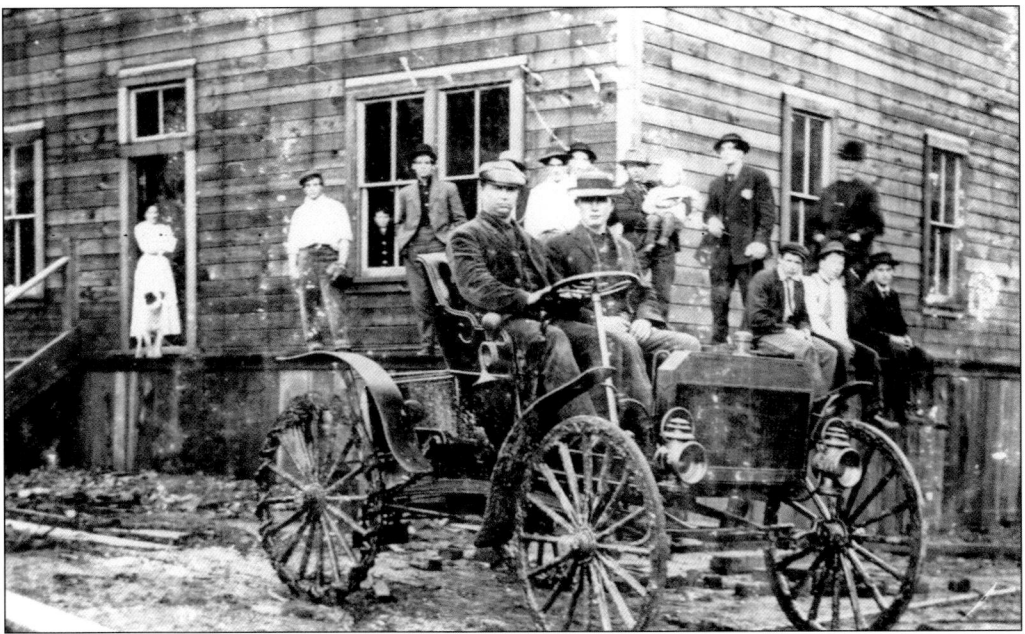

The driver of this 1906 Schacht automobile at Union Landing had the envy of the onlookers, but the driver and passengers might anticipate problems reaching their destination. Notice the rope entwined around the hard rubber tires in the rear; this was an attempt to improve traction on muddy roads.

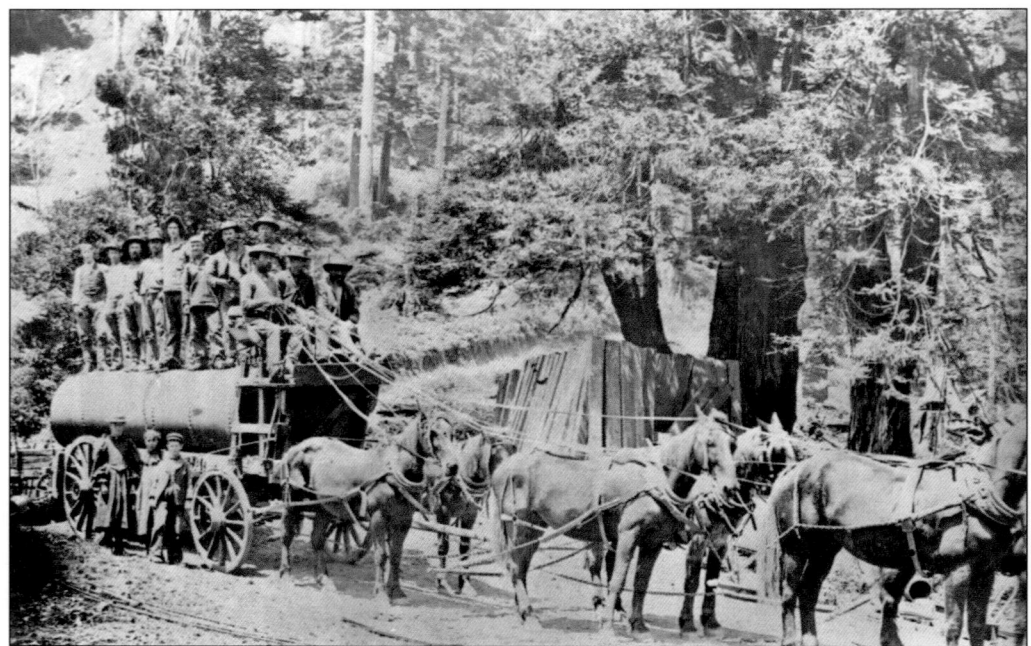

The Hardy Creek Lumber Company was organized in 1896. Here a new boiler was being delivered to the mill with a dozen men balanced on top for a photograph. The boiler came in by ship to Union Landing. The mill burned in 1911. Old mill sites up side canyons of the Shoreline Highway are invisible now due to the regrowth.

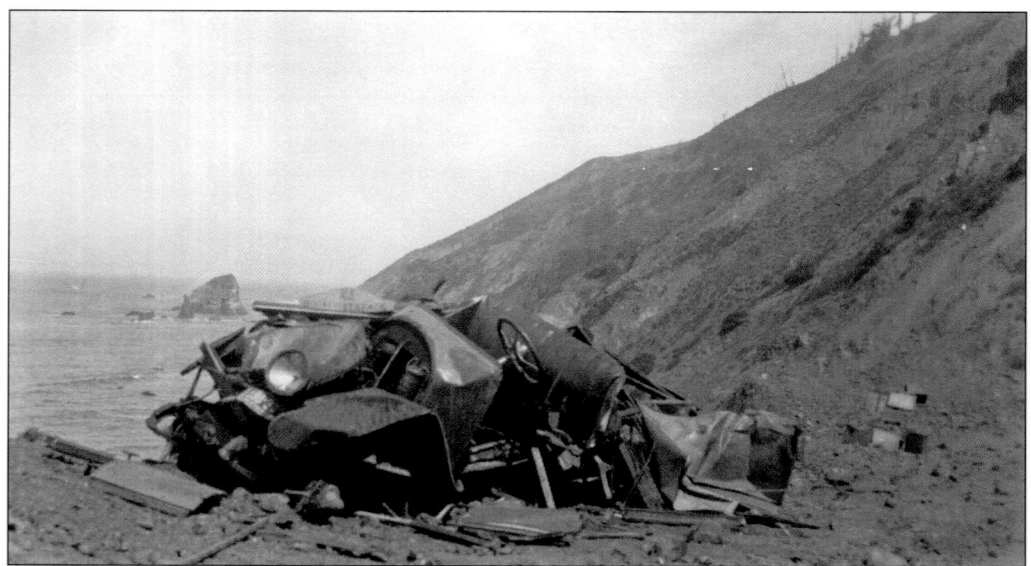

A minute's inattention on a twisty road was as deadly 90 years ago as it is today. The auto stage left the road at Hardy Creek, and the condition of driver and passengers when it hit the beach is unknown. If today's drivers want to admire the view, they should advantage of the turnouts—pull off and stop. Don't go too close to bluff edges!

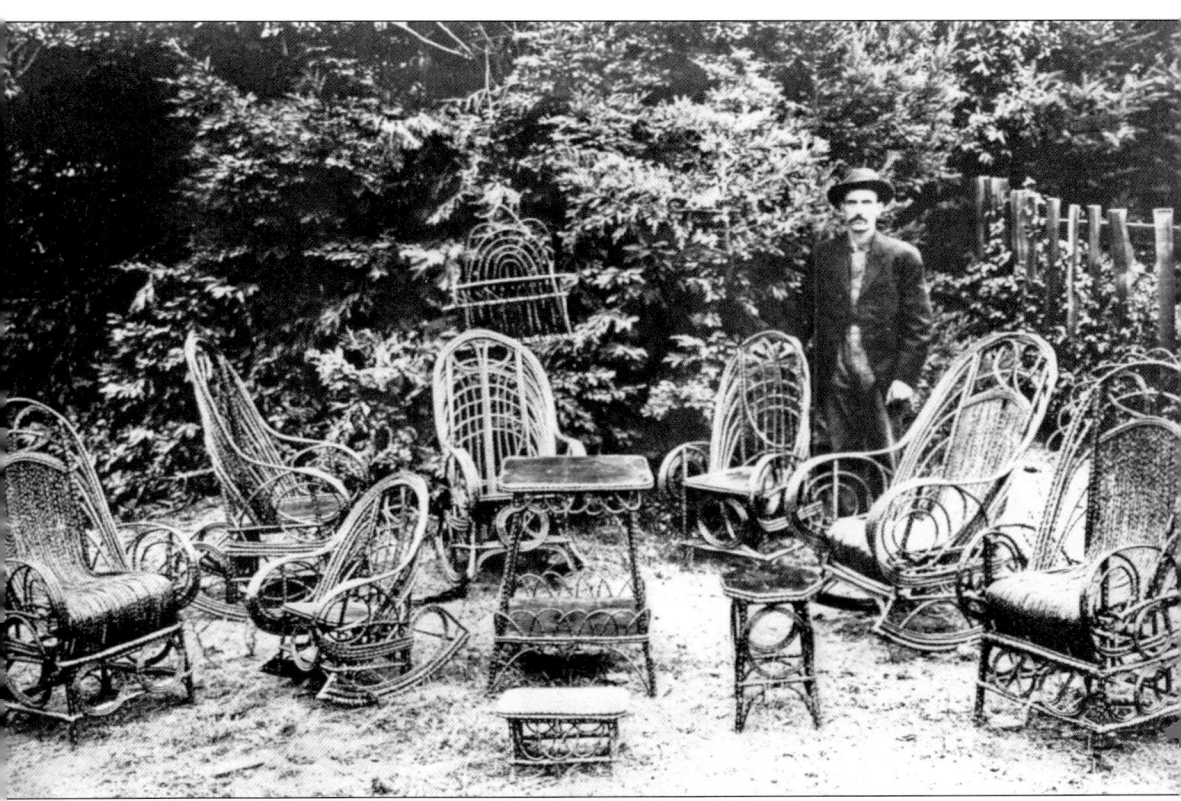

Always looking for a way to make an extra dollar, this fellow took flexible willow and made tables, chairs, stools, birdcages, and rocking chairs as a sideline occupation. Ideas could have come from a Montgomery Ward or Sears and Roebuck mail order catalog featuring illustrations of furniture. Any object a craftsman could produce from free materials and sell equaled money in the pocket.

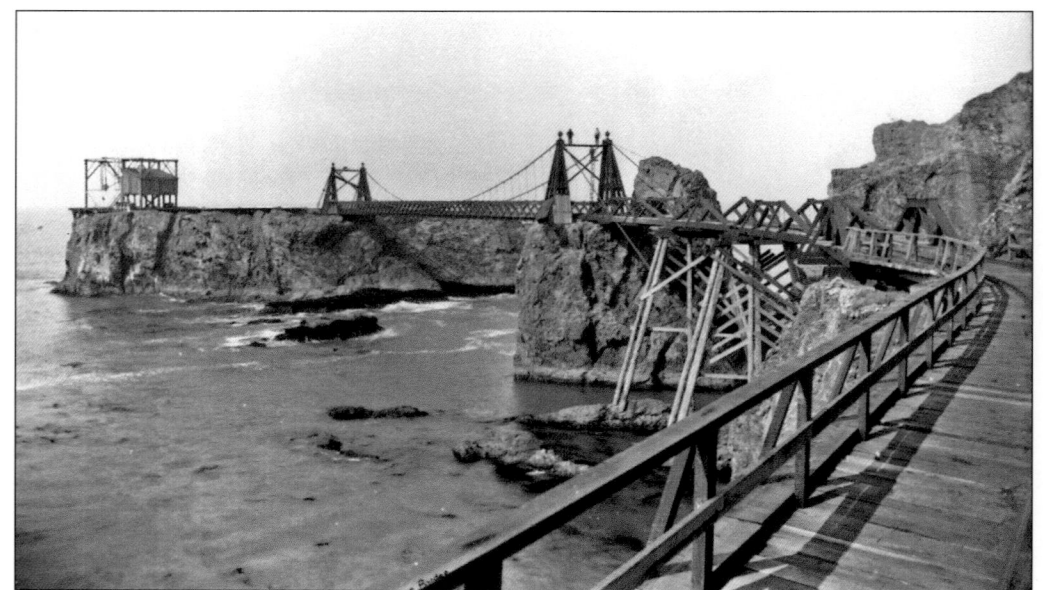

Today the site of Rockport is invisible to motorists at the mouth of Cottoneva Creek, but in 1877, the town possessed an architectural marvel: one of the first iron suspension bridges on the West Coast. It gave access to offshore rocks and a wire loading chute. The sawmill here went through boom-and-bust cycles before finally closing in 1957.

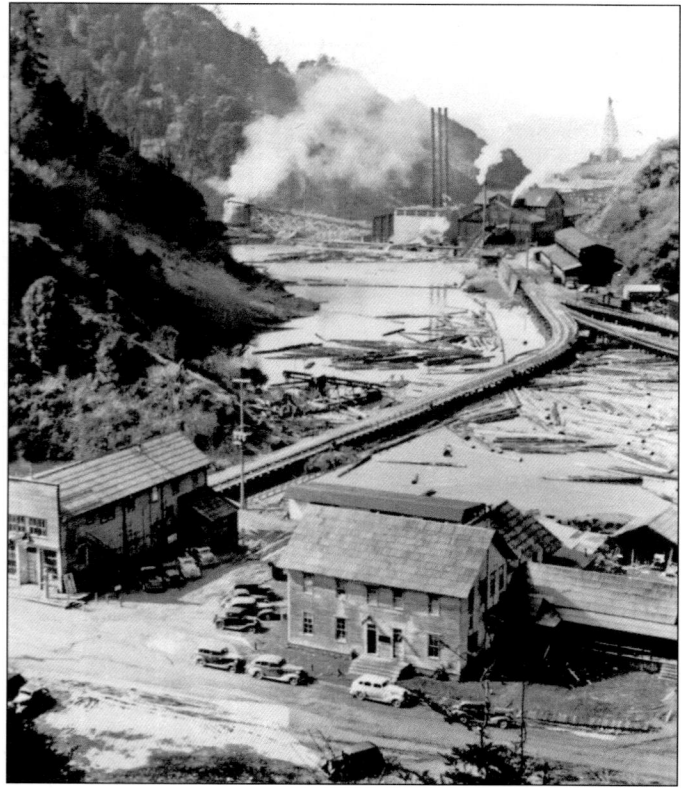

On the left is the Rockport Company Store and offices, and on the right is the hotel with the mill visible in the background. Automobiles surrounding the building include a 1938 Buick, 1939 Dodge, 1936 Ford, 1934 Graham, and a 1933 Plymouth.

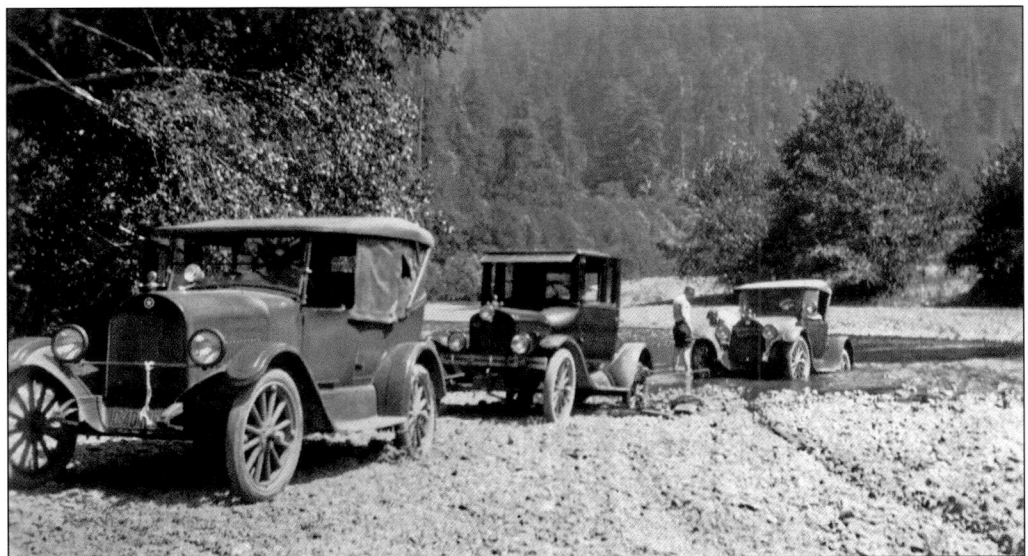

When no bridges existed, motorists found shallow fords to cross creeks and rivers. They also carried two ropes and traveled together in case disasters occurred. Swimsuits indicate that the stop on the river bank is intentional. Just as Central Valley residents came west in summer looking for cool ocean breezes, coast folks drove east looking for sunshine and heat.

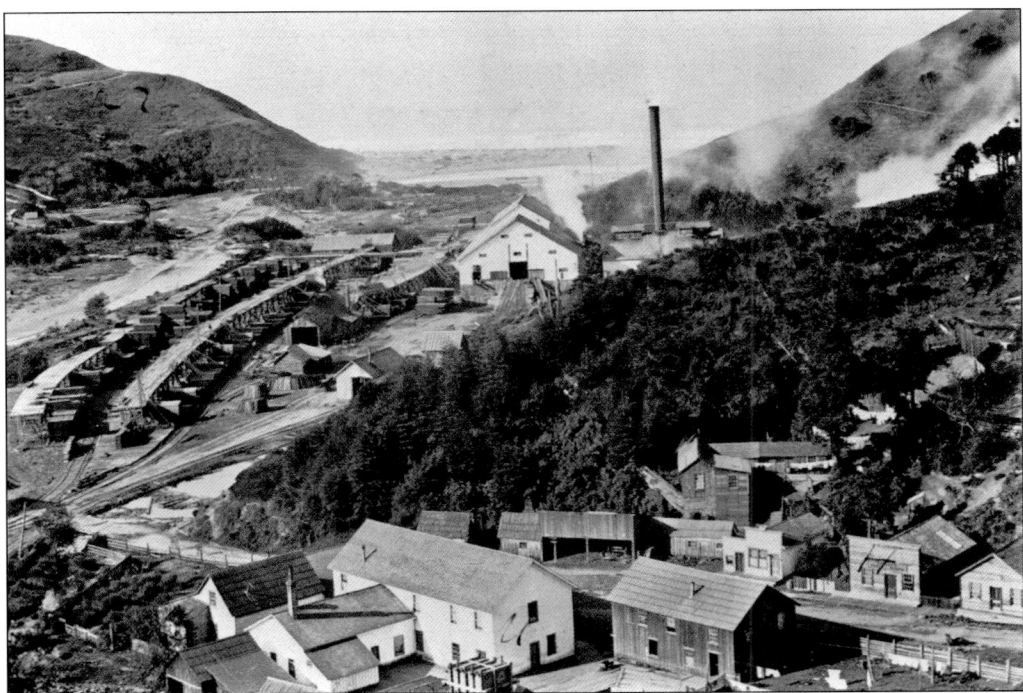

Thirteen miles north of Westport, at milepost 90.88, the road to Usal and the Lost Coast turns to the north. To travel the six miles to Usal is not a problem. Beyond that point, travelers should have gas, food, a map, and all day to spend on dirt roads. From 1900 to 1902, Usal had a sawmill, hotel, hospital, photographic studio, and 300 workers. Today Usal has a beach and camping.

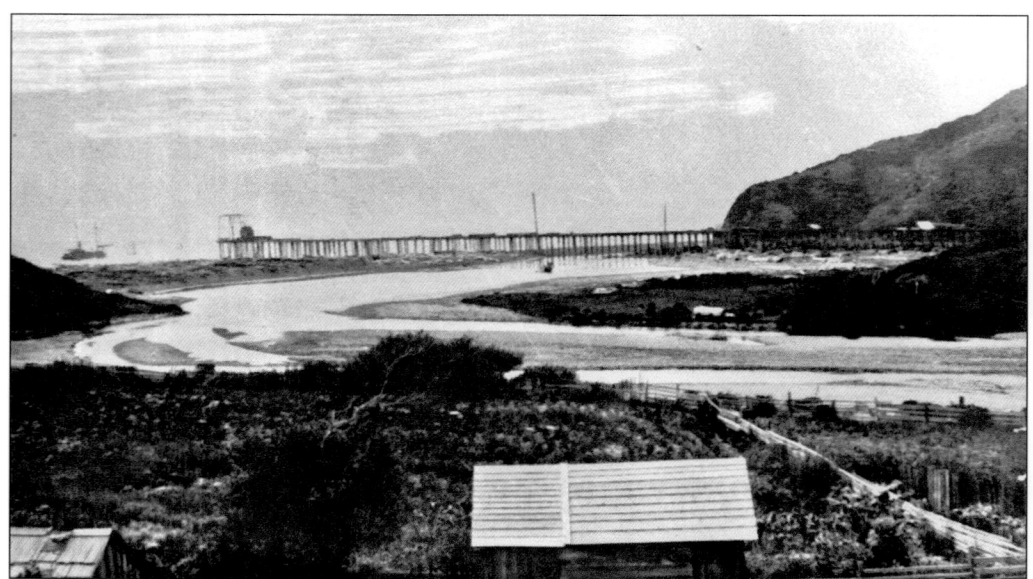

In 1895, carload after carload of tan oak bark awaited shipment on the Usal wharf. A chute lowered bark to the deck of the Rio Rey. Today it is possible to walk from Usal Beach to Bear Harbor on the Lost Coast Trail system. The book *Hikers Hip Pocket Guide to the Mendocino Coast* by Bob Lorentzen tells how.

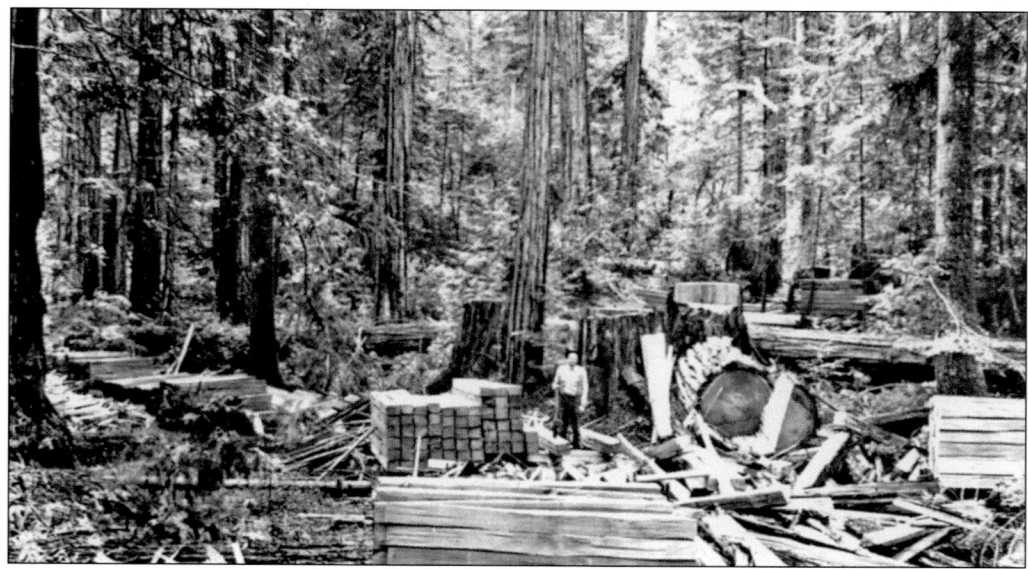

Railroad-tie making was lonely work, but it was something one chopper could do by himself as this man was doing around 1920. An 8-foot-by-7-inch-by-7-inch tie was worth less than 50¢ at that time. "Tie whacking" was the name given to this line of work.

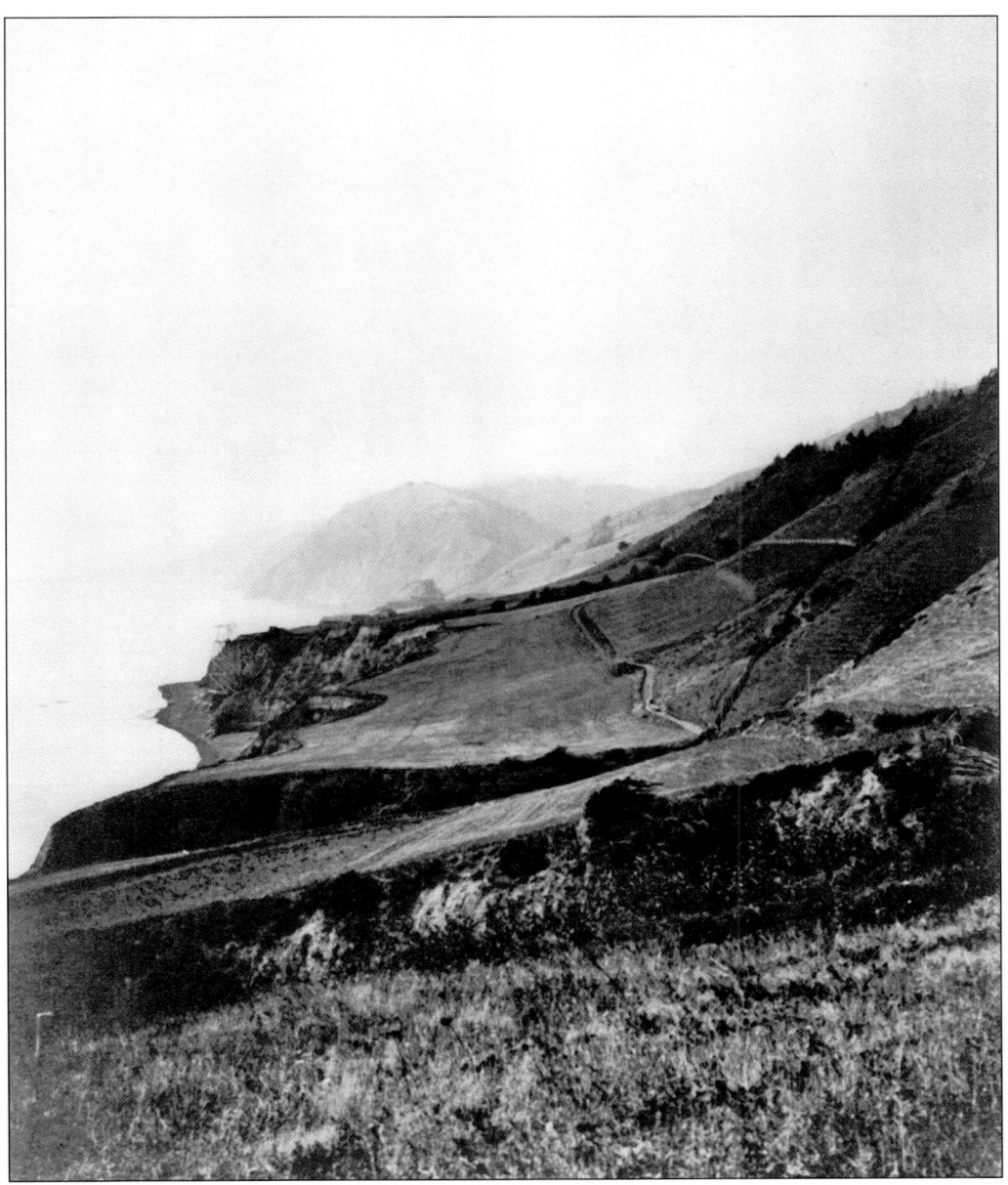

How many places can visitors go on the California coast today and look at a landscape almost identical in appearance now to 100 years in the past? Here it is. If drivers venture north out of Usal or approach the area from paved roads west of Garberville and Highway 101, they reach the Four Corners intersection. Turning west leads travelers to the Lost Coast. The old Needle Rock ranch house is now a visitors center for the Sinkyone Wilderness/Kings Range National Conservation Area. Visitors can inquire about the road to Bear Harbor, watch the waves and the wildlife, and enjoy the total lack of people. The dirt road here is a last remnant of the Mendocino Coast's Shoreline Highway.

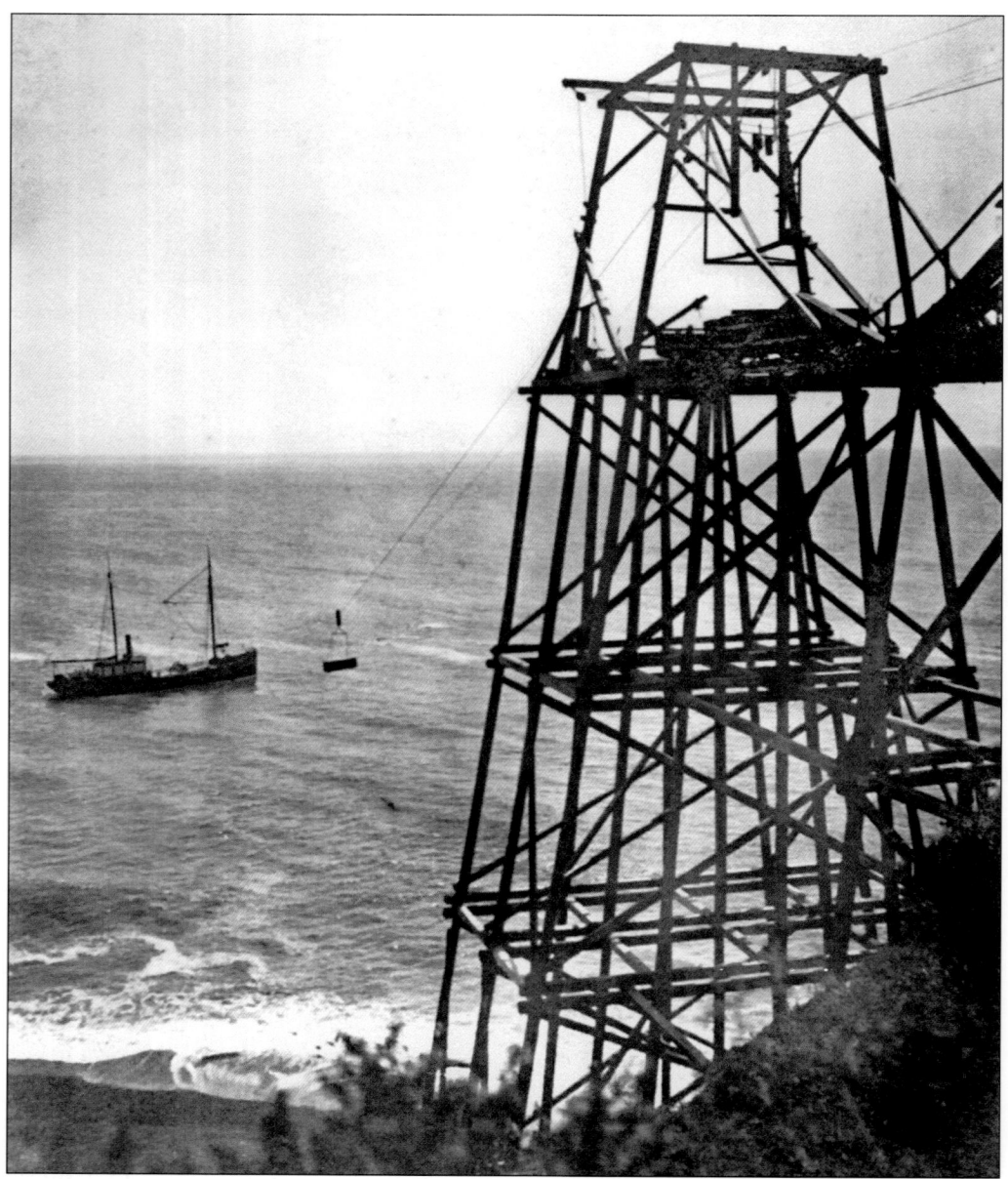

In the 1890s, the Needle Rock chute was always busy sending off wood products and the surplus from farming and ranching operations on the wide-open headlands. Here a traveler holds a load sliding down to a steam schooner. Needle Rock land form lost its point in the 1906 earthquake, and the chute operated until about 1920.

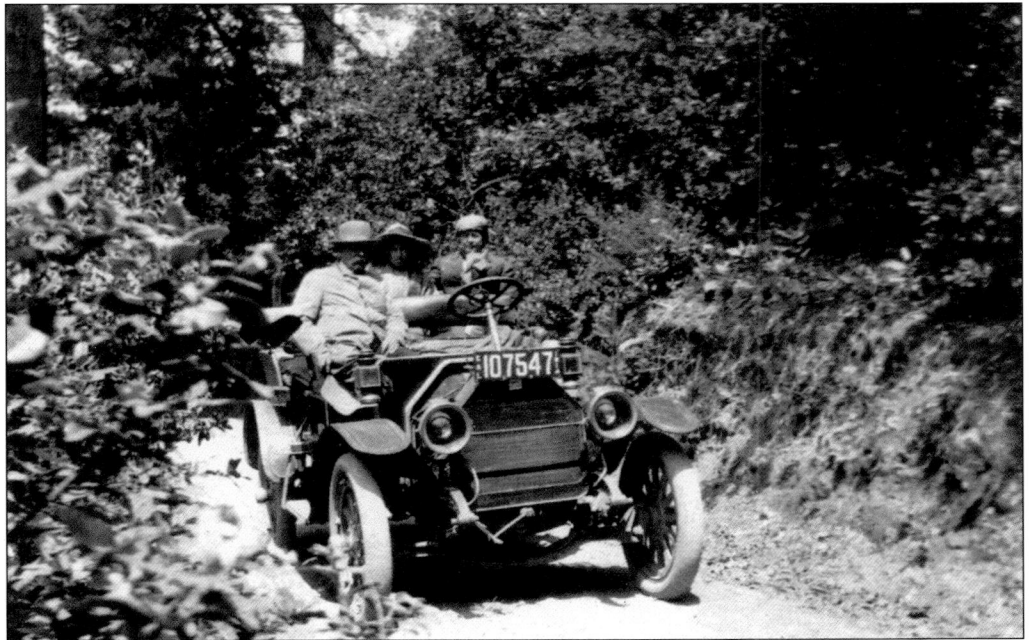

Motorists can drive on the road between two now nonexistent towns, Usal and Kenny. In 1914, these two places were busy enough to have a maintained road in between that went on north to Four Corners then out to the coast. Kenny had an 18-room hotel, a saloon, stables, and a post office in the 1880s.

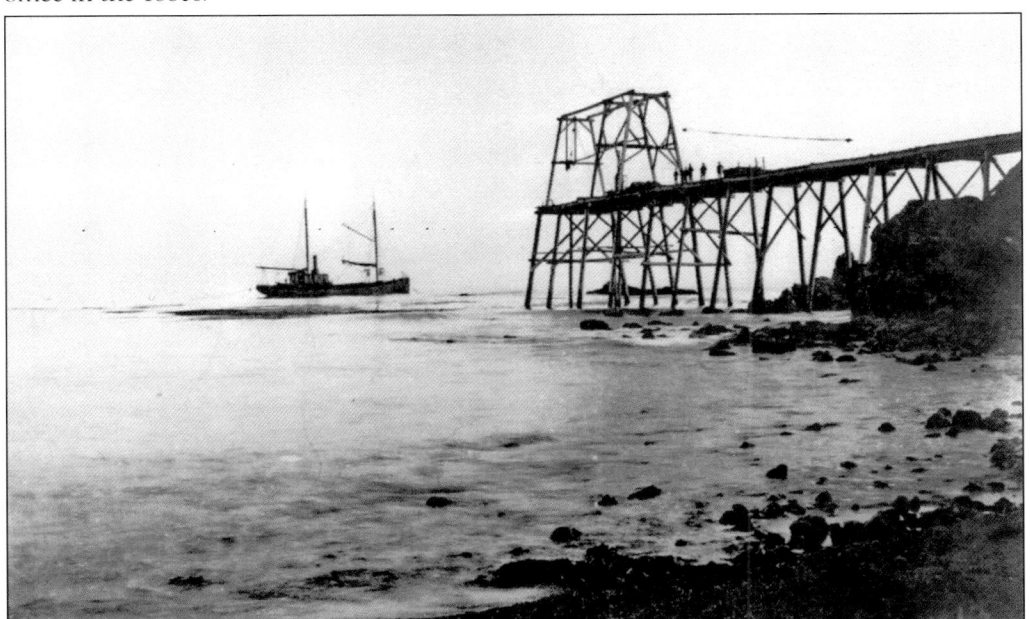

The steam schooner *Cleone* approaches the Bear Harbor shipping point and wharf around 1900. There were grand plans for a railroad to connect to Humboldt County in Andersonia, but it never happened. In 1899, a tidal wave destroyed this shipping point. Only foot trails extend along the coast south now.

Discover Thousands of Local History Books
Featuring Millions of Vintage Images

Arcadia Publishing, the leading local history publisher in the United States, is committed to making history accessible and meaningful through publishing books that celebrate and preserve the heritage of America's people and places.

Find more books like this at
www.arcadiapublishing.com

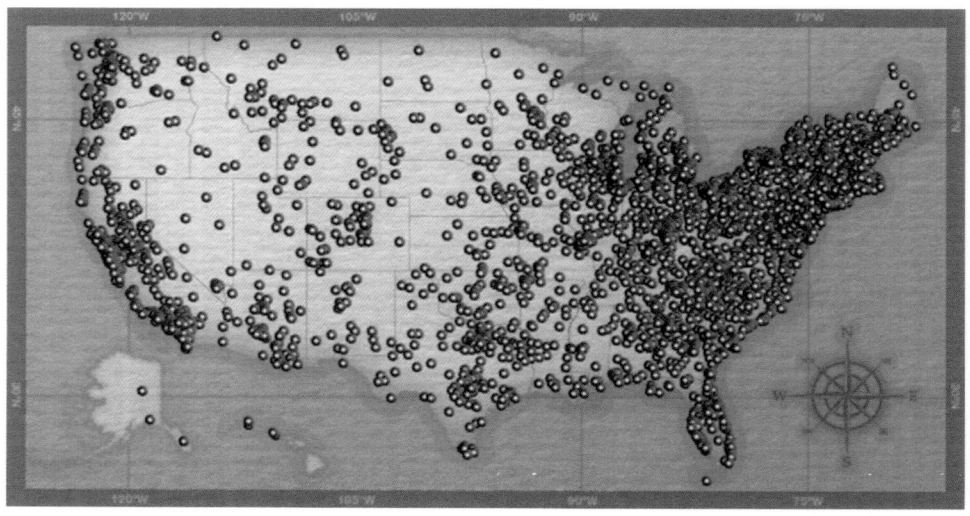

Search for your hometown history, your old stomping grounds, and even your favorite sports team.

Consistent with our mission to preserve history on a local level, this book was printed in South Carolina on American-made paper and manufactured entirely in the United States. Products carrying the accredited Forest Stewardship Council (FSC) label are printed on 100 percent FSC-certified paper.

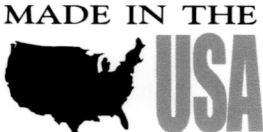